Unfinished Dream

# Unfinished Dream:
## The Musical World of Red Callender

Red Callender and Elaine Cohen

Quartet Books
London Melbourne New York

*Dedicated to all musicians everywhere*
*– past, present and future*

First published by Quartet Books Limited 1985
A member of the Namara Group
27/29 Goodge Street, London W1P 1FD

British Library Cataloguing in Publication Data

Callender, Red
Unfinished dream: the musical world of Red Callender.
  1. Callender, Red
  I. Title
  785.42'092'4    ML418.C3

  ISBN 0–7043–2507–1

Typeset by MC Typeset, Chatham, Kent
Printed and bound in Great Britain
by Mackays of Chatham Ltd, Kent

# Contents

# Acknowledgements

Red Callender's life has been and continues to be a marvel. I first met this modest and huge-hearted gentleman briefly in Los Angeles in May 1983, and again in October in San Francisco, where he surprised me by asking if I would work with him on his life story. A few months later we began the first of several two- to four-day interview sessions which are the substance of the book. It has been a joy, a privilege and a great challenge to weave Red Callender's stream-of-consciousness recollections into a chrono-logical narrative.

Through Red, I have been fortunate enough to meet some of the wonderful personalities who populate this book, including his gracious wife Mary Lou Callender, Buddy Collette, Bill Douglass and, through telephone interviews, Lee Young, Gerald Wilson, Al Viola and Gerry Wiggins. A heartfelt thanks to them as well as to Art Sato, who broadcast a two-part, three-hour interview with Red and his music on radio station KPFA, Pacifica Radio in Berkeley. Thanks also to Bill Schweitzer, owner of the Record Finder in San Francisco, who simplified my discographical research by offering access to his copy of *Sixty Years of Recorded Jazz*.

There are a few individuals without whose help this book would never have been written and our gratitude towards them is great: Eya Yellin of Oakland for her invaluable advice, assistance and moral support; Gail Cameron for her hospitality and humour; Lillian Dawson and Lynn Cronin. Earl Watkins, Daniel Blanc, John Carter, James Newton, Charles Owens, John Nunez, Sir Charles Thompson, Howard Johnson, Stanley Dance, Miriam Cohen, Richard Simon, Shirley Christy, Sally Shaw, Horace

Tapscott, Marsha Rosser and Rebecca Bruns are among the many friends and relations whose encouraging words and deeds provided a great deal of sustenance. We would also like to thank Mark Kantor for privately screening several films in which Red Callender appeared; Sharron Callender Craig for retyping the discography and the Haight Ashbury Training and Education Project for the use of their dictaphone machine. To Dr Samuel Browne of Los Angeles, our gratitude, for his articulate vision of Central Avenue in the 1920s and '30s which informed some of the prose found in this book. Perhaps the greatest thanks are due to fate, which provided the chance encounter that grew into a beautiful collaboration. And, finally, our special thanks to Chris Parker of Quartet Books for actualizing this book.

Elaine Cohen
25 January 1985, San Francisco

Note: My apologies to the numerous musicians, artists and friends not mentioned. No reflection on your talent or our friendship is intended.

Red Callender

# List of Illustrations

# Foreword

I read this book in manuscript with increasing pleasure. It told me much about my friend, Red Callender, that I did not know, but what was more important was the extent to which it expanded upon the rather scanty existing picture of jazz in Los Angeles.

Having lived in Connecticut for twenty years, I shared the opinion, common in the East, that Los Angeles was a wasteland dominated by the bad taste of the movie industry. Jazz has, however, often thrived under seemingly inimical conditions before, in Chicago and Kansas City, for example. Jazz musicians who made a large part of their livelihood in the Hollywood studios undoubtedly derived satisfaction from good crafts-manship there, but they found their artistic satisfaction in other activities outside or, as it were, underground.

Red Callender's graphic and unflinching story is unique. His association with great artists like Lester Young, Art Tatum and Erroll Garner makes it particularly valuable, and his insights are those of a *real* insider.

Stanley Dance
March 1985, Vista California

# Chronology

| | |
|---|---|
| 1916 | Born 6 March 1916, Haynesville, Virginia. |
| 1919 | Moved with family to Atlantic City, New Jersey. |
| 1928–1932 | Attended Bordentown School, Bordentown, New Jersey. Began musical training under Professor Alexander Valentine on alto horn, then tuba. Studied bass; joined school dance orchestra. Summer vacations spent in Atlantic City playing tuba in Elks Band and touring with Banjo Bernie playing for dances. |
| 1932 | Graduated Bordentown, moved to New York City to join mother, Hattie Callender. Played tuba in Elks Band, NYC. |
| 1933 | Bass playing with Eddie Hunter's Black and White Review in Harrisburg, PA and Cleveland, Ohio. |
| 1934–1935 | Cleveland, Ohio with Jimmy Darrow Band. House bassist at Henry's Furnace. Roderick Ray Band at Gloria Nightclub in Columbus, Ohio. Trans-Canadian and west coast tour with Blanche Thompson and the Brownskin Models. |
| 1936 | Arrival in Los Angeles, joined Buck Clayton's band, played bass with Papa Mutt Carey, C.C. Caldwell, Happy Johnson, C.L. Burke and other bands. Began arranging for choreographer Llewelyn Crawford at Sebastian's Cotton Club and other LA theatres. |
| 1937 | First two original tunes 'Lost Love' and 'Bogo Jo' recorded by Lionel Hampton. Began period of intensive bass study with Herman Rheinshagen and Leon Ziporland. Played Vogue Ballroom with Louis Armstrong and first record date with Armstrong, 'Sunny Side of Street', 'Once in a While'. Married Emma Priestly. Gave bass lessons to Charles Mingus. |

1938–1939    Gigged with Fletcher Smith, Ike Bell, Carl Johnson, Herschel Coleman; sidelined in movies and recorded with Nat Cole, Lee Young, many others.

1940–1943    Member of Lee and Lester Band at Billy Berg's Capri and Trouville Clubs in LA, and Cafe Society Downtown in NYC. Met Jimmy Blanton, Billy Strayhorn, continued composing, arranging and recording. First daughter, Sylvia, born 27 July 1941.

1944–1946    Formed own trio in NYC with Sir Charles Thompson and Louis Gonsales; north-east and cross-country tour. In LA, trio personnel changed to Duke Brooks, Willard McDaniel, Jack La Rue *et al.* on piano, Lucky Enois on guitar. Extensive recording with trio and Red Callender Sextette featuring Maxwell Davis, Harry Edison, Howard McGhee, Jack McVea, Lucky Thompson *et al.* Recorded with Red Norvo Nine.

1946–1947    Appeared in *New Orleans* with Louis Armstrong and Billie Holiday, joined Erroll Garner Trio with Doc West, recorded the Dial sessions with Charlie Parker. Extensive recording with Garner, Dexter Gordon, Wardell Gray, Benny Goodman. First recorded bass solo on Gerald Wilson's 'Dissonance in Blues'.

1948–1950    Toured Hawaiian Islands with Cee Pee Johnson Band. Had own trio in Honolulu and Pastel Sextet with Charles Mingus in San Francisco. Joined Honolulu Symphony and wrote 'Pastel Symphony'. Formed international sextet at Lai Yi Chai's in Honolulu, wrote and arranged for numerous bands.

1950–1953    Returned to LA, joined Vido Musso Band. A & R for Dolphin's of Hollywood, extensive arranging for early rock'n'roll dates. Involved in LA Musicians' Union struggle to amalgamate segregated Locals. Joined Jerry Fielding Band, television appearances with Fielding and with Gerald Wilson Orchestra. Second black in history to be hired for television studio band on 'Life of Riley' show. Divorced Emma Priestly, married Toni Craig. Second daughter Sharron born 1953.

1954–1956    Worked in trio with Art Tatum and Bill Douglass. Recorded with Tatum, Fielding, Buddy Collette, Billie Holiday and own sextette featuring Maxwell Davis, Bumps Meyers, Chico Hamilton *et al.* Continued television and film studio work.

1957–1958    Recorded *Callender Speaks Low*, first album to feature tuba as solo jazz instrument; *Swingin' Suite*, first album of Callender originals; and *The Lowest*, featuring both bass and tuba. First son Craig Callender born 1956, third daughter April born 1958.

1959–1971    First black man to go on staff at NBC in California in 1964. Also staff on CBS. Featured on 'Danny Kaye Show', 'Carol Burnett Show', 'Gunsmoke', 'Dinah Shore Show', 'Joey Bishop Show', 'You Asked for It', also numerous game shows. Performed 1964 Monterey Jazz Festival with Charles Mingus; recorded with Lalo Schifrin, Dizzy Gillespie, Percy Faith *et al* and numerous film scores.

1971–1979    Divorce from Toni Craig, marriage to Mary Lou Lyons. Destruction of new home in Sylmar by 1971 earthquake. Attended First World Tuba Symposium in 1973, featured on 'Flip Wilson Show' 1971–1974, 'Emergency', 'Policewoman'. Toured Europe with Legends of Jazz Louis Armstrong Memorial Tour in 1978, 1979.

1980–present    Recorded with James Newton and the Wind Quintet, toured Europe with Wind Quintet. Founded the Wind College in Los Angeles with John Carter, Charles Owens and James Newton. Duo with Gerald Wiggins. Teaching, television appearances, recording, playing in clubs, composing, arranging.

# PART ONE

# Blessed

A boy of ten stood on the sidewalk of Baltic Avenue in Atlantic City – me. My feet were riveted to the ground; passers-by had to skirt me; I couldn't move. Music was pouring from the entrance of the Blue Kitten Cafe, music so unusual, so fascinating and alive that it flooded my whole world, swept me up in its current. Someone inside the Blue Kitten kept feeding the jukebox, kept punching the button that read 'East St Louis Toodle-oo'. My ears fastened on to the lowest notes and wouldn't let go. So I stood there drenched in Duke Ellington's music until the sky began to darken. When I finally hurried homewards, I told myself, 'This is what I want my life to be.' Then and there I started out to be a musician. I never wanted to be anything else.

Soon the way became clear. The same year my parents took me to the recently rebuilt New Jersey Avenue School, the school I would be attending. The mayor of Atlantic City gave a dull speech, then a band played, the Bordentown School Band. Sitting up on tiers in the auditorium were boys not much older than I with clarinets, trumpets, trombones, alto and bass horns, dressed in brown uniforms decorated with flashy gold trim. Impressive as this was, my mouth dropped open when they began to play. Such wild sounds were coming from that brass! By the end of their concert I was ready to say goodbye to my parents and get on the bus with the band. I pleaded with my parents to let me go to that school. There was only one thought in my mind – to play in that band. Mom and Dad listened, saw my keenness, hunger and passion, and sent for the school brochures. Yes! I could go to Bordentown School, but would have to wait two long years until I turned twelve.

From the time I was big enough to wind up my parents' Victrola, I was entranced by music. At three, it was a violin solo which turned me on. Every day I'd crank up the machine and place the needle on the heavy shellac disc to hear strains of what I later found out was 'Meditations' from Massenet's *Thaïs*. Paul Whiteman's Orchestra was another great favourite, as was Bert Williams, the first black comedian to play in the Ziegfeld Follies. Though his jokes went right by me, I laughed out loud at the strange and funny sounds made by the piccolos, bassoons and oboes. This was when we lived on the farm in Richmond County, Virginia, outside a town called Haynesville where I was born on 6 March 1916.

It was my grandparents' farm and I remember roaming through the orchards to the 'crik', raiding the vegetable garden and wandering into the dark, silent smokehouse where sides of bacon hung from the ceiling. Or, during the canning season, standing in the kitchen where my grandmother, Amanda Tolls Spense who was part Cherokee, stood over immense steaming kettles. She'd shoo me outside to feed the chickens and ducks. Once I watched a colt being born in the barn. Death was a less pleasant mystery. I'll never forget how my grandmother would choose a chicken from the yard and spin it by the neck until its head twisted off. Then the headless bird hopped around in the dust until it mercifully conked out. She'd sear and pluck the feathers, cook it and serve it for dinner.

My father, George Callender Sr, worked at the garage in Haynesville which he owned with a neighbour, a white man called Will Oliver. People were just people in those days; there was no black, no white. Despite the fact that Virginia was considered part of the South, my family experienced little racial prejudice there. People treated each other gently in those days, with respect.

My father was born in Barbados. He was a descendant of one of five Callender brothers who left Scotland in the eighteenth century and settled in the Caribbean. These adventurous Callender brothers intermarried with all the island women – Ashanti, Yoruba, white and mulatto women – creating a mongrel mixture which accounts for my red hair, freckles and my light-brown eyes with purple rings. Slavery was abolished in Barbados a hundred years before it ended in the United States. The British, who colonized the island, made education universal and compulsory. My grandfather was a skilled tradesman, a carriage-maker and carpenter. He and my father came to blows during an argument when my father was nineteen. Since there was only one way to leave an island then, my father caught a ship out of Bridgetown, destination Panama. When he met my mother in Boston, he was a merchant seaman. Several years passed before I discovered his true origins because his reminiscences had more to do with Panama than Barbados. He spoke fluent Spanish and was a boss cook, chief chef on the merchant ships.

When I was still a wee baby, my parents tried living in Boston. Their apartment had a separate room for me, but I'd raise holy hell when they left me alone, shaking the sides of my crib and yelling until they took me out of there. When they found out someone had been murdered in that room, they decided to go back to Virginia to live with my mother's folks on the farm. They were a very loving couple as I was growing up and used to sing together in the evenings. My father had a nice baritone voice and told me that he also played C melody saxophone, though I never once heard him play. My mother, Hattie, had a guitar, played a little, took lessons, but it was her brother, Uncle Elijah, who lived with us, who really played the guitar. When his day's work was done, he stretched out his long legs on the farmhouse porch steps and played the blues, the first blues I ever heard. With his huge hands strumming the guitar, he'd sit there making up verse after verse of the blues. Sometimes the sad blues, sometimes the happy blues. Whatever he happened to feel at the moment was what he'd play.

Uncle Lee lived on the farm too. He was really my cousin, though the same age as Elijah, so they were both 'Uncle' to me. Uncle Lee and Uncle Laj would get drunk and mess with my mother by stealing her stockings to put on their big calloused feet. Outraged by this, I'd try to scold them, but they just laughed. All my folks were very kind people who knew how to enjoy life. I was the apple of my grandmother's eye even though she was the one who'd grab a switch from a convenient bush if I needed to learn a lesson. And I did too – almost burned the barn down once, tied firecrackers to my dog's tail. To this day my mother cannot be convinced I actually did these things – or anything wrong. She scoffs and says, 'Why, you never did anything of the kind!'

My folks used to tease me, saying, 'He's happy as long as his stomach is full.' My grandparents ran a small grocery store out by the road. If, during the summer, an ice delivery failed to come, they'd let me run amok in the ice cream and Coca-Cola. Cornflakes were my favourite; my father always brought them in from town for me. One day when he drove up in his Model T, I jumped on the running-board of the car, slipped, fell off and scared everybody half to death. They thought I'd fallen under the car, but I'd only fallen in the dirt and cut my lip. That's been my Achilles heel; another time I fell and my two front teeth went all the way through my bottom lip. As soon as I grew old enough to shave, a small goatee disguised the spot.

When I was about four years old, my grandfather Edmond Spence, who was well into his eighties, decided it was time to retire from the farm. My Aunt Annie was living in Atlantic City, New Jersey, and my parents went there to investigate the possibilities. Soon my parents, grandparents and I were living at 1007 Baltic Avenue, Atlantic City. Uncle Lee and Uncle Laj moved in with Aunt Annie. Before leaving the farm, I sold my toys to the neighbours' kids for three cents. That was a big deal then. It helped compensate for leaving the first paradise I ever knew.

Atlantic City was a different world. Grandpa was so disoriented by the move he insisted on lifting the globes from the gas lamps and blowing out the flame. That was fine when we used kerosene on the farm, but here we had gas jets in the wall. Everyone had to keep an eagle eye on him to save the family from asphyxiation.

Our first Christmas in Atlantic City my parents bought me a shining new orange scooter. Gleefully I hopped right on it, rode all the way to New Hampshire Avenue. There, at the corner, a voice challenged me: 'Nigger! What you doing with that new scooter?'

There was a group of boys crowding in on me, trying to grab the scooter, jeering, pointing, yelling in hateful, degrading voices. Somehow I managed to snatch my prize from them and escape. It hurt and confused me, this mockery and ridicule. We kids called each other 'nigger', but always in a playful way. I didn't understand it, couldn't fathom how people could be so mean.

A few years later I learned what the comedian Bert Williams said when asked if he resented being black.

'No,' he answered, 'not really. It's just inconvenient at times.'

When I first went to school, all the public schools in the State of New Jersey were integrated. Then a group of black doctors campaigned to get separate schools for blacks, which unfortunately was granted. I skipped kindergarten and entered the first grade at age five. That first day at school was the loneliest day of my life.

My first musical instruction was given to me in the fifth grade by Miss Ghoul, who carried a long pointer with her at all times. She had a pinched face, her hair in a topknot and wore black stockings, altogether like a stereotype in the movies. I was terrified of her. She'd march you up to the piano, strike a note. 'Sing what I play, boy,' she'd command, wielding her pointer. If you missed the note, you'd get it . . . WHACK . . . right across the palm with that pointer. That's how we were taught ear training, singing and solfeggio and – needless to say – we all learned quickly.

As intimidating as Miss Ghoul was, she never spoiled my dream of becoming a musician. I had a tin drum which I called 'my band' and in the evenings I curled up with it under my parents' Majestic radio and listened to broadcasts of Duke Ellington from the Kentucky Club. That was Duke's 'jungle period'. I was thrilled with what Bubber Miley was doing with his plunger mute, though it was the low sounds which appealed to me the most. Perhaps I was born with a hearing spectrum lower than someone who would naturally gravitate to violin or flute. I heard the high notes, but felt no urge to reproduce them. I was too in love with low sounds. The Mills Brothers had started their live broadcasts and I felt a real affinity for John Mills who sang bass. The Paul Whiteman Orchestra was also featured on broadcasts. Whiteman had two basses and a tuba in his band. He'd position the basses on either side of the stage, which was great for publicity photos, but ridiculous as far as sound is concerned. To play well together, basses must be in close proximity for intonation and tempo. Whiteman, who never played a lick of jazz in his life, was being celebrated as the 'King of Jazz'. Jazz or no, I enjoyed listening to his band. Music was just music. All the labels and criteria cooked up by critics and publicists made no difference to me. I was going to be a musician, able to play it all.

During the 1920s you could hear radio broadcasts from as far away as Chicago and Kansas City. I soaked up Earl Hines, the Coon–Sanders band, the Isham Jones Orchestra. I'd sit at the dinner table humming, keeping time by drumming my fingers on the tabletop until my mother reprimanded me. Oh, I'd stop -- out loud that is – but inside, the rhythms and tones continued as if they had a life of their own. Even in church, which my mother made sure I attended every Sunday, it was only when the Baptist choir sang hymns like 'Rock of Ages' or the 'Negro National Anthem' that I'd wake up and try to find a note in the harmony.

My dad belonged to the Methodist Church, but attended the racetrack far more faithfully. When we moved to Atlantic City he got a good job as a chef at Saul's Restaurant. Whenever I was hungry I'd slip on down to Saul's to get something to eat. One of my dad's prize-winning stunts was to bone a chicken so that the bird would stand upright on the platter as if its skeleton were still intact. Then he'd slice through it like butter. He did quite well financially in Atlantic City, so well that my mother was able to buy him a new Oldsmobile for his birthday when I was eleven.

Momma had training as a nurse, but during those first years in New Jersey she stayed at home where her services were needed. My grandfather had become ill, and Momma took care of him until the end. A year later almost to the day, my grandmother followed him. Losing them was about the only sadness I experienced in my childhood. I was blessed. Life was full of love from parents, grandparents and relatives. Francis Matthews, a cousin on my mother's side who later played baseball with the Newark Eagles, was born the same year as I. Marcus Callender, a cousin on my father's side, was much younger, but having Francis and Marcus nearby was the closest thing to having brothers. Both of their fathers had also been born in Barbados. Marcus shared my interest in music and later became a bandleader and warrant officer in the army. Some of my schoolfriends from those days became lifelong friends, like the artist Cal Bailey. I remember how as kids we used to watch the airshows and barnstormers over Atlantic City. Together we breathlessly followed Lindberg's miraculous thirty-six-hour flight over the Atlantic. We'd eaves-drop on my Uncle Lee and Uncle Laj when they got to talking about smoking hemp or tea. In our innocence of these matters, we'd sneak Orange Pekoe or Salada tea from the cupboard, roll it up, thinking we were smoking 'tea' like my uncles did.

There were no laws about marijuana then; nobody thought much about its use, even in public places. 'Viper's pads' were the thing. Someone would offer their house as a place to get high and lie around. No booze was allowed. There was a popular saying then: 'Whiskey will turn you around, whiskey will bring you down . . .' Whiskey-drinkers had a bad reputation for stumbling all over your feet. But a viper? A viper was cool! Many popular songs on the radio referred to marijuana. One of Louis Armstrong's first hits contained the line: 'I'll be standing on the corner high when they bring your body by . . .'; Don Redman's theme song on the radio was 'Chant of the Weed' and Stuff Smith had a big hit called 'The Viper': 'Dream about a reefer five foot long, the sky is high and so am I . . .' Reefer, hemp, tea, weed or bush – that was the lingo. The terms pot and grass weren't used until the 1940s and 1950s.

Cab Calloway's 'Minnie the Moocher' was about a cocaine user:

> Let me tell you a story 'bout Minnie the Moocher
> She was a lowdown hootchie-cootcher
> She met a guy in Chinatown
> Who taught her how to kick the gong around . . .

The original Coca-Cola soft drink actually contained cocaine. No wonder it made me sick when I was allowed to gorge on it back in Virginia – that cured me of drinking Coca-Cola for the rest of my life. Heroin and morphine were standard ingredients in cough medicine for children. It's interesting to note that the word 'heroin' was originally copyrighted by the Bayer Aspirin Company many years ago. It was said that hemp could be easily purchased at tobacconists' shops in New York City. After Prohibition was repealed, all these drugs became illegal. Liquor, once again, became the acceptable vice.

Smoking Salada tea didn't harm me, but I nearly lost my life by drowning. The beaches in Atlantic City had a wicked undertow. Our little gang of kids was always egging someone on to tempt the fates. One of us would say, 'Hey – you're a sissy if you can't swim from the end of the steel pier back to the beach.' No one dared be considered a sissy, so in we jumped, little fools that we were. One day I practised this swim by myself, got caught in the undertow and barely made it back to shore. Not long afterwards, Randolph Snowden, another red-headed kid who played saxophone, was drowned there.

We used to go to the circus. Everyone was getting their initials tattooed on their arms, so I did it too. When I went home to get more money to have a wreath put around the initials, my uncles said, 'Boy, you better never do anything wrong because they'll always be able to identify you.' This was before fingerprinting was common. Knowing I was easily recognizable probably kept me from a life of crime. How many brown kids have you seen with freckles, flaming red hair and a tattoo? I didn't get the wreath.

Everything began to shape up; I was going to Bordentown. My folks had managed to scrape up the heavy forty dollars a month for tuition and had me measured for uniforms. The summer before going away, I came across a book at home entitled *The Art of Selfishness*. It wasn't about being stingy, rather about cultivating patience, learning what you want to do in life and going after it, no holds barred. From this book I understood that if you learn your craft well, there'll always be a place for you no matter where or who you are or what the competition. It gave me enormous confidence to know this, and it's proved itself true. You can find great bass players in every nook and cranny in the world, but there's always been a spot somewhere for me to play.

Finally, September 1928 arrived. My parents packed me and my uniforms into the car and we drove up to northern New Jersey, about nineteen miles from Trenton, to Bordentown. Nervous and excited, I walked through the door of the main building of Bordentown School to register. That was the door which opened all the doors I've walked through my whole life.

Professor Alexander Valentine at Bordentown School was the teacher who awakened me to the possibilities in the world of music. Bordentown was lucky to have him. He was absolutely brilliant and could write music like most people write a letter. Valentine was a veteran of Jim Europe's band, the first all-black band to tour the continent during World War I. He wasn't much taller than an upright piano and had such thick chops you'd wonder how he made those beautiful sounds stream from his trombone and trumpet. For four years I was lucky enough to be in the presence of this unknown genius.

Of course Bordentown wasn't primarily a music school. Rather, it was a heavy-duty military school, with ROTC training, rifle drills, marching and strict discipline supervised by Colonel Watson, a regular army martinet. Demerits were passed around like candy and it only took three demerits to get sent home. At one point I climbed the ranks to top sergeant, had my own room in the dormitory, all the little privileges of rank. Then I was caught smoking a cigarette. They busted me back to private so fast I could hardly catch my breath. After that I was cool.

Not everyone was in the music department. Valentine wouldn't fool with you if you didn't have talent. Everyone had a chance to join the band, but if you weren't adaptable or didn't show talent – you were out. I was one of the lucky ones because Professor Valentine saw something in me and took me under his wing.

First he gave me an alto horn, often called a peck horn. The alto horn is closest in sound to a french horn, but it's built in E flat, fingered with the right hand and alto saxophone parts can be played on it. Within a few weeks I learned enough alto horn to play in the band, third or fourth alto chair. When Pinkie Morris, the first alto horn player, moved over to tuba, I was moved up to first alto. Still, my natural affinity was for tuba, or bass horn as we called it then. Valentine saw my heart's desire and soon he gave me the opportunity.

Each morning for three hours all students in the music programme studied music theory, harmony, composition and had band practice. Afternoons were for academic classes. I was so in love with the music that I developed the habit of getting up at 4 a.m. every morning to practise for a few hours before beginning the daily routine. That's how progress was made. The band played light classics like Rossini's 'Semiramidi', Ravel's 'Bolero' Tchaikovsky's 'March Slav'. Professor Valentine challenged me right away by giving me a tuba solo from 'Barbarossa', a rather difficult piece of music. I protested: 'This is written for E flat horn, I can't . . .'

'Hey, little round-head boy, I know you can play it. Just try We begin like this . . .'

With Valentine's help I mastered 'Barbarossa' and played my first solo with the Bordentown School Band. I was scared at first, but with every concert my confidence grew, as did my love of performing and touring all over New Jersey in our specially outfitted bus.

Everything I've pursued in my later life began that first year at school. On Saturdays all the kids would get passes to walk down the highway to White Hill, a small nearby settlement which had a soda fountain that served great banana splits. One day I got to talking with a classmate, Dwight Boone, a day student who lived just down the road from Bordentown School. He was telling me about a contrabass that was just standing around in a closet at his house. 'Oh, yeah?' I said. It wasn't long before Dwight Boone was lugging that bass down the road to the school. I latched on to it fast – for fifteen dollars. Dwight pointed out the strings to me, Professor Valentine gave me an instruction booklet. Since I'd been playing the tuba, the bass wasn't any great mystery to me. Both instruments have relatively the same range. The first thing I learned was the popular hit 'Careless Love', which could be played all in the first position, key of F.

The day I joined the dance orchestra with my bass and tuba, my whole career began. I had tried playing basketball, but never was very good. My tongue would be hanging out – if I made a basket it was pure luck. I tried track, too. Then football, mainly to impress girls with the big shoulder pads. During the first scrimmage someone stepped on my finger. Valentine gave me the ultimatum: football or music. There was hardly a choice. I never did learn to dance very well, but up there on the bandstand, I felt at home.

All that was necessary to play the popular dance tunes were the first two positions. A few years elapsed before I studied the instrument to learn the first six positions. My fingers were so sore, I kept them wrapped in tape. Bass strings were still being made of gut then and to play loud and strong enough to be heard over the drums required a toughness that I had to develop. Strength in the fingers, especially the fourth finger of the left hand, took years to build. Bass drums and press rolls were then the musical fashion; it was easy for a bass player to be swallowed. If I was going to play the instrument I didn't want all my efforts to be drowned out by the drummer.

Soon I had a nickname, 'Indispensable Red'. 'Reds' is what the kids always called me in Atlantic City; at Bordentown the 's' was dropped. Indispensable was all about being the first one to show up for class, rehearsal, one hundred per cent punctual, ready, eager to learn. Improvising didn't come as easily as I thought it might. Valentine had trained me to be a reader, so I had to analyse each tune, investigate its structure to discover the inner workings. My ear was good, but improvisation takes knowledge as well as freedom.

A Mrs Whetsol was one of my academic teachers. One day she asked me, 'Ever hear of my son, Arthur Whetsol? He plays trumpet with Duke Ellington's band.' At that time I wasn't aware of Artie Whetsol. Her question made me pay attention to each band member, which is the only way to listen to Duke's band because Duke wrote for the individuals. Duke made them all stars; each had his speciality: Bubber Miley, the plunger mute king on trumpet; Lawrence Brown who joined the band when I was at Bordentown. Even though Brown had been featured with Les Hite, with Duke he became a sensation on the trombone. Duke knew exactly how to bring out the best in his men. Tricky Sam Nanton, a trombone plunger expert; Juan Tizol on valve trombone – individually they were distinct, yet their blending in ensemble passages was miraculous. In the reed section: Johnny Hodges, without peer; Otto Hardwicke playing first, the top voice in the chord; Barney Bigard on clarinet and tenor and Harry Carney on baritone, whom you could hear no matter how loud the band played. In the rhythm section, fabulous Sonny Greer on drums, Freddy Guy on guitar and the man who first made me aware of the bass – Wellman Braud from New Orleans. It gave me great satisfaction to recognize each man's sound on the radio broadcasts.

With the knowledge I'd gleaned from Valentine, I was inspired to try my hand at writing arrangements. I had intended to become a classical musician, a thorough musician. I didn't think it was possible to play in the innovative style of the musicians in Duke Ellington's band. But as my comprehension of harmony increased, some of the mystery vanished and I could see it was possible after all.

During my third year at Bordentown, I received an important letter from my parents explaining that they were going to separate. Being a fairly wise kid, I had an inkling something along those lines might happen. The news didn't tear me up too much because I loved each of them very much. Dad was a man who loved racehorses and women, and scored pretty well with both. He bet on tracks all over the country, was a real handicapper, knew all the details. He dressed sharp, was very handsome, the kind of dude who attracted women – and he didn't resist. Momma was an outstanding beauty, but conservative, never smoked or drank, a real homebody. She believed in God's power to manage everything. My father was more of a realist and far more gregarious than Momma. He enjoyed hanging out with the guys, playing poker, coon-can, whist, gin, all the games. He took a taste of liquor now and then, used to keep a case of Canadian Club under the bed. They both loved life and each other, but their means of expression were miles apart. I confided in my friend Bob Bowers, who later became a psychiatrist.

After they separated they each moved to New York City. The Depression had hit hard by 1930. Momma found a job as a housekeeper for Sam Jaffe, the actor who played Krinolin in the Broadway play of *Grand Hotel*. Jaffe saw to it that Momma and I got box seats for the performance. My dad, who had always been a *Little Caesar* fan, went to work for Edward G. Robinson as his cook. Momma and Dad tried getting back together again, tried to make it work. He moved in with her, then out again. To me it seemed he was slightly ashamed of his failure in the marriage, his weakness for other women. Yet as far as I was concerned, it didn't matter. By then I had my music and nothing could make me feel insecure.

Summers, I'd return to Atlantic City and live at Aunt Annie's house. Jazz was always playing on her record-player, Louis Armstrong and His Hot Five, Ethel Waters, all the latest hits. My first heartbreak was experienced there; I fell head over heels in love with a young lady friend of my aunt. Her gorgeous black eyes enchanted me, but it was unintentional on her part. Those eyes were for no one but Mr Benny Carter, who was about nineteen or twenty then, and just had his first success with 'Blues in My Heart'. At least I can thank that young lady for turning me on to a great musician.

The summers at Aunt Annie's house were busy. She lived next door to a baseball park where Josh Gibson, Satchell Page and other future Black Hall of Fame baseball players used to play ball while I watched. I once held down a job as a dishwasher in a restaurant for two weeks and spent the whole time listening to the cook bellow 'Carolina Moon' in a raspy voice. My main activity, however, was playing tuba in the Elks Band. Atlantic City was a big hoopla town, conventions, parades, plenty of activity for a marching band, which was what the Elks Band was. Word must have got out about a kid playing tuba in the band because Banjo Bernie found me. He just appeared one day and asked if I'd like to do a little travelling with his band playing the tuba. That was my first real gig at thirteen, riding up and down the Jersey Shore in Banjo Bernie's raggedy old bus, playing for small-town dances.

Duke Ellington knew Banjo Bernie; they were in the same age bracket. Banjo was a real con man. Very neat and clean in appearance, stocky build, moustache. He'd gather young musicians from all over the state to play in his band and pay them very little. Banjo was a taskmaster; you had to play good to stay with him, he was swinging on banjo and guitar. He was also a skirt-lifter *par excellence*. I mean Banjo Bernie would ball anything that wore a dress. Being a kid, a woman of forty looked ancient to me. I was aghast at how Banjo Bernie would snatch these old broads and up-away with them, even while the band was playing.

Banjo introduced me to nightclub life and I'll forever be grateful to him. The band played a speakeasy at the corner of Broad and Lombard in Philadelphia. One of those places where you say, 'Joe sent me', before they let you inside. This particular place was called the Golden Dawn. I loved it immediately – being around all that sophisticated smoking and drinking, those low blue lights, those smooth brown legs, the glitter and laughter and dancing. This was the life I wanted to be involved in always, or so I thought then.

The band played tunes like 'Christmas Night in Harlem', 'Careless Love', arrangements by Jimmy Dale, Archie Blyer. Banjo used to write some himself when he wasn't out chasing skirts. He was an excellent musician, just a Fagin-type guy. All summer long he'd tell us he never made any money, lay a little change on us, give us a meal ticket and take care of our rooms.

That was it, but he gave me a chance to see the road, to see how life was being lived, gave me that glimpse of what was ahead.

After Labor Day, I'd be packed, eager to get back to school. In spite of the rugged discipline, I loved it. 'Old Ironsides' is what everybody called the school, after the battleship USS *Constitution* anchored in the Delaware River below. Once I knew the ropes, Old Ironsides and I got along fine. The days of music, the pre-dawn hours of practising, the knowledge and wisdom of Professor Valentine – all this was ingrained in me from the first week until the day I graduated from Bordentown School. Total immersion in music was total joy.


Since I had never intended to be anything but a musician, the idea of being a busboy didn't appeal to me. Jobs were scarce during the early 1930s; people stood in breadlines, souplines, took handouts, anything to keep from starving. Times were grim, yet I was fortunate. I never went hungry. I even got to witness how the rich folks lived when I accompanied my mother to a party she was catering at George Gershwin's apartment. His place was all done up in white: walls, furniture, rugs, a fabulous white grand piano. That's how the composer of 'I Got Rhythm' lived.

Of practical experience other than music, I had little. When I was a kid I sold papers, mainly because I liked to scream: 'GET YOUR *EVENING NEWS*, READ ALL ABOUT IT', like the other kids. Never made a penny's profit. I tried parking cars, lasted only a day at that. But I had an ace in the hole, or so I thought. Alexander Valentine was a friend of W.C. Handy and had written me a letter of introduction to him. I was proficient at copying music – even back then being a copyist was a veritable profession. So I presented myself in Handy's office at 1619 Broadway in the Brill Building. Handy himself received me. He was a bald, stocky man, ensconced behind a big oak desk. He still had his sight then, was very cordial, inquired after Alexander's health. After he read the note he sat silently for a moment. Clearly I was bubbling with enthusiasm and hope.

Handy let me down easy. 'Son,' he said, 'I've got to tell you that this office is just a front to get me out of the house. I've been living off the "St Louis Blues" for the past twenty years . . .'

So much for my career as a copyist!

New York City was a fascinating place to be in the early 1930s. You could ride the subway all day for the same nickel, before the A train got going, the old inter-borough rapid transit. My friends and I would get up by the engineer's box and lean on the wind, get off at 42nd Street, cross over the tracks, ride back up to Harlem. On Sunday afternoons when I was supposedly going to church, I'd go instead to the Apollo Theatre when it was still a burlesque house, and sit in the balcony watching the dancers swinging their tassels. I went to see a Maurice Chevalier picture filmed in Paris, the picture where he sings, 'Louise . . . and the birds and the bees'. New York had a few sidewalk cafes like the ones in Paris. That's where I learned to drink black coffee. I'd sit there by myself, order a black coffee and a vanilla ice cream and watch the parade go by. I played stickball with my friends in the street; we'd ride our bicycles through Central Park, stopping to watch political speeches, preachers, prostitutes, crap games, chess games, bocci ball, swindlers hooking suckers into shell games – the old hand-is-faster-than-the-eye routine. Our favourite thing was standing in front of the Rhythm Club on 7th Avenue in Harlem where all the great musicians congregated. Chu Berry, Pops Foster, Jimmie Lunceford, Coleman Hawkins, Fletcher Henderson, Cab Calloway, all the famous cats. Once in a while Chick Webb would notice me and say, 'Hi kid, nice day . . .' or something like that. The thrill lasted for hours.

Being tall for my age, getting into the clubs was no problem since I never asked for a drink. When I first saw Duke Ellington's band in person, I planted myself directly in front of Wellman Braud, Duke's bassist, really listening to every note. All the music was for dancing. It was a beautiful sight to watch the people swirling around on the dance floor, but my eyes rarely drifted from my idols on the bandstand. I frequented the Savoy Ballroom – the 'Home of Happy Feet' and saw such greats as Chick Webb, Benny Carter, Don Redman, Claude Hopkins, Baron Lee's Blue Rhythm Band, McKinney's Cotton Pickers, Cab Calloway, Jimmie Lunceford, Erskine Hawkins, Fletcher Henderson, as well as the Santa Domingans, a Latin band that was really swinging – all the bands I'd heard on the radio and more. In person was much better, truly inspiring.

The name of Claude Hopkins's bass player escapes me, but I'm sure I borrowed something from him. He played high up on the neck of the bass, which was very unusual for the times. Most bassists were stuck lower down in the first two or three positions. Often bassists just made sounds, the lower the better, and they slapped the bass. That's something I've always refused to do and have lost more than one gig because of it. Nothing musical about it, it hurts your hand – and where was the sound?

Tuba players were still plentiful in the bands. The Coon–Sanders Band featured their marvellous tuba player as did Isham Jones. I was playing tuba then in the Elks Lodge Band on 137th Street and wanted nothing more than to join one of these great dance bands. Not one leader was ready for me yet. By the time they got ready for me, I was going in another direction.

My mother often used the phrase 'divine order' to explain how faith works in this world. Others may call it luck, some call it destiny. I prefer to call it positive thinking. Positive thinking is the key that opens doors. Positive thought produces positive action, positive responses. If you dwell on the negative, you're sure enough going to reap negative consequences. Things rarely work out the way you think they might, but they do work out. Scatman Crothers and I always say to each other, 'Keep your eye on the sparrow, keep marching, one foot at a time.'

It was my mother's trust in the divine order of things, her profound faith that God would manage everything, that led to my first experiences in the Midwest. Benny Booker, a friend who was playing bass in Eddie Hunter's Black and White Review Band, wasn't allowed to go on the road with the show. His dad put his foot down and told him to stay right in New York City. So I was offered the job. My mother's reply when I asked her permission to accept?

'Why yes, God will take care of you.'

It was 1933 or '34; it was the dead of winter. Our broken-down bus chugged across the snowy mountains of Pennsylvania headed for a one-night stand in Harrisburg, PA. The actors, dancers, singers, comedians and musicians on the bus clowned and gambled their way through the blizzard. When we reached Harrisburg, we played to an empty house. Hardly anyone was willing to brave the snowstorm for our novel form of entertainment. The Black and White Review was really two shows in one, two segregated contingents performing separate acts, both accompanied by an all-black band. This was my first taste of the vaudeville circuit and it made me hungry for more. Nothing dismayed me, not even the complete collapse of the bus on the road between Harrisburg and Cleveland. By the time we pulled into Cleveland, the show for that night had been cancelled. We lasted there a week at best. Then, Eddie Hunter melted into thin air with the bread. To put it mildly, we were stranded.

No one panicked. People were very kind to us, let us stay on in the rooming house on 'credit'. My dad made a quick run from New York to Cleveland and back again to lay some cash on me. I remained where I was and fed the band. Food was cheap; you could get a meal for fifteen cents. Sunday dinners, which included three or four vegetables, meat, salad, dessert, cost only thirty-five cents. With the money my father gave me, we bought ham hocks and a sack of beans. Our trombone player had a talent for making cornbread as well as for producing good weed to smoke. What great meals we shared . . . food has rarely tasted so delicious! After a few weeks of this lifestyle, I caught a Greyhound bus back to New York City.

Not quite a year later I was in Cleveland again, this time playing in Jimmy Darrow's big band. Darrow was a high-note trumpet player without a lot of business sense. We were all just youngsters starting out, so when I was offered the job of playing bass in the house band at Henry's Furnace, I grabbed it. The Furnace was located inside the Majestic Hotel, the main hotel in the black neighbourhood, comparable to the Theresa Hotel in Harlem. The management gave us rooms there, paid us a salary and we did pretty well on tips. The dancers in the show made good tips as well, only they had to dance up to the tables and pick up the dollars between their legs. The hours were something else – from nine or ten in the evening to nine or ten the next morning, whenever the last person went home. We didn't care, we could sleep all day. It didn't matter to us at all. Fletcher Henderson's band was in town with Pops Foster on bass, Roy Eldridge on trumpet, Coleman Hawkins on tenor saxophone. Lonny Simmons, the great guitar player, was in town, too. They all came in to Henry's Furnace to jam when their gigs were over, after all the paying customers went home. I became a Coleman Hawkins fan right there on the spot, still am, always will be. Never had I heard anything like that before. When I was still in New York we used to hover around his big Chrysler parked near his apartment on St Nicholas Terrace. His horn and music would be lying on the back seat and no one ever touched it. Try that now . . .! There I was, still a kid, sitting two feet away from him night after night, two feet away from the Master, hanging on to every note, really carried away.

Roy Eldridge was about nineteen then; he and I struck up a friendship. We wore long overcoats that dragged along the ground, but never wore a hat. That was considered 'sissified'. Roy carried his trumpet in a case slung over his shoulder by a strap, and I'd trail along with him all over town. He was a bundle of energy, effervescent, entirely wrapped up in music. Everyone called him 'Little Jazz'. Louis Armstrong reigned as the King of Jazz, but as far as trumpet players went, Roy was *it* then. No one played as high or fast as Roy. No one, that is, until Dizzy Gillespie found himself and dethroned Roy as king.

Roy was always ready to go into a club and blow everybody down, though his ego never got out of proportion. Roy was the person who took me to Mamie Louise's Chicken Shack to see Harry Edison. 'This is one cat you've got to hear,' he told me.

Harry Edison was playing in the band of another great trumpet stylist, Chester Clark. Neither player was any competition for Roy, they each had distinct styles. Harry Edison's style was fully developed even at age eighteen. It wasn't until he went with Basie and Lester Young named him 'Sweets' that the world got to hear what I heard at Mamie Louise's. Chester Clark's band also had a tuba player named Slim Waters who really inspired me. He played tuba like a big trumpet. Since being at Bordentown, I'd been playing melodies like 'Stardust' on the tuba, thinking melodically, why not? Just because the tuba was used primarily in the rhythm section didn't affect my notion of the instrument's possibilities. Hearing Slim Waters affirmed everything I'd been thinking, and took it in new directions.

Roy Eldridge also took me to Jimmy Owens's Club, right down the street from the Majestic Hotel. That's where Art Tatum, who was twenty-three then, was playing every night, upstairs at Jimmy Owens's. Lanny Scott and a whole raft of excellent piano players used to come by there, trying to cut Tatum. None of these pianists had the least fear of Art; they'd try over and over again to wipe him out. They never gave up trying. Apparently, they had no idea of Tatum's true stature; to them he was just hometown.

'Sweets' told me the story about Teddy Wilson being in Cleveland during this period, hanging out with Coleman Hawkins. Wilson asked Hawk if he had ever heard of a piano player named Art Tatum. Teddy was obviously cocky in those days and he said to Hawk, 'I think I'll go over to Jimmy Owens's and wipe him out.'

'I wouldn't do that if I were you,' Hawk warned, 'I think you'd better go listen.'

There was nothing vicious about these cutting sessions. They used to call it ass-cutting, before the term jamming came into use. To cut meant to outplay, and all this competitive playing resulted in much wonderful music. During my free time, I'd take my tuba over to Jimmy Owens's to sit in with Tatum. I'd go anywhere and everywhere there was music to play until the last person went home. Often I couldn't believe my ears, especially Art Tatum on 'Tiger Rag'. His hands were a blur. I just couldn't believe what I was hearing and seeing.

We dressed sharp in those days. Now that I was one of the musicians I had to live up to the image. Believe me, when you're poor you pay far more attention to how you're dressed than when you've made it. On my salary of nine or ten bucks a week, I could make a down payment and have a suit tailor-made for only $14.95 at Woolmouth's, a chain store. Unbelievable. Once I messed up a terrific blue suit when I got loaded on some booze called 'white lightning'. All I remember is waking up with my head hanging in the commode. White lightning was fierce – far worse than the home brew I was once served at a party at (of all places!) Miss Ghoul's house in Atlantic City. White lightning would really knock you on your ass. So that was my first drink . . . but it wasn't my last. I was a shy guy with the ladies and I used to find that having a drink would loosen my tongue.

Jimmy Darrow came on the scene again with a new band that had an engagement in the thriving city of Mansefield, Ohio. Adventure, travel – I was easily tempted. Predictably, the money got scarce with Darrow in Mansefield, but I had made friends with the piano player, Logan 'Lord' Hawkins, whose home town was Columbus, Ohio – a short bus ride away. Logan got us work in a joint on the outskirts of Columbus. It wasn't too glamorous but I was glad to be working.

The words of Professor Valentine kept coming back to me while we were up there playing for sparse houses. He'd said: 'It doesn't matter where you're playing – even if there's no one in the house, there might be someone listening right on the other side of the door.' Every night before I went to work I remembered that. When I got to work, I made sure to give it my best effort.

Logan had connections in Columbus so we weren't scuffling for long. Roderick Ray, a drummer and vibraphonist, had a band playing the Gloria Nightclub, a big fancy roadhouse owned by Italians. Ray hired both Logan and me to join the three saxophones and three trumpets. I stayed with Roderick Ray almost a year. We were a very commercial little band, playing all the latest tunes like 'A Quarter to Nine' and 'With Every Breath I Take'. All the stock arrangements. When we did 'Two Cigarettes in the Dark', they'd extinguish the lights. All the band members lit matches before the lyric, 'gone is the flame and the spark', then we'd dramatically blow them out. Tricks like that went over big. I enjoyed working there immensely even though the owners only allowed blacks on the bandstand, never in the audience.

Logan's home in Columbus was on Long Street and I rented a room nearby on Garfield. Whiskey had just become legalized. After work we hung out together in all the after-hours spots, jamming and drinking 'shorties' – booze served in cream pitchers with a set-up of ice and water. On the way home we'd each get a half-pint of whiskey to fortify ourselves against the cold, stand on the sidewalk, drink the half-pint down in one swallow and go to bed, zonked. That might kill me if I tried it now – terrible stuff, that bourbon. It was so cold in Columbus, Ohio, we'd do anything to keep warm.

There was a piano in the rooming-house that pulled me like a magnet. Professor Valentine had taught me about the keyboard, all the elements of harmony. Here was the chance I'd been waiting for – time to sit down at the piano to compose. My first effort was called 'Unfinished Dream', very influenced by Don Redman's use of augmented and major 7 chords:

One of the main reasons I wanted to become a proficient writer was to disprove the then popular myth that bass players and drummers didn't know anything about music. It altered in time, but some people thought the rhythm section was pretty ignorant – musically, that is. I was determined to set them straight.

My love life in Columbus had become complicated. The girl who had ensnared my heart was married. Not that I knew she was married! I had always been very choicy about girls as Mr Ray, my gym instructor, had drummed the dangers of VD into all of our heads. 'Keep it in your pants, boy, unless you know for sure . . .' that sort of thing. I knew she was *clean*, yet it never occurred to me she might be *married*. One night this lovely Mrs was in my room; we were having a good time until we heard a loud, insistent knocking on the downstairs door. She started getting nervous. 'Don't worry,' I told her, 'I haven't done anything illegal.'

Then there were voices: my landlady's voice, firm and persuasive, and the enraged threats of a man.

'Now don't you wave that gun at me,' said the landlady. 'You put that gun away. There's no one here by that description. You came to the wrong place, Mister . . .'

'I'll kill that bitch who calls herself my wife! I'm gon' kill him too!'

'I told you there's no one here who looks like that . . . Wait . . . across the street about an hour ago I saw a strange woman go into that house, yes, that yellow house over there . . .'

We heard the door shut and the safety bolt being drawn.

Bless that landlady! I could have been a has-been in a cold grave in Columbus. Fortune stayed in my corner because the next day I received a telegram from Blanche Thompson in Minneapolis, asking me to join her show, the Brownskin Models, at thirty dollars a week plus hotel. That was good bread for then and the show was heading to California. How Blanche Thompson ever heard of me I'll never know, but at that point I wasn't asking questions, just thanking my lucky stars. I checked with Roderick Ray, who agreed to such short notice, wired back YES, packed up my stuff, went to the Greyhound station. Within a few hours, me and my bass were on our way to Minneapolis to join the Brownskin Models.

From Minneapolis the Brownskin Models played East Grand Forks, North Dakota. Vaudeville was still king; this was years before television. A vaudeville troupe could travel across the country doing the same show for a year, delighting small-town audiences, linking them to the glamour of the big cities of the world. We performed mainly in motion-picture theatres and were featured following the picture, sometimes doing as many as four shows a day. It was a great adventure . . .

'Ladies and Gentlemen, from NEW YORK CITY the Bijou Theatre proudly presents . . .' Up went the curtain with a fast, flashy fanfare from the band. Kid Lips Hackett, the drummer, was the showstopper. He'd throw his drumsticks up in the air, catching them behind his back, in his teeth, do anything for effect. Comedians of the slapstick variety were next, Mantan Morlan and his straight man. They'd do the money bit.

Mantan would say, 'Hey – you got twenty, and I got twenty too.'

Then the other one would complain, 'How come I got twenty and you got twenty-two, huh?'

'No, idiot! You got twenty and I got twenty too. Also! . . .'

For their graveyard bit they'd use fluorescent white gloves and lights. There was a universal fear of passing a graveyard at night so the comedians played on it, running in slow motion with arms moving fast. The lights flickered over their treated gloves, creating the illusion that they were really hustling. Every night I'd see this corn and laugh loud and long. Even though I knew the lines by heart I couldn't help myself, Mantan Morlan was a comic genius. As soon as we got to Hollywood he was snatched up by the motion-picture industry.

A singer followed the comedians, then the chorus line came on, all sequins, shimmy, sparkle and legs. Blanche Thompson, the star, never appeared until the last act when she'd pose on a pedestal behind a gauze curtain, not exactly nude, but very scantily clad.

The band was featured between the acts. Eddie Heyward Sr was a terrific arranger and pianist and our band was excellent. Jimmie Beard and Guydner Paul Campbell were on trumpets. Campbell later joined the Lee and Lester Young band and went on to join Count Basie. Tommy Kyle played guitar, Billy Childress saxophone and Kid Lips Hackett was on drums. I had a ball with that show. Being the kid, some of the pretty chorus girls had eyes for me, the head chorus girl especially. She was the one who, like Pearl Bailey, returned onstage after the chorus line's exit to crack a joke, do a few extra turns and get a laugh. Pearl Bailey was doing that at the Apollo in Harlem when her amazing talent was discovered.

After East Grand Forks we headed into Canada, played Winnipeg, Calgary, Saskatoon, working our way west to Victoria, BC. The show travelled by bus. Blanche and Eddie rode up ahead in Blanche's big Cadillac. She was a contemporary of Josephine Baker, had the same charisma, as well as being quite an eyeful. Since I was the new guy, the pet so to speak, she often invited me to ride in the Cadillac. The honour had its drawbacks because Eddie Heyward Sr drove like he spoke and he was a stutterer. He'd drive a way, take his foot off the gas, coast, start up again, lurch forward, all through the vast Canadian forests like the car had hiccups. Often I'd opt to ride in the bus, which was far more fun anyway, much looser; there was always some sort of game going.

In Canada the accommodations were much better than in the States. You could rent a room in any hotel you could pay for, with no restrictions other than financial. We encountered no racial problems, no segregation. Apparently many Canadians had never even seen people of colour and an all-black travelling show was a real novelty. We enjoyed success in every town. In Victoria I remember walking down the street when some small child exclaimed to his mother, 'Mama, Mama – look! A red-headed *niguerre*!'

During the ferry ride from Vancouver to Seattle, somebody cooked up the idea of a stage wedding to enhance the show. I was elected to be the groom; Jessie Mae Tanner, the youngest chorus girl, was to be my bride. We were both about seventeen or eighteen. Everyone thought we were the cutest ideal couple, fawned over us, dressed us to the hilt. It was a great gimmick for drawing the crowds in Seattle, a swinging town at the time. Phil Moore, who later became famous as Lena Horne's arranger, used to come by the show with his latest arrangements. Every night we went out on the town after work, heading for the nearest joint to listen to the players and sit in. An old dude criticized me one night by yelling out, 'Hey kid – you're playing sharp!' Of course I didn't agree with him, but it gave me pause for thought. Ever since, I've been hyper-conscious of intonation.

We also ran into a guitar player named Banjosky – no relation to Banjo Bernie – who played octaves on the guitar, played jazz with classical technique, no pick. Years later when I heard Wes Montgomery, I remembered the innovative Banjosky in 1935.

Our band was a super show band, displaying lots of teeth, lots of personality. My thing was to spin my bass around like a top. This was before the days of amplification and there were no wires. It was all muscle then – that's how and why I developed a big sound, playing in those drafty theatres with a drummer who was as loud as can be. Merely to be heard over the bass drum and the press rolls was a struggle. Kid Lips Hackett, though always a showman, was a swinging drummer. A complete musician, Eddie Heyward Sr played great piano and was surprised at how well I could read his arrangements. To me it was no big deal – that was my training.

After Seattle, the show slid down the west coast, playing Yakima, Washington; Eugene and Portland, Oregon; Eureka, California. Then we arrived in San Francisco: a wide-open town, sunshine in December, ferries running across the bay. We played the Golden Gate Theatre for two weeks. That's when I almost blew it. The band was situated on high tiers above the stage. I'm spinning my bass, smiling, the audience loving it. I stepped back and fell off the stage. Luckily the curtain broke my fall. All of me disappeared from view except one arm, still holding on to my bass. The house came down! They wanted me to repeat that misstep for every show – but no way would I ever do that on purpose.


On New Year's Day, 1936, the Brownskin Models rolled into Los Angeles. Everything I'd seen in Laurel and Hardy and Chaplin movies was real – the palm trees, the clear skies, the warm temperature, the rugged mountains in the background. Luxuriant tropical beauty was everywhere; flowers were blooming, fruit hanging on the trees – I could hardly believe it. I wasn't quite twenty years old, yet I knew I had arrived in the place I'd dreamed of all my life.

'This is it,' I told myself. 'This is where I jump off the bus.'

# PART TWO

# Baby, I'm Gone

The Brownskin Models moved into the Torrence Hotel at 56th and Central Avenue for our two-week engagement at the Lincoln Theatre. Central Avenue was the main stem; everything flowed into Central Avenue and everything flowed out of it. From 5th Street where the red caps and porters came in from the Southern Pacific all the way out to Slauson, beyond which was the hinterlands, Central Avenue was a carnival of life, music and action. Every kind of cafe, restaurant, tailor shop, real estate, insurance broker, dance hall, social hall, beauty shoppe, music store -- every kind of business numbering into the dozens was there. One of the great crossroads was at 12th and Central where Reb Spikes and his brother ran a record store that magnetized all the elements. Across the street was the Hummingbird Cafe and Adams Sweet Shop where you could sit and watch everyone pass by. It was common to meet celebrities on Central Avenue, celebrities like Jack Johnson, or view parades marching past, parades given by the Elks, Foresters or Masons. Another great crossroad was at 41st and Central where the Dunbar Hotel stood, next to the Club Alabam. That's where Sy Oliver, Jimmy Mundy, Jimmie Lunceford, Don Redman and all the musical luminaries would stay when they were in town, there or the Clark Hotel on Central and Washington. Walking up and down Central Avenue, one saw everything and everybody: people going to church, people going to dances at the Parish Hall or to the Egyptian Hall at 28th and Central where Les Hite's big band played and small groups led by Jake Porter, Alton Redd, Pepe Prince, Roy Milton, Sammy Franklin and many, many others played. Lorenzo Flennoy had a big band at the Club Alabam with the great

drummer, Oscar Bradley. Lear's was an after-hours joint where
Jackie McVea and Don Byas used to jam. Day or night, dusk or
dawn, Central Avenue was jumping.

Buck Clayton's band had just returned from eighteen months
in Shanghai and most of the members were staying at the same
hotel we were, the Torrence. I struck up a friendship with the
band's percussionist who played vibraphone and tympani as well
as drums, Baby Lewis. He introduced me to Buck and the rest of
the band: Arcima Taylor, Eddie Beal, Caughey Roberts. Their
bass player had remained overseas and I was invited to join
Buck's band. After the two weeks at the Lincoln Theatre, I gave
Blanche Thompson notice. I worked two more weeks with the
Brownskin Models at the Million Dollar Theatre in downtown
Los Angeles. After that, the show went back on the road with a
new bass player.

Hubert 'Bumps' Meyers and Arcima Taylor played alto
saxophone in Buck's band, Eddie Beal piano, and Caughey
Roberts played marvellous clarinet and tenor. Alan Durham was
on trombone and Lionel Hampton's main threat on percussion –
my friend Baby Lewis. Buck was as great an arranger as he was a
trumpet player; it was Buck who wrote 'One o'Clock Jump',
though Count Basie usually gets the credit. Buck was a Parsons,
Kansas native and soon after he organized his band in Los
Angeles, Bill Basie from Kansas City called him. Buck and
Caughey Roberts left for Kansas, offering to take me along.
Kansas City? Or Los Angeles? The choice was obvious. I was in
paradise and going to stay put. KC had overtones of the South
anyway. Colour line, Jim Crow – who needed it?


Los Angeles was a big, rambling country town, that's how I
perceived it then. I was the hip New Yorker among all the
squares. No one in Los Angeles had heard of either Roy Eldridge
or Art Tatum. I took great pleasure in prophesying, 'Hey – you
*will* hear about these guys, I know you haven't yet but you *will*.'

Bumps Meyers (Hubert, but they called him Bumps) and I
became tight friends. One day I was walking down Central
Avenue near 47th Street and saw a woman who resembled my
mother so closely that I began to follow her. Happy coincidence –
the woman who could have been my mother's twin sister was

Bumps's mother. Who knows, they could have been related since they both originally came from West Virginia and so many families during slavery were split apart in those days. Bumps and his mother shared an apartment near where I'd seen her, and since Bumps and I were friends, Mrs Meyers graciously invited me to come and live with them. She treated me like a second son, gave me free rein in the house. Always, I'll be grateful for the way they took me into the fold. Bumps was like a brother, very gregarious type, very sensitive. He fell deeply in love with a singer, married her, and a happier man couldn't be found. That is, until his wife was offered a job singing with Lionel Hampton. We all thought Bumps would be hired too, but he wasn't. That was the beginning of the end of Bumps's happiness because his wife took up with another musician in Hamp's band and divorced Bumps.

Eddie Beal was also close, like a brother. He was a great human being, a giver. He's done more for people than they could ever repay. If you wanted to rehearse, Eddie would be available; if you needed something, Eddie would be the first to offer. We later rented an apartment together. I wasn't freeloading exactly with Bumps and his mother, but being the extremely independent type I am, I needed to have my own set-up. Eddie never moved into the apartment we rented – within two weeks he was married to a singer, Rene Gonsales. I arranged a few tunes for her. She did an act with a top hat and cane, wore a little tutu. Actually she resembled a Mexican version of what Judy Garland looked like years later. Eddie, Rene and I hung out together. Once, I stuffed myself into the rumble seat of their brand-new 1936 Ford and drove all the way to San Francisco in the baking sun. When you're young, you can survive anything.

Towards the end of that first year, Nat Cole came to town with the King Kolax Orchestra and Show, which was really another version of the Brownskin Models. Nat decided to stay in Los Angeles. We became good friends, and we both became tight friends with the drummer, Lee Young, brother of Lester Young. Nat was an astonishing pianist and arranger. It was only by a fluke that he became a singer; a patron at the Swannee Inn on La Brea requested that he sing 'Sweet Lorraine'. The rest is history. In those early days, Nat, Lee Young and I all joined the Thomas Waller Masonic Lodge, eventually becoming thirty-second-degree Masons. We also used to sideline in pictures. We'd get calls to do bit or extra parts, or to mime playing music while recorded music was being played on the soundtrack.

Fox, Paramount, MGM, Universal, Warner Brothers – we worked all the studios. Within a few years, Lee Young would be the first black to be hired by Columbia for their staff orchestra. He would also coach Mickey Rooney how to mime playing drums for an MGM picture, *Strike Up the Band*. But then we were just extras, reporting to the studio early in the morning. First thing, they'd send you to wardrobe to outfit you for whatever part you had to play. If it was a Southern picture, all the blacks would be dressed in raggedy clothes, shabby straw hats. If it was a classy nightclub you were supposed to be in, you'd wear tuxedos. Lee and I used to wear our own tuxedos and get extra money for providing costumes. Sidelining paid about $42 a day, not bad for the times.

It was a kick being seen by people all over the world on the screen, even though we were only miming the music. I'd write my folks back east to tell them I was in this or that picture. The family would go see it, stand up and yell, 'There he is!' One second later I'd be gone. Lee, Nat and I once worked in a picture where we had to play the part of Africans. Nat had dark skin, but both Lee and I were of lighter hue so they stuck us way, way in the back. That's the way it was.

The first picture I appeared in was *Think Fast Mr Moto* with Peter Lorre. Lorre had a wonderfully distinctive sound. He wasn't stuck-up, had no prejudices, which is something I can't say for all American actors with whom I've worked. Being on the inside of picture-making was slightly disappointing. Some of the magic, the belief in the reality of what's going down on the screen was forever lost. What I gained was a certain insight into the personalities and temperaments of the people making the pictures, the mechanics of it all, the infinite takes. There were so many sideline jobs I can't remember all the titles. There was one with Bette Davis, and I worked in *Broadway Melody of 1936* with Jack Benny. Benny was someone I learned from; he always surrounded himself with the best available people. When he started his radio show, everyone was great. He chose Eddie Anderson to be Rochester. Anderson and Johnny Taylor had been doing a hilarious comedy duo at the Club Alabam. Of course their act broke up when Anderson became 'Rochester', a character who was Benny's servant, but the role the way Anderson played it was never demeaning. I guess I learned that when you get top people to work with you, their sheer talent transcends anything negative. After I worked in the band with Louis Armstrong, Elmer Fain began calling me for jobs where I actually played the music which was used in the soundtrack, either on screen or behind the scenes. But now I'm getting ahead of myself.

Elmer Fain was the business agent for the Musicians' Local 767, the black segregated Local which I'd joined. Fain had an 'in' at the studios; that's how we got all those picture calls. He must have liked me; he knew I was the kid in town, and he knew I could play. The business agent's job was to check out everything and everybody. Fain was constantly hanging around the clubs making sure that neither musicians or club-owners were doing anything illegal, like having too many musicians on the stand. They were trying to protect musicians, but it was a Catch-22 situation. The only way to learn to play was to sit in and jam, pick up on what other people were doing. The union figured if a club-owner hired three or four guys and there's seven or eight musicians on the stand, the club-owner is getting more than he paid for. Somehow both musicians and club-owners found ways to skirt the rule – to everyone's benefit.

Jobs were plentiful during those first few years in Los Angeles. I often worked around with older guys like Paul Howard of the Quality Serenaders, a great tenor saxophonist who was also an official in the union. Papa Mutt Carey, an old New Orleans trumpeter, was another. They all liked what I did but weren't used to it. They'd say things . . . 'Play the low notes, boy. Stop playing that piccolo bass . . .' An old dude by the name of Fess White told me, 'Any low note is a good note, any low note is bass.' Even with my so-called 'modern' sound, I always had a gig. For a while I worked with Happy Johnson's band, then with C.C. Caldwell's band, then with C.L. Burke. It was great to be garnering all this experience and my confidence swelled enough to try my hand at arranging.

Sebastian's Cotton Club in Culver City was the hub for travelling name big bands. Frank Sebastian, the owner, was an Italian guy who dug black musicians. He kept a black band at his

club, which was popular then. He featured both black and white
bands at the club – Artie Shaw, Tommy Dorsey, Les Hite, Lionel
Hampton – all the great names. He was the first one to bring
Louis Armstrong to the West Coast in the early 1930s. Louis had
a record date then with Lionel Hampton; they were doing an
arrangement of 'Memories' that Eubie Blake had sent out for
Louis to record. Lionel told me the story about how they're in the
studio and there's a vibraharp sitting around which the radio
station used to sound their station breaks. Pops said to Hamp,
'Hey, can you play that . . .?' So Lionel walked over to it, made
an introduction in E flat and 'Memories' got recorded. Lionel had
played orchestral bells, but had never touched a vibraphone
before in his life.

I used to go out to the Cotton Club to ask if anybody needed an
arrangement. Then, I'd write it up; that's how I got my start. I did
some arranging for Lionel Hampton; two tunes that I wrote,
'Lost Love' and 'Bo-Go-Joe', Lionel recorded on RCA with
another bassist, my friend Vernon Alley from San Francisco. I
played with Lionel's band briefly in 1937. Llewellyn Crawford,
who was a very popular and talented choreographer, was always
in need of arrangements for the floor shows. He choreographed
shows most often at the Paradise on Main Street in Los Angeles
and he gave me a start writing for the chorus lines. Once, for a
show at the Paramount Theatre, he needed an arrangement for
the chorus line which the Duke Ellington Orchestra was going to
play. I was so excited to be writing an arrangement for the Duke's
band that I put far too many notes in it. Duke had to take out all
the fat, just use the lean.

That taught me a lot about the use of space. What I knew then
was the range of the instruments, knew things about what the
instruments could do, but I was a beginner. I'm still learning
about the possibilities of instruments and what *not* to write. Back
then, I'd overwrite like crazy. Always had the trumpeters playing
far too long and high. They would have to be monsters to play
what I wrote. So I learned, the brass section needs a rest to get
the blood back to their chops. Saxophone players can play a
whole arrangement without taking the horn out of their mouths,
but the brass chops must rest. From my experience playing the
tuba I wasn't aware of that, as the tuba has a much larger cup
mouthpiece than the rest of the brass. The tuba was usually in the

rhythm section and tuba players generally played from top to bottom.

Working around the shows was not only stimulating my creativity, but my interest in dance as well. Sometimes I could hardly take my eyes from those dancers, their pulchritude overwhelmed me. I used to gaze at all the fine girls like Lois Bright, Ronnell Bright's sister. The girls in the lines thought I was cute, nicknamed me 'Little Boy Red'. After some time had passed, my eyes kept settling on one particularly beautiful girl, Emma Priestly. She winked back, too.

We started spending a lot of time together. People would say to us, 'You're such a handsome couple, why don't you get married?' I was twenty-one at the time and hadn't the vaguest notion of what love and marriage were all about. We were having fun, were having a ball together, so we thought, why not get married? A few days later we were at the altar, 13 December 1937. At that point in my life I was blindfolded from inexperience – no regrets – that's the way things happened. When you're a kid, you're stupid, you don't think far enough ahead. If you slept together you had to get married and obviously I loved her enough to marry her. It's only with hindsight I can say, live a little before you get married because you've got to get that living in sooner or later.

Emma was a real family girl. She had a three-year-old son, Ronald, when I married her. She insisted that her parents move in with us when we bought a house on Newton Street, not far off Central Avenue, next door to the police station. I guess I wasn't too strong in forbidding it, thought it would work out all right, but it just never should have happened. Her parents were from Mississippi, where they must have got a lot of flack. Her mother was as light-skinned as any Southern belle, and pretty; her father was very dark. He was about sixty years old then, had a job with the city of Los Angeles. He was lovable, but he had a drinking problem. So Emma and I and her parents set up housekeeping together. Since Ronald was three, and our daughter Sylvia came along a few years later, it wasn't too bad a situation. Emma's mother gave Emma and myself some freedom to pursue what we wanted to be doing by providing care for the children. Emma always liked to be working, always kept a job of some kind. Then, she was still kicking high in the chorus lines.

While Emma and I were courting, I was working around town

with the pianist Fletcher Smith on a 'freelance' basis, though the word hadn't come into vogue yet. Fletcher was and is a funny little guy. Gerry Wiggins and I still joke about Fletcher, we say we're going by Fletcher's to study how to be evil. Although he's one of my best friends, he can be the most cantankerous guy in the world. Once he had a gig with Benny Carter, they were playing 'Have You Met Miss Jones?' Evidently, Benny had added a change here and there. Fletcher would only play the tune the way it was written on the sheet music. He couldn't care less about Benny Carter or anybody else – if he thought he was right, he was right. Wouldn't budge an inch. So Benny Carter said, 'Look, I don't want that chord there . . .'

Fletcher says, 'Man, I'm playing the music the way the man wrote it!' The next night he comes in with the sheet music to show Benny Carter. Benny, the ultra-gentleman type, didn't say a word – except from then on, Benny's nickname for Fletcher became 'Funky Butt'. Fletcher is a down-to-earth cat whose convictions are locked in by steel. I get along with him, love him; he's my kind of guy. We just never argued about music. I was the first one to show him a 13th chord. He looked at it and said, 'That can't be did!' So I explained, a 13th is simply a 6th chord over a 7th . . . six and seven make thirteen . . . At that time a 9th chord was heavy. You'd hear runs on the piano and the modern thing was to finish up on the 9th.

Fletcher and I went over to Yuma, Arizona, where the temperature registered 110 degrees in the shade, to work in a group led by the trumpeter Ike Bell. Between sets I used a bass stand to prop up my instrument. One evening Wilma Chevalier, one of the singers in our group, swished by and unintentionally knocked over the stand. Down went my bass with a broken neck. We rushed a carpenter to the scene, and he bolted it back together, but it was never the same. On my return to Los Angeles, Yuli Apfeld, the salesman at Lockie's Music on lower Broadway, called me, excitedly describing a Morelli bass from Germany that had recently arrived in the store. 'I think you should have it, kid,' he said. When I saw it, I instantly agreed with him and signed on the dotted line. Although it took me three years to pay for the instrument, I'm still playing it today.

The night after I got my new bass, Elmer Fain, the business agent, called me. 'Hey kid' – (everyone called me 'kid' then) – 'you want to play with Louis Armstrong? You want to be in the band?'

'What happened?' I asked. Louis was playing in the Vogue Ballroom, fronting a band conducted by Luis Russell.

Fain says, 'Pops Foster is sick. They need a bass player right away.'

Who wouldn't want to play with Louis Armstrong? Louis had been our idol in high school; we all used to scream and get our voices hoarse so we would sound like him. Wearing a white tuxedo, I practically danced all the way to the Vogue with my new bass. The salary was $85 a week. This was my entry into the big time.

Louis Armstrong was about thirty-seven years old then, right in his prime. It was like heaven, getting a chance to play with the legendary New Orleans guys: Paul Barbarin on drums, J.C. Higginbotham and George Washington on trombones, Charlie Holmes alto saxophone, Bingy Madison on clarinet, Luis Russell, the leader of the band, on piano, Sonny Woods vocals and Shelton Hemphill and Red Allen trumpets. To distinguish the two Reds for the announcements on the national broadcasts we were doing from the Vogue nightly, Louis called me 'California Red'. The first evening I played, the wires holding the tailpiece on the bass snapped during the broadcast. So I carefully laid down the bass and played tuba for the rest of the night.

I was one of the lucky ones who happened to be in the right place at the right time. Imagine my elation when I learned the band was going to record a few days after I'd joined them. That was my first record date ever, 13 November 1937. I'll never forget walking into the Decca studio at 5500 Melrose, seeing the big sign over the doorway – a portrait of an American Indian and the slogan 'Where's the Melody?' Louis Armstrong always gave the people what they wanted, played for the people. He took popular songs, played them in his own way, and the public called it jazz. The songs we recorded on that session, 'Once in a While' and 'The Sunny Side of the Street' became big hits. Suddenly I was on two hit tunes, in the US and in Canada, for we had done a separate version of the tunes for distribution north of the border. Suddenly the name 'Red Callender' became known to thousands.

A few weeks after the recording session, Pops Foster got well, but not before Louis Armstrong's wedding to Lucille, which all the band attended. Louis was an absolute prince of a guy. He didn't care about money, he'd give away anything he had. His manager was Joe Glaser, who'd been a gambler and hustler around Chicago before he started managing Louis. They had a deal. Louis told Glaser not to bother him with details. 'Just give me *x* amount of dollars,' Louis told him, 'I don't care what you make.' He didn't want to be worried about taxes or anything – 'I'll play the horn and you take care of business.' I don't know how much it was, but Joe Glaser became a multi-millionaire, a big stockholder in the Chase Manhattan Bank. Big money was being made off Louis Armstrong, even way back then.

Shortly after the Vogue Ballroom gig, my phone started ringing and has never really stopped. Right away I was called to join C.C. Caldwell's band at the Gloria Nightclub, located in Gardena, near Los Angeles. When I arrived at the rehearsal, there was already a bass player on the stand. 'What's going on?' I demanded.

C.C. Caldwell said, 'Sorry kid, but we got Al Morgan.'

'OK,' I said, and tucked my tail between my legs and left. Al Morgan was a famous bass player, a real showman, who had just left Cab Calloway's band. Even though I had recently been with the King of Jazz, it didn't mean as much to them as to me. So I said to myself, 'I'll show them!' My ego, of course, was slightly punctured. I kept my vow by really going to work studying.

First I went to the premier bassist of the day, a German teacher named Herman Rheinshagen. He pointed me in new directions, advised me on what to practise, demonstrated alternative positions. He was an advocate of the German bow style which wasn't too comfortable for me, given my anatomy. A German bow has a large frog, it's held cupped in the palm of your hand. Nevertheless, I practised with it, learned that technique. Next, I went to a teacher named Leon Ziporland, who played things like 'Flight of the Bumblebee' on the bass at rapid tempos. Also, I studied with another German teacher who showed me how to get power when using the French bow, a bow that's held like a violin bow, the one I prefer. My studies continued three or four years. From each teacher I learned something. I had decided to master the technique of the instrument and know exactly what I was doing at all times.

During this period, calls to perform music in pictures, not just sideline, started coming. I had the good fortune to work in a movie with Fats Waller before he died; he was only thirty-eight. Fats was barrels of fun, always keeping everybody in stitches, always had his schnapps, a ham or turkey and various goodies on a sideboard near the piano. The real Fats was a very brilliant, serious musician, a great stride pianist. I was such a kid then, about twenty-one, totally in awe of him. In his presence I'd immediately become tongue-tied. Working on that film led to another job doing the soundtrack for an all-black picture produced by Leo Poppin featuring Nina Mae McKinney and Lawrence Criner. The picture had an eight-week run at the Million Dollar Theatre in downtown Los Angeles.

Lee Young and I used to drop by the theatre on our way to other gigs to chat with girls in the show. The band that played the show was comprised of high-school kids, a good band that featured Buddy Collette on saxophone. That's when I first met Buddy, that was the beginning of our lifelong association. Through Buddy, I met another young bass player, Charles Mingus.

Mingus had been hanging out with Buddy since he was thirteen or so. Charles had a reputation around Watts for being different. One day Buddy sees a guy who fits the description the kids had been passing around: a crazy-looking guy, kind of fat, bow-legged, kind of a tough guy but not really – hit you in a minute even if he couldn't win a fight. He was carrying a shoeshine box that was almost four feet tall with legs on it like chicken legs. Buddy decides it's got to be Mingus; no one else was that unusual.

'How do you know that's me?' asks Mingus when Buddy approaches him.

'It's got to be you; nobody else would have all this wild stuff,' meaning the shoeshine box with chicken legs.

Mingus explained that the shine box worked when his customers sat on a car bonnet. He liked Buddy right away for being straightforward and they became friends. Mingus had been playing cello, and, on Buddy's suggestion, switched to bass when he saw there was an opportunity to play in Buddy's band with kids from Jordan High School. They used to ride the old Red Car together, the local streetcar from Watts into Los Angeles. Mingus would always take the cover off his bass and urge Buddy to jam with him during the ride. Instead of being bothered, the passengers loved it, looked forward to hearing them play. When Buddy was in the band at the Million Dollar Theatre, he had memorized the soundtrack. The bass had a strong pickup on it and Buddy convinced Mingus that Red Callender was *the* cat who was getting the sound. Mingus followed through and tracked me down.

One morning there's a knock on the door of my house on 20th Street, where I was living with Emma and her family. It's Mingus, saying he wants to study with me. He was seventeen, still in high school. I told him I was no teacher, that I was still studying myself, but he persisted. That was typical of him; Mingus would go through walls to get what he wanted. He was very nice, intense, eager – we had a rapport from the very beginning. So I decided to take him on as a student, only charging him two dollars a lesson. After each session, we'd go out and buy ice cream, go to the five-cent hot-dog stand, or go to the Rosebud Theatre to see the latest picture with the two bucks.

At that time, Mingus knew little about the bass, even though he'd been playing it. Mainly, he'd been fooling around with trombone and cello. I showed him the rudiments, the proper way to finger the instrument, gave him a direction. My inspiration had been Duke Ellington, so naturally I was conscious of where the beat was, the rhythm, and I could demonstrate how to approach it. He had some concept of jazz from Buddy Collette and Britt Woodman already. What I taught him primarily was how to get a sound from the instrument. However, even then, he knew exactly what he aspired to be – the world's greatest bass player. That was his all-consuming passion.

To prove that genius is hard work, Mingus practised seventeen, eighteen hours a day. I'd drive by his house early in the morning and there would be Mingus out on his front porch practising. That's the secret of his greatness: the hours he put into it. Once he learned how to play the instrument, he figured he was ready for anything – even studio auditions. He had nerve, but he wasn't that great a reader. He could play note values in the book. Yet it takes years of experience to scan a musical score, psyche out the difficulties ahead so you can deal with them when you get there. I like to think I imparted some of that ability to him. He always credited me . . . called me 'Teach'.

A more loyal guy couldn't be found. There's a story about Charles Mingus beating up some fellow he'd seen hanging around my wife Emma. In a way, I became his father-confessor. He was always on an even keel with me, never in those well-documented dark and violent moods. Throughout the years it was me he would call, myself or Buddy Collette, to extricate him from various sticky situations, usually self-created. Like when he came to Los Angeles, already having made a name for himself in New York, and checked into the Ambassador Hotel, private cabin, first-class all the way. Despite his name, he was broke. Who'd he call? Buddy Collette and Red Callender to the rescue. We were the ones he trusted all the way down the line. He knew that if he was anywhere near us, everything would be all right.

After a few years with me, I suggested that he study with Rheinshagen and my other teachers. By then he was also into composing; I might have influenced him there too, since I was very involved with writing. His object in music was to astound everyone, his idea about writing was to intimidate the players with shit so hard it was almost impossible to play. He'd expect them to play it anyway, get furious and punch somebody out if they didn't do it exactly the way he had conceived it in his head. On analysing his written music, it's clear to me how much simpler it could have been. Certainly one of my main objectives was and is to write music that musicians can play the same way more than once. And to write things for instruments within their proper range so the players aren't constantly extending themselves to the utmost limit of their ability. But Mingus had his own way of doing things.

In 1939, it was time to visit New York City and see what was happening. By then I was affluent enough to have purchased another new bass. I had a trunk made for it and sent it to New York City by ship via the Panama Canal, thinking it would arrive in New York about the same time I did. Cozy Cole, the drummer, was going to ride the train back east with me. He had just finished up an engagement with Stuff Smith and Jonah Jones at the Famous Door in Hollywood on Vine Street. We were in touch with this cat who said he would come down to the train station to bring us some weed, pot, or whatever we were calling it then, for the trip. The train was about to pull out of the Southern Pacific Station, the conductors were yelling ALL ABOARD, and this cat still hadn't shown up. Five minutes, four minutes, three . . . and at the last minute the dude runs up to the train to lay a Prince Albert tobacco tin full of weed on us. We give him the bread, the whistle blows, and we're on our way.

Cozy and I are laughing at the close call, congratulating ourselves, thinking about what a ball we're going to have, laying back high digging the scenery all the way to New York. We get as far as San Bernadino. Cozy and I look at each other, nod, then head out to the vestibule to roll up some of that herb. We open the tin – 'What's this, man? Don't look like . . .' Alfalfa. Nothing but alfalfa. A whole big tin of alfalfa. We got took.

The rest of the trip was uneventful. We pull into Grand Central Station and the first thing I do is head for my relatives in Brooklyn, to a big four-storey brownstone with the welcome mat out. Then I took a side trip to Atlantic City to visit my mother, who had returned there to live. The restaurant which she'd opened was a big success. I spent time with Jim Hosick, the clarinet player whose father was a lieutenant of the Atlantic City Police. Talk at their dinner table centred around that 'devil weed', marijuana. Obviously I never let on that I was hip to it. Jim's father warned us anyway – 'stay away from that stuff'. Cocaine and junk hadn't really taken over the drug scene yet. People did it, but to me cocaine was just a name in a song.

On my return to New York, I checked in at the shipping office, as my bass still hadn't arrived. Too bad, because I would gladly have lugged it up to Harlem, to Mack's on 139th Street where I was spending my evenings. Bedbugs would be crawling all over the joint, but Thelonious Monk was sitting at the piano. The first tune I heard him play was 'Sphere'. Before the advent of so-called bebop, I'd hear all Monk's licks and be thrilled with it. After his sets, we walked around Harlem together. Years later when I saw him again he didn't remember me. Though I remembered him, never forgot what I heard at Mack's. Last time I saw him, he was into his crazy way of spinning around, completely off his nut. People who knew him better than I saw another side of him. That nutty side disappointed me because he was a gigantic talent, an inventive genius.

Finally, my bass arrived in New York City just as I was preparing to leave for Los Angeles. I picked it up, got back on the train. Emma was waiting for me in Los Angeles . . . sort of. When you're that young, it's easy to be married and not married at the same time. I was so glad to be back in California that when the train arrived I took my bass out of its custom-made case right in the waiting-room of the station. Left the case there on the floor, never did go back for it. Dumb, but I did it.

Many of my musician friends didn't think it was possible to be a success or to make a living in music. On my return from New York in late 1939, I went into Billy Berg's Capri on La Cienga and Pico in Hollywood for the first time to play an engagement with Herschel Coleman, a very talented musician who played beautiful trumpet and alto saxophone. Coleman was a heavy drinker, carried a half-pint of gin or vodka with him at all times. He passed away early in life, at thirty-eight, before giving himself a real chance. He was a guy who thought that if you hadn't made it big by the time you were thirty-five, you should quit. Being a youngster then, I used to think that too. After all, what are all these old-timers doing trying to play? Everyone except Louis Armstrong, that is. Time goes by and I see how foolish that was. You don't begin to be a musician or anything else until you *do* approach thirty-five. It takes that long to find out where you really want to go. In the early 1940s I was only beginning to get started.

There was an upstairs place at 8th and Figueroa called the Skyline where I worked with Luke Jones, one of the better altoists around LA. Oscar Bradley, a superb and underrated musician, was on drums, and my down-to-earth friend Fletcher Smith on piano. Way before Charlie Barnet came out with his hit 'Skyliner', I had written the theme song for our band, entitled 'Skyline'. The discographers are still confused about that.

We're playing one evening and a guy comes dancing in front of the bandstand and says, 'Hey, can you niggers play "Way Down Yonder in New Orleans"?'

I put my bass down and went out to grab him. It turned out to be one of the most embarrassing moments of my life because the fellow with the request was Wingy Manone, a one-armed musician from New Orleans. What match was a one-armed man for me – a 200-pound, six-foot-two-inch so-called giant? My temper was terrible in those days. I couldn't stand anybody using the word nigger. When I heard it, I'd get so pissed I'd go blind. Later, when I got to know Wingy, I found out he was a real New Orleans character who thought nothing about using that word all the time. To him it didn't hold the derogatory connotations it held for me.

Luke Jones was as good a barber as he was an alto saxophonist. He used to come over to our house on 20th Street to cut my hair. In those days we were using what was called 'gas' – an acid substance that made your hair straight or curly or whatever you wanted. Luke came by once to give me a 'gas'. That stuff was so potent that it fried your head if you left it on too long after it had done its work. My mischievous stepson Ronald, Emma's son from a previous marriage, snuck under the house that day and shut off the water main. So I emerged from the 'gas' with a few bald spots.

Perhaps Ronald, who was about seven or eight years old at the time, was undergoing some pangs of sibling rivalry for he had a new baby sister. My first daughter Sylvia had just been born. Ronald's father was still hovering in the background; used to drive by the house and take Ronald out for a ride in his big Buick occasionally. Many years after the fact, I discovered all the other practical jokes Ronald played on Sylvia. Being an only child, I never had the pleasure or displeasure of having brothers or sisters. Two kids around the house makes things a lot more lively!

During that period I was working not only with the Sammy Franklin Band, but also out in Long Beach at a place called Papa Pagone's in a group with the drummer Carl Johnson, George Crawford on piano and Frank Pasley, guitar. This was in the days before the freeways were built and the twenty-one miles to Long Beach seemed a great distance. Carl Johnson's father was Prez Johnson, president of the Musicians' Union Local 767, located on Jefferson across the street from Jefferson High where Dr Samuel Browne was busy training the next generation of musicians.

The Young family lived right next door to Local 767 after it moved to 18th and Central. Mr Young Sr gave music lessons on all instruments. He was a hard taskmaster, a no-bullshit type of man. Apparently he'd experienced some hard times and vowed that none of his children would ever be porters, waiters or maids; they would all be musicians. Lester, Irma and Lee Young, Jimmy Talbert and a nephew, all spent many years playing in the family band. In the late thirties, Lester was with Count Basie, and Irma had for the most part given up playing alto saxophone to pursue a career in dance. A thorough musician, a marvellous drummer, Lee Young's career was beginning to soar. Lee organized a band which became the house band at Billy Berg's Capri. Every day we rehearsed at his house on Adams Boulevard to prepare the band for the engagement and in anticipation of Lester's joining us.

We had Arthur Twyne on piano, Guydner Paul Campbell, who was in the Brownskin Models band, on trumpet, my buddy Hubert 'Bumps' Meyers on tenor. Louis Gonsales on guitar was the Latin contingent in the band. Lee played drums, led and sang; Lee was the glue that held the band together for the next few years, and I played bass. We were all contemporaries who dug each other's sound. I did some writing for the band, Nat Cole contributed some arrangements, as did Dudley Brooks and Gerald Wilson whom I had met along with Snooky Young when they first came to Los Angeles with the Lunceford band in 1940. When our pianist Arthur Twyne died, Jimmy Rowles came into the band and also contributed arrangements. We'd memorize every ensemble part completely, wanted no music on the stand. It was the thing to do because the show at Billy Berg's Capri was perfection.

Billie Holiday and Joe Turner were the featured singers we accompanied. A very uninhibited group, the Spirits of Rhythm were in the show, with Teddy Bunn playing finger-style guitar and Leo Watson, one of the greatest scat singers of all time, playing trombone and drums. Watson was a genius; he could do anything musically. Slim Gaillard and Slam Stewart were also on the bill, singing the songs they'd made famous like 'Cement Mixer' . . . putty, putty . . . and 'Flat Foot Floogie' with the floy doy . . . floy doy, floy doy, floy doy, floy doy . . .

Slam Stewart's arco bass playing is still unbelievable; he has absolutely perfect pitch. When Lester Young finally left Count Basie and returned to Los Angeles, he became our 'guest' artist. The Musicians' Union had a rule about musicians being in town six months before they could work regularly. So we featured

Lester at the end of every set, like a singer. Night after night, the
most amazing musical entertainment was broadcast live on
national radio. Yet no airchecks of it are available today, no
records were made, only the memory remains, indelibly etched in
my brain.

After Prez came to LA, Lee started organizing after-hours jam
sessions. They began at 2.30 a.m. when the customers were gone;
then the Capri would be packed with show people and musicians.
Once, both Basie's and Lunceford's bands were in town at the
same time – they all came over to the Capri when their gigs were
finished. Everyone played and Lee also featured Nellie Lutcher's
Trio, Lorenzo Flenoy's Trio and the Nat Cole Trio – with Lee on
drums and myself on bass. When the union got wind of these
goings-on, they fined Lee $500. Of course he never paid it. Since
he lived next door to the union, the officials were always checking
up on him; fining him left and right. He was known as 'Peck's bad
boy' of the union.

Duke Ellington's Orchestra spent several months in Los
Angeles when *Jump for Joy* was running at the Mayhan Theatre
on L Street. The band members would come by Billy Berg's when
their show was through for the evening to check us out and
mingle with the jazz-loving clientele that hung out there. Billy
Berg didn't care who his patrons were – big-name stars or obscure
street people – as long as they spent their money. Howard
Hughes would appear in the audience wearing his tennis
sneakers, Mickey Rooney was a regular, Jackie Cooper, John
Barrymore. One night, Jimmy Blanton came in, Charlie Christian and Lionel Hampton . . . this was when Hamp and Charlie
Christian were with Benny Goodman. Naturally I got off the
stand and turned my bass over to Blanton. Lionel got up and
played that two-finger piano he does. Charlie Christian was about
twenty-two or so, same age as Blanton. They played the blues,
things like 'China Boy', 'Liza', 'Honeysuckle Rose', all the
standard jam tunes. It was an orgy of good music.

Prior to Charlie Christian and Lester, tunes were pretty static;
eight bars on eight, then an eight-bar bridge, then the last eight
bars. Or maybe it was sixteen on sixteen. When Charlie Christian
played and got to the bridge, he'd start running the changes in the
bridge, really fiddle through those chords. Most other guys would
fake the changes – you can hear it when listening to old records.

Charlie Christian changed all that. He was inspired by Lester, as was Bird. Lester deserves more credit than he gets for his influence on many musicians.

The most impressive bass player I ever heard was Jimmy Blanton. When I first heard him, I said, 'This is the way the bass is supposed to be played.' Blanton inspired all of us musically. He became my major inspiration and my close friend. We'd hang out together . . . we'd stay up all night long. I'd lug my bass around anywhere he wanted to go so I could hear him play. What technique and what beautiful fingers he had! He could play anyone's instrument; that's something not many people can do. Fletcher Henderson used to live in LA on Hoover Avenue on the east side. One morning Blanton and I went by his house and he played bass with Fletcher's piano for hours. I'd just sit and marvel at them. It was completely free music.

We'd also go to Lovejoy's and other after-hour spots. The town was full of jazz. All the bands were coming through and all the movie stars went 'slumming' on Central Avenue because that's where the jazz was happening. You'd see Mercedes-Benzes, Cadillacs, Bentleys; people like Mae West, Barrymore, John Steinbeck. Stepin' Fetchit was big then, he'd drive up and down Central Avenue in his chauffeur-driven Rolls-Royce with a washtub full of champagne on ice. He liked living it up. Bill 'Bojangles' Robinson, who worked in pictures with Shirley Temple, was on the scene. All the stars, both black and white, came to Central Avenue. We might arrive there at two or three in the morning, hang out until ten or twelve o'clock the next day. We rarely got tired; it was too much fun . . . Jack's Basket Room, Milamo's on Western, Last Word, Club Alabam, the Turban Room, the Brown Bomber, Brothers . . .

Blanton must have been quite young when he switched from violin to bass because he was only twenty-four years old when he died. I think he'd been playing bass about ten years when he went with Duke. Before Duke, he played the riverboats in Fate Marable's band. I believe it was in St Louis that Ben Webster heard him and took Duke to see him. Ben Webster loved Blanton dearly and the love was mutual. Yet one of the factors in Blanton's early demise was hanging out with Ben. When you play bass it's very physical; when you play bass with a big band you might have to change shirts or undershirts a few times a night,

you perspire so much. This is how Blanton first contracted TB –
improper care. Working in Chicago or some northern city, being
wringing wet from playing all night, then going out on the town
with someone who drinks like Ben – you get wiped out. Blanton
was very frail; I don't think he weighed over 130 pounds.

Lee Young and I went to see him in Duarte, at the City of
Hope Hospital, the day before he died. He was wasted away, he
lay in bed strumming a guitar to keep his long beautiful fingers
agile. He didn't really know that he was going to go. The day
after our visit, he was gone.

Blanton had introduced me to Mercer Ellington, and it was
through Mercer that I first met his father, the Duke. I was
tongue-tied at that initial meeting. After Blanton died, Elmer
Fain, the same business agent who'd called me to work with
Louis, rang again to ask if I wanted to go out on the road with
Ellington to replace Blanton. But I had no penchant for going on
the road, even though Duke's band was the most glamorous band
in the world. I didn't want to play 'Jack the Bear' and all those
things Blanton had made famous. I wasn't even sure I could fill
Blanton's shoes. There was my tuba playing, my composing,
arranging and recording activities to pursue. Knowing that Duke
actually wanted me was quite enough for my ego.

The Capri was such a fantastic place – I don't think we realized
it at the time. Billy Strayhorn was coming in there every night
after *Jump for Joy* along with everyone else. When I think about
Billy Strayhorn, and a tune called 'Take the A Train', I have to
close my eyes. People think it was written in New York City, but
it wasn't. Sweet Pea – that's what Lena Horne had nicknamed
him – Sweet Pea came into the Capri one evening and brought us
some music scratched out in pencil which we played on our
nightly broadcast. It was 'Take the A Train' before Duke had
seen it; when Duke heard it, he adopted it for the band's theme
song. Billy Berg, a very personable Jewish fellow, used to
announce for the broadcasts. He said on the air, 'Ladies and
gentlemen, now the boys will play "Take a Train".' Lawrence
Welk usually gets the credit for that slip, but it was the
club-owner, Billy Berg. Strayhorn also brought in an incredible
arrangement on 'Flamingo' and another tune of his before Duke
heard it, 'My Little Brown Book'.

Strayhorn was a quiet introspective guy, small in stature, like a miniature. An absolutely brilliant musician, he and Duke's musical rapport was so close that it was hard to tell where one left off and the other began. One night, Strayhorn's at the Capri, disappears for a while and comes back during our break. 'I just lost all my money,' he says, quite calmly, though his eyes revealed how he felt. He had gone to the can and when he got up his money fell into the toilet and was flushed away.

Strayhorn and Lee Young became very good friends: Lee got close to Strayhorn like I gravitated to Blanton. Lee and I had been buddy-buddy since my early days in Los Angeles. We're both Pisces; he was born 7 March, me on 6 March. We've shared so much through the years. I remember our excitement mounting as we waited for Lester to leave Basie's band and join ours. Everyone in the band knew Lester's music from his hits with Count Basie. Who didn't? Lester was our musical hero and playing with him kept us at the top of our game. The six months' residence required by the union passed quickly. When Lester joined the band as a full member, we really started to swing at full throttle. We loved playing Sweet Pea's tunes . . . in fact, playing in that band was like being involved in an intense love affair. Naturally we played many Basie hits like 'Lester Leaps In' and 'Tickletoe'. We were a crowd-pleasing band, playing tunes like 'Stairway to the Stars' as well. Lee had a fine voice; the audience loved his vocals. Our theme song was a tune I wrote called 'On Again, Off Again' and Lester played my tune 'Pastel' as a solo. Billie Holiday always had requests for 'Strange Fruit'. She'd sing it, but she told Lee how much she hated to do it because it made her cry every time. Apparently, her daddy had been strung up in the South. She wanted to sing 'Pastel' as a solo and stupidly, to my detriment, I didn't let her do it because I wasn't satisfied with the lyrics. So that one passed me right by.

Billie and Lester were very close friends, totally enamoured of each other's artistry. He played the way she sang; she sang the way he played. Everyone fell in love with what they were doing together. They always had plenty to rap about, having been in New York and in Basie's band together. Both of them were true innovators. Neither vocal style nor tenor-saxophone style were ever the same after Billie Holiday or Lester Young.

Billie had nicknamed Lester 'Prez' and Lester nicknamed her 'Lady Day'. He had a way of naming everybody, so Holiday became Lady Day to him. Many people thought Lester was 'strange' but that's completely erroneous, nothing could be further from the truth. That was just Lester. Everyone was Lady this, Lady that. He called me Lady Red. Along with Jo Jones, Lester invented many words we have now like 'the fuzz' or 'Bob Crosby' for the police. 'Orrin Tucker' was what he called a dirty guy – you can imagine what Orrin Tucker rhymes with. Everything Lester said was almost in code; he had his own private language. 'Where's your pound cake?' meant where's your wife or girlfriend. To Lester, pound cake was so rich, you couldn't get any better than that. Wearing a hat meant having sex. If he saw a fat lady go by on the street, he'd say la de da de . . . which meant all ass and no body. If he liked what he saw he'd say 'peaches and cream'. He'd comment on everyone, though he never poked fun at people in a cruel manner. Lester was an extremely sensitive human being who bruised easily. His gestures and manners were so exact, they became classic. He also had a distinct little whistle. When the band members heard it, we knew it was time to play.

I loved Lester dearly, enjoyed hanging out with him. He was a soft-spoken man who wouldn't hurt a fly. We mostly rapped about music and his experiences on the road. After he came out of the army, in 1945, he became quite close-mouthed. I knew the army had affected him negatively, had turned him inside instead of out. He was an introvert by nature and the army had darkened his view of humanity. He'd been incarcerated in an Arkansas or Mississippi prison for having a tiny bit of pot on his person. So when he was finally discharged he never touched pot or any drugs; he literally drank himself into bad health. At the time, I lived a few blocks away from him and would go over to his house in the morning to mix his morning concoctions for him. The recipe was a quart of gin and a quart of sauterne mixed together in a punchbowl. A horrible blend, but he dug it. That was how he lived, he didn't eat properly, sometimes not at all. He was sort of heartbroken because he knew he was the real innovative stylist. 'Stan Getz gets the money for playing me,' he said.

Funny, I never thought of Lester as an alcoholic. Lester never had a smoke or a drink until he was thirty, came from a very strict and close family. Lots of the guys drank. Some could handle it and others couldn't – I was in the latter category. That fact that someone else drank all the time never bothered me; I just thought they wanted a drink. Several musicians drank in the daytime; it was no big deal then. Bumps Meyers, who was like Lester's soul brother, was one of them. Both were Sagittarians, they really dug each other, played different tenor styles and never got in each other's way. Both could drink and handle it. You'd never see either of them stagger or fall. The booze didn't affect their playing, but it ultimately killed both of them.

Lee Young and Lester Young were like night and day. Probably the only thing they shared in common except their musical family background was their love of sport, particularly baseball. Lee was, and is, a leader, an extrovert, a consummate businessman, dependable, organized, health-conscious, a terrific golfer, a great drummer – 'a drum college all by himself' as Sir Charles Thompson puts it. Lee's only vice was ice cream and malts. Other guys would be sitting around sipping booze while Lee would be sipping a milkshake. Though Lee never censured anyone for what they did, if they were smoking pot or whatever, Lee was cool. He's a very clean-cut person with a broad spectrum of interests. When the band finally split up, Lee went on with the Nat Cole Trio for several years. At the height of his career, he decided he didn't want anybody saying 'you should have heard Lee Young in 1954 or whatever year'. So he went into the record business, worked for Liberty, ABC, Dunhill and for Motown two separate times. It's the genius of Lee Young you hear in the 'Motown Sound' and in many of the hit records of the late fifties, early sixties and seventies.

A young college student used to come into the Capri frequently. He always wore sneakers, dressed casually, was of medium height and build, had light sandy hair. By day he worked as a film cutter at MGM; by night he was a fixture on the jazz scene, particularly at the 331 Club. This unassuming young man was to have a profound effect on the world of jazz. By now you might have guessed I'm talking about Norman Granz. When he was in his early twenties he began to hire different halls around town for Sunday-afternoon jam sessions. Norman took special delight in inviting selected musicians to come and play: Joe Comfort, myself and Johnny Miller on bass, Nat Cole, Phineas Newborn, Art Tatum, Lee and Lester Young . . . and many more. We did it for the love of making music, for the joy of playing. There certainly wasn't more than a few dollars involved in those days. Art Tatum always insisted on playing for free. Then Norman got the idea of having a jazz concert at the hall where the LA Philharmonic Orchestra played. The building was owned by a Baptist organization which eventually frowned on presenting jazz in their territory. Before Norman got the word to get out, several of those sessions were recorded. I played on the very first, with Illinois Jacquet, Howard McGhee, Gene Krupa, Willie Smith, Charlie Ventura, Joe Guy, Garland Finney and Ulysses Livingston. Later, he took Jazz at the Philharmonic on the road with the best musicians available and all the new hot ones who were coming on the scene. His intense love for jazz has kept Basie and Ella Fitzgerald in the public eye for years and years. Norman kept recording great jazz even when other companies had dropped it. He knew he wasn't going to sell millions of records, but that wasn't what Norman is all about.

Back in 1942 Norman had the bright idea of recording Nat Cole, Oscar Moore who played guitar in Nat's trio, Lester Young and myself. One Friday afternoon we all got together in Glenn Wallach's little studio on the corner of Sunset and Vine. All of us, that is, but Oscar Moore. We waited for hours but Oscar never showed. 'Let's go on ahead and do it,' I said, since I was the rhythm section. So we got a balance and played, having no notion it would be for posterity. 'Indiana', 'Tea for Two', 'Body and Soul', 'I Can't Get Started' – those sides are collectors' items now. For years, Norman made sure we got royalties on that date, he was always fair with musicians. Now that the sides have been bootlegged in Europe, we don't get a nickel.

Nat Cole was a very organized pianist, concise in his introductions. He'd say, 'OK, I got four bars.' And it would be four bars; he had a way of letting you know exactly when to enter. Nat was a thorough musician – that's why everything he did came off so well. Though he was heavily influenced by Earl Hines, his chord progressions were more pianistic than Hines's famous 'trumpet style' of playing. To my ears, more musical. Few people know how truly great he was as a pianist because he made his sensation singing. Nat was the kind of guy who would do anything he said he would do – even if he had to break his butt to do it. Once, we were going to one of the Norman Granz Sunday sessions. Nat came by our house on 20th Street in his Studebaker with one side of the car completely crushed. There had been a big storm and a tree had fallen over his car. Something like that would never deter Nat Cole. I climbed in the car from the driver's side, hanging on to my bass all the way to the gig. That was the Nat Cole I knew . . . a funny guy, beautiful guy.

His first wife Nadine was equally lovely. He often used her name as an alias to avoid contractual problems on record dates. 'Shorty Nadine' certainly got around. The Coles lived on 42nd Street then, right off Central Avenue. Many was the time that Emma and I would go over there and share red beans and rice with them. We were all poor together, though not starving poor. We enjoyed ourselves.

In '43 I had an offer to be in an MGM movie. *I Dood It!* starred Red Skelton and Eleanor Powell, and contained a segment which featured Hazel Scott and Lena Horne. Lee Young and I were part of Hazel Scott's trio. Here was another marvellous pianist; she played the hell out of the piano. In those days they sold sex more than they did music. The cameras panned in on her beautiful bust, ignoring her dancing fingers for the most part. They just couldn't realize how great musicians can also be female. *I Dood It!* also featured a number called 'Jericho' with Lena Horne and Jack Trainor on trumpet fronting a truly great large band. Trainor was supposed to blow a wall down and he looked the part – he was built like a halfback. The story, according to the Hollywood press releases, was 'a song-sprinkled adventure comedy of a glamorous footlight's favourite's spite marriage to her saucer-eyed pants-presser swain'. But, for the musicians, the story was about the greatness of Lena Horne and Hazel Scott.

Another film opportunity came along the following year. Norman Granz was co-producing *Jammin' the Blues* with cinematographer Gjon Mili. This was a short feature with Lester Young, Jo Jones, Big Sid Catlett, Barney Kessel, John Simmons, Harry Edison, Dickie Wells, Marlowe Morris, Garland Finney, myself and one of my best buddies, Marie Bryant, who sang and danced. Marie loved Louis Armstrong so much she sang 'Sunny Side of the Street' exactly like Louis, note for note. I played on that tune as well as a blues in B flat. When Marie was singing she kept looking at me. I was smiling back at her behind my dark glasses. In those days my eyes would be a little pink and I thought shades would hide it. Lester's smoking a cigarette through the whole film, holding up his horn to the side. That way he had of holding his horn was his trademark. Most people think it's for effect, but he started doing it back in the days when he was playing carnival shows with the Young Family Band. He had to hold his horn up to one side to keep it from getting kicked if one of the dancers on the line kicked too high.

Soundies were popular then too; quick five- or three-minute films that one viewed on a small screen – kind of a jukebox movie idea; put in a quarter and see a moving picture. Recently I was pleasantly surprised when I saw a soundie I'd entirely forgotten I appeared in – a club scene with Roy Milton's band. Camille Howard played some dynamite piano and the blues singer, June Richmond, was really shaking up the set. It's difficult to remember all the many and various things I've done through the years. Often I went from one date to another, and inevitably you lose track of some. Memory is strangely selective. But the more I remember, the more it opens up.


Business was so good at the Capri that Billy Berg decided to move the whole show to a much bigger, posher place on Beverly and Fairfax in Hollywood, the Trouville. Where the Capri could seat only ninety people the Trouville comfortably accommodated 250. It was decorated in 'Hollywood' style and the opening was a true gala event. Again we had the Spirits of Rhythm, Joe Turner, Billie Holiday, Slim and Slam and the Lee and Lester Young Band on the bill. Not long after the opening I received a letter from the government I'd been dreading – my draft notice. It was 1943 and America was fully involved in World War II. There was no alternative but to report to the Draft Board. After being in military school I *knew* what the army was like – when somebody said 'JUMP' – you jumped. I never did dig that kind of discipline so before going down to report I had chewed my fingernails off in an attempt to appear neurotic. At the place I twitched and tried to act nervous; it wasn't hard, I was nervous. But I passed the physical anyway and was classified 1A. They put me on leave, gave a twenty-one-day furlough, said they would call me. I omitted mentioning my ROTC training.

My luck didn't fail; I managed to stay on that twenty-one-day furlough for the entire war. They just never called. Of course I didn't call them, either. A lot of the guys, Bumps Meyers, Eddie Beal, called them up to inquire when they had to report. They were given a definite date. Buddy Collette and some other musicians had already joined the navy because they were able to get into the navy band. Recruiters came down to Local 767. Whenever a musician was drafted, these recruiters would see to it that they were funnelled into an army band. The drummer I worked with so often in the 1950s and after, Bill Douglass, wound up being the drum major of the 144th Division, the contingent that marched through Italy to liberate Rome. Bill tells a great story about his experiences running army jeeps on Italian cognac instead of gasoline, but my destiny took me in another direction. The Lee and Lester Young Band had an offer to play Cafe Society Downtown in New York's Greenwich Village, 2 Sheridan Square.

Emma, my stepson Ronald and our three-year-old daughter Sylvia came with me to New York. We stayed with a friend of my mother's, Miss Pearl Tilman. She was a great hostess and cook; I'll never forget her warm hospitality. We remained somewhat incognito because my relatives in Brooklyn were too square (or so I thought then) to accept my musician lifestyle. They had made it clear when I visited in '39 that I'd be much better off with a nice safe job in the post office – a far cry from what was happening at the Cafe Society Downtown.

There were two Cafe Society clubs – one uptown in the 50s, the other in the Village. Leonard Feather, newly arrived from England, lived in an apartment over the Downtown club. The uptown club was plush, catering to the bigwigs. Downtown the clientele consisted mainly of the numbers-racket dudes and their chicks; pimps, hustlers and lovely black sporting ladies, dressed to the nines in their diamonds and minks. Some uptown bigwigs passed through when they went 'slumming'. You had to be doing something to go to that club; the tariffs were high. New Yorkers were wild about boogie-woogie pianists and two of the best opened the show: Pete Johnson and Albert Ammons. A hilarious avant-garde satirical group called the Reviewers with Adolph Green, Judy Holliday and Betty Comdon peformed between the musical sets. There was also a classical pianist, Sam Reichman Lewis – something to please everybody, including the original tenor-saxophone stylings of Lester Young.

All the musicians who were in New York at that time came by to dig Prez. Everybody would try to cut him, but Lester blew them all down. Ben Webster would try to keep up with Lester both on the bandstand and out in the alley drinking booze. Unfortunately Ben couldn't hold his liquor the way Prez could and he ended up frustrated, drunk and beaten down by Lester's horn. Even Coleman Hawkins would come by the Cafe Society to hear Lester because his sound was so unique. At the time, 1944, Charlie Parker's alto playing was upsetting all the alto-saxophone players – all the disciples of Johnny Hodges, Benny Carter, Russell Procope knew their days were numbered. Parker was a breath of fresh air back then, just as the flautist James Newton is today. When I first heard Dizzy Gillespie play with Parker it was a revelation to me that guys could play together like that. From that period on the whole style of music changed.

It was quite an experience to be there, just bad on the health. The only drag about the Cafe Society Downtown was the hours. In LA, we worked from 10 p.m. to 2 a.m. In New York, we're making more bucks, but the hours were from 8 p.m. to 4 a.m. which is too long a stretch to be involved in music; the money should have been twice as much and it wasn't. By the time you get off, you're exhausted. During our breaks we'd go out the back door to the alley, stand around drinking, smoking weed, chewing bennies – anything to keep going because the gig was so long. Lester turned us on to his version of a boilermaker. The bottom layer was 151-proof rum, topped off with Rainier Ale. We'd drink these down and it was a bomb.

Jimmy Rowles, our pianist, had been snatched by Benny Goodman before we arrived in New York. Who could refuse Goodman's bread? We were fortunate enough to get Clyde Hart for our pianist, and I was doubly fortunate because I became Clyde's friend. He opened new worlds to me by inviting me to his house to listen to Stravinsky recordings. We followed the scores to 'Petrouchka', 'Firebird Suite', 'The Rite of Spring'. Uptown,

Bird was the new sensation, yet I was far more taken with
Stravinsky's unusual harmonies, his use of polyrhythms, the way
he fitted atonal and polytonal passages together. By listening
closely I discovered that Duke Ellington was a Stravinsky fan too.
That was the beginning of my love affair with the modern classics.

On nights off, I went to the Village Vanguard to play with
Willie 'the Lion' Smith. Mezz Mezzrow was in his band. He
wasn't the world's greatest clarinettist, but he always had a job
because he provided the very best weed to smoke. Albert
Ammons had taken a liking to me; he invited Emma and me over
to his house for dinner. He was a soul-food fanatic . . . they'd
serve ham hocks and butter beans, red beans and rice, greens,
cornbread, black-eyed peas, sweet potatoe pie . . . mountains of
food. Maybe all the home-style cooking reminded Emma of
something she was missing back in LA. I can't say I blame her,
what with the hours I was working – I hardly saw her or the
children. I had a pretty strong notion, too, that there was
someone back on the West Coast she was homesick for – and it
wasn't her mom and dad.

Then one night I began to feel very weak. My throat was sore, I
was feeling terrible, I had no idea what was happening to me; I
lost my desire to eat or drink. The Cafe Society blurred before my
eyes. I was stumbling around in a daze, barely alive. It occurred
to me that here I am, twenty-eight years old and I might die.
Somehow I got to a hospital to ask for help. They put me in a
wheelchair and straight to bed. Pneumonia, that's what it was,
from going out in the cold between sets while I was damp with
perspiration from playing the bass. Walking outside in the ice and
snow and getting loaded. Same kind of thing Blanton did and I
knew better. Fortunately my recovery was rapid. I went right
back to work and thanked Lester Young for saving my life – I had
stopped kidding myself. No way could I ever drink while playing
a gig. Meanwhile, all the guys were going on blithely, as though
nothing had happened.

Emma saw me through my illness, but by that time homesick-
ness was written all over her face. I put her, Ronald and Sylvia on
the train heading west. Clyde Hart, busy New York musician that
he was, had committed for another engagement. Lee hired Sir
Charles Thompson, who was known then merely as 'Chase'.
Within a few weeks the engagement was over. I had been doing a

lot of thinking, thinking about my life, what was I doing with myself, trying to feel out my true desires. I had always liked the trio format – Nat Cole's group had been my inspiration. Before all the guys in the band headed back for California, I asked the guitar player, Louis Gonsales and Charles Thompson if they would like to join the Red Callender Trio. They both said yes, though I found out it was now 'Sir Charles' I'd hired, not Chase. He said, 'There's an Earl, a Duke and a Count – you might as well have a knight.'

The trio became a reality when a patron of the Cafe Society, a rich heiress, offered to buy us uniforms and set us up with a booking agency, the Harold Oxley Agency, the same outfit which booked the Jimmie Lunceford Band. No romance was involved, nothing personal with this kind lady; she simply took an interest in me and she could afford it. The Harold Oxley Agency had us pegged wrong; they must have thought a trio would be playing cornpone, because they booked us in some weird, some very inappropriate places. We were playing jazz, singing hip little songs; Louis Gonsales was a great singer. We all sang – that was the draw, the entertainment aspect of our trio. I did most of the arrangements and composed a new tune for the woman I'd recently put on the train to LA: 'Baby I'm Gone'.

We played upstate New York during the blizzard season, then were booked into Lord Landsdowne's in Toledo, working our way there through western Pennsylvania. Lord Landsdowne's was memorable, as Cab Calloway's band was in town. It was there I met the trumpeter Freddy Webster as well as Milt Hinton who used to practise his bass constantly, even during the breaks between shows.

The next gig was Kenosha, Wisconsin, a short train-ride from Chicago. During our time off, we'd go straight to the Club DeLisa in Chicago where Red Saunders was leading a great band. That's where the black folks hung out; the Grand Terrace where Earl Hines played was too expensive. Chicago had wonderful after-hours spots; we had a ball visiting there. The three of us would rent a hotel room, then catch the train the following day back to Kenosha. One day Sir Charles and I hurried down to the train station to catch the last train that would get us back in time for our gig. Louis had disappeared. I knew he had no money in his pocket; I had all the money. We figured he might turn up

EXCLUSIVE

MANUFACTURED BY EXCLUSIVE RECORDS, HOLLYWOOD, U.S.A.

MASTER
SERIES
202-B

INSTRUMENTAL

"SKYLINE"
(Red Callender)
RED CALLENDER TRIO
Lou Gonzales - Guitar
Duke Brooks - Piano
Red Callender - Bass
RR-9955-1

ONLY FOR NON-COMMERCIAL USE ON PHONOGRAPHS IN HOMES. WE HAVE AGREED THIS RECORD SHALL NOT BE RESOLD, OR USED FOR ANY

SRC 10056
THESE FOOLISH THINGS
Strachey-Link-Marvel
THE RED CALLENDER SIX
Harry Edison - Trumpet
Herbie Haymer - Alto Sax.
Arnold Ross - Piano
Paul Leslie - Guitar
Red Callender - Bass
Shadow Wilson - Drums

SUN-114

Sunset
RECORDINGS

B&W
BLACK & WHITE

NOT LICENSED FOR BROADCAST

782-B
(BW 268)

Inst.

RED BOOGIE
(Red Callender)
RED CALLENDER TRIO
Red Callender, bass
W. McDaniel, piano
L. Enois, guitar

eventually; actually we were worried about him. That same night, as Sir Charles and I were performing as a duo, in strolls Louis with his guitar, having walked the railroad tracks all the way from Chicago to Kenosha. Louis was something else. He would drink up all his money as fast as he got it, bourbon or whatever he could get his hands on. Sir Charles was and still is a real card, a real character, very garrulous type. When he was travelling in the trio he used to get loaded on nutmeg. With Sir Charles high on spice, Louis drunk on whatever, I had to be cool because I was handling the bread. We worked a few more gigs together in the Midwest before Sir Charles decided to return to New York. Louis and I caught a train for Los Angeles.

The trio idea stuck; we simply regrouped. Duke Brooks came in on piano. Los Angelenos were as crazy about trios as New Yorkers were for boogie-woogie pianists. Exclusive Records signed us and we recorded some of my tunes like 'Skyline' and standards like 'How Come' and 'Everything about You Appeals to Me'. We were never without a gig but Duke Brooks was kind of a gypsy and decided one day to hop a freight back to St Louis. He was never heard from again. Much later I learned he'd been killed.

I also formed a sextet called the Red Callender Six to record for the Sunset label. Harry Edison, my old friend 'Sweets', played trumpet; Herbie Haymer on alto saxophone; Arnold Ross, piano; Les Paul on guitar and Shadow Wilson on drums. The trio received a new burst of energy when Louis Gonsales finally got a straight job to support all his children and Lucky Enois became the guitarist. Lucky gave our group a lot more drive with his Kansas City guitar and vocal style, a whole new feeling. Willard McDaniel, a powerful two-fisted piano player, was now with us. We recorded for the Black and White label and played all over; the Casa Blanca in Los Angeles, Slim Jenkins's in Oakland, and a long stint at the Rite Spot in Glendale. We even had a minor hit around town with a tune I wrote based on a kid's game, called 'Red Light' . . . 1, 2 – 3, 4 – 5678, 9, 10 . . . and into the blues. The LA columnists were writing about us and Barry Ulanov paid me a back-handed compliment about my singing. We were playing for the people with tunes like 'By the River St Marie' and 'Red Boogie'; we were having a ball.

That trio also played intermission sets at the Casa Mañana,

which was the old Cotton Club. The bandstand there was huge, large enough for two bands, each to one side, with the trio set up centre stage. One evening we remained onstage to have a jam session with the two bands on the bill – Duke Ellington and Charlie Barnet. It probably lasted half an hour or so – an incredible high. We jammed on some tune like 'Cottontail', some tune based on the 'I Got Rhythm' changes with a new melody. I could have jammed on and on that night for ever.

PART THREE

# Pastel Kaleidoscope

In 1946 I got a call from New York, from Joe Glaser, who was Louis Armstrong's manager and a pretty gruff fellow.

'Hey kid,' he growls, 'want to do a picture?'

They were making a picture at the Hal Roach Studio; the name of the picture was *New Orleans* and the cast included Billie Holiday and Louis Armstrong. Having worked with Louis at the Vogue Ballroom in '37, and sidelined with him in *Every Day's a Holiday* in the early 1940s, Louis remembered and asked for me, had Glaser call to hire me for the picture. I think it was about $600 a week.

Naturally, Billie Holiday and Louis Armstrong weren't the stars, they were just the musical interest. Woody Herman and his big band were in it also – they played the big theatre – we were just the street band in New Orleans at the time. As great a singer as Billie Holiday was, her part was just a maid. Louis was some sort of handyman who happened to play trumpet. The band had Zutty Singleton on drums; Charlie Beal, Eddie's brother, on piano; Barney Bigard on clarinet; Bud Scott, who played guitar and kept a cigar in his mouth all the time; Kid Ory on trombone and me, Red Callender, the kid again. I was the bebopper in the old-timer's band, but who cared? I had fun and to me music was always music; I didn't care what style it was as long as I could handle it.

The stars, Arturo de Cordova and Dorothy Patrick, weren't too memorable, nor was the plot. Cordova played a gambler and Dorothy Patrick was a society girl, a budding opera singer whose parents didn't want her to associate with this guy. That's where we came in; we played at the gambling joint. We weren't exactly

61

street urchins but we wore ragged-looked clothes, we were supposed to be poor New Orleans musicians who played on the tailgates of wagons.

The picture was being made at the beginning of the McCarthy era when the witch hunt was really getting under way. When we started shooting everything was real cool, we began on a happy note. It was a gradual thing the way it seeped in; eventually things became more and more uptight. Jules Levey, the producer, and Herbert Biberman, the writer, were suspect because they were so-called liberals. We were supposed to have worked much longer than we did; the picture was brought to a hasty finish. Our part was cut short. In the original script Louis's band was slated to appear on the same bill as Woody Herman's at a big stage concert. We had our tuxedos and everything, filmed it, but thanks to McCarthyism it was never shown. Later, in 1947, Biberman was one of the 'Hollywood Ten'; he refused to testify in front of the House Un-American Activities Committee and was sent to jail. Around this same period I was on a record date with Red Norvo and Red Nichols. 'McCarthy will get you guys,' my friends joked. 'Three Reds on one date?'

Hollywood had certain hiring tactics. There was a general consensus that black people should only be allowed to play subservient roles. The only acceptable alternative role for a black person was as an entertainer. You'd never see a black doctor or lawyer in a picture even though at that time there were plenty. Anybody with intelligence was anathema to the decision-makers. When we were playing at the gambling joint, the bandstand was located next to the kitchen. Being the bass player, I was in the back right next to the door where the food came through. The waiters brought out crêpe suzettes and the director wanted me to bug my eyes and lick my lips. I refused to do it; I looked on with appreciation but that's all. I wasn't very popular with the director, Arthur Lubin, but I wasn't going to Tom for anybody.

Billie Holiday was naturally teed off, having to play a maid. She dealt with it gracefully given the circumstances. She was a big star who never considered herself a star. Musicians were her favourite people. Nothing stand-offish about Billie Holiday, she would talk and joke like she was one of the guys and she was. She was still so beautiful and striking then. But that's the way the script was written; if it hadn't been written that way, we might never have been in the picture at all. I think the fact that Louis and Billie were in the picture saved it from utter banality.

The call would be for eight or nine o'clock in the morning to take advantage of the sunlight for the street scenes. When you're shooting a picture you stay there, even though you might not get called to do a bit until late afternoon. Or they call you to do a bit, shoot from different angles, then you go to your dressing-room and wait until you're called again. During those days, Lady Day was a freak for tonk, a fast card game she loved to play. She would wander off by herself frequently; at other times when she was feeling blue she would come out and play tonk with the guys. I might have won once or twice but she was the real pro.

Lady Day would wear the long gloves; everybody knew she had a habit. When she'd try to be straight, these people whom I call leeches would always seek her out and lay some drugs on her to get her going again. Being like she was, she was an easy victim. They'd allow these leeches on the set, they'd let them into her private dressing-room.

So during the breaks we'd sit around and play tonk or whatever. Several of the guys would have a drink. I no longer drank while I was working, or smoked pot even though the best pot was always available. I'd learned about smoking pot while working when once I arrived at a picture call high. I just barely got there on time, loaded and utterly miserable because of the pressure. I found out, to my good fortune, that when you're high, you're paranoid. You think everybody's noticing you and it's not necessarily so. I was lucky enough to discover I couldn't handle pot and play a gig. That was the end of that.

Some good music came out of this picture, the best thing being 'Do You Know What It Means to Miss New Orleans?' Billie Holiday sang it; since then it's become a standard. Composers Eddie de Lange and Louis Alter had hurriedly scratched it down in pencil; we rehearsed it and recorded it all in the same day. It was great fun. Nothing ever bothered Louis; he just took life as it came. Many people associate Louis with singing and hitting the high notes on the trumpet, but Louis could really swing. When we weren't shooting we had little get-togethers playing tunes like 'Lady Be Good'. On a break during the shooting of *Every Day's a Holiday* I remember standing around with my tuba playing Hoagy Carmichael's 'Stardust'. It amazed some people that a

tuba player could think melodically. Louis comes over and says,
'Give me some of that!' We traded licks until the man screamed
'PLACES . . .' We had a ball. There was a part in *New Orleans*
where Louis introduces all the members of the band with rhymes
he, de Lange and Louis Alter made up like:

> Let me introduce Mr Charlie Beal
> Piano man, can he steal
> Only got two hands, but that's plenty
> When he plays, it sounds like twenty . . .

Charlie Beal had come back from a tour in Italy to make this
picture, he's always been a world-traveller type. I didn't know it
at the time but Charlie had played with Louis when Louis was a
young man. Kid Ory, the great composer of 'Muskrat Ramble',
who must have been in his sixties at the time, came out of
retirement to make the film:

> Here's Kid Ory on the horn
> Greatest slide man ever born
> Plays trombone with laughing notes
> No human being ever wrote . . .

   Zutty Singleton was a real fun guy as I knew him. We might be
playing 'Stardust' or any other tune and Zutty would want to take
one on the snare drum, he'd rap out the melody on the snare,
which a lot of people thought was pretty corny, but that's the way
he felt about it . . .

> Everybody knows Zutty Singleton
> Can beat them sheep skins like no one
> Cymbals, bells and all that stuff
> Give out a chorus and treat 'em rough . . .

> And here's Barney Bigard on the clarinet
> You ain't never heard nothing like it yet
> When he cuts loose I know you'll roar
> Mr Bigard, please give us more . . .

> Now here's Bud Scott and his old guitar

Always smokin' that big cigar
He's the rhythm man of a great renown
Give a listen while he goes to town . . .

Red Callender, meet him face to face
He's the one who plays that old slap bass
He started out with a violin
But the doggone thing grew up on him . . .

After Louis introduced me the music had to go into another key. I was given either a two-bar or four-bar break to set it up. It happened to be quitting time for the day so I had a whole night to think about what I wanted to play. I figured out a modulation which I thought was pretty hip. Actually it was bebop. The band didn't notice a thing . . . although all my friends said, 'Man, what were you doing putting bebop in there . . .?'

When Louis got to himself he said,

And then there's me, excuse my crust
Introduce myself I must
I'm Satchmo Armstrong don't forget
I've got to give out on the old cornet . . .

Louis was beautiful. If there had never been a Louis Armstrong we never would have reached the point in jazz where we are now. In my estimation Louis was the first father of modern jazz. Aside from his humour, strong personality and great musicianship, he was also a great entertainer. People often get entertaining and music mixed up, but Louis could do it all. His energy came from the audience and he gave it back to them. I was elated to be making the picture with him, with all these New Orleans musicians who had made history. Totally elated.

Not long after the picture was finished, Sarah Vaughan was working at Sardi's on Hollywood Boulevard near Vine Street. Her bass player got into an automobile accident, and her pianist, Ronnell Bright, called me to sub for him.

One evening Joe Glaser comes into Sardi's, sits down, sees me and says, 'There he is now, the godamn fool. I tried to make him famous and he turned me down.'

The story was this – after *New Orleans* they formed the Louis

Armstrong All Stars. Of course they called me for it; I had just worked with him. Frenchy, Glaser's road manager, called and said, 'Hey kid – we're gonna start to work in a couple of weeks. We want you.'

I said, 'What kind of money does it pay?'

Frenchy says, 'Well, what do you want?'

'I figure I'm worth at least $450 a week.'

'WWWWHHHHAAAAT???? For a *bass* player?'

So I said, 'Well, you don't need me . . .'

I was doing that well or better with the studio scene, working when I wanted, had my own trio going. I never played the same thing two days in a row. I really didn't want it in the first place knowing that I'd have to play 'Sleepytime Down South' every night and the few other things they played over and over again. I just didn't see any progress there.

Everyone knows the rest of the story, the fame of the All Stars. They were getting $25,000 a night for that aggregation. I figured what was $450 a week? It wasn't so much the money, and it hasn't ever bothered me. I'm still in the learning stages of music, I never relegated myself to one kind of music. I like to be able to do it all, so I turned it down with no regrets.


After a day of being on the set of *New Orleans* I'd be glad to get the hell out of there because that's when Erroll and Doc and I would hang out and play music . . .

I first met Erroll Garner in late 1945. My trio was working in a joint on San Pedro near Adams called the Casablanca. It was a place owned by Elihu McGhee, whom everyone called Black Dot. Prior to this, Norman Granz had been telling me about this wild little piano player from Pittsburgh. 'Just wait till you hear him,' he said, 'then you'll hear the ultimate piano.'

At the Casablanca, the trio consisted of myself, Lucky Enois, my great Kansas City guitarist and a piano player named Clay Savage who called himself Jack LaRue. Willard McDaniel had gone on to other things, and I'd hired LaRue. He was a feisty little guy, a real showman. One night Erroll walks into the club and we invite him to sit in. Never had I heard anything like it, but I spied his whole card from the very first note. He had that lagging, delayed style, being a natural southpaw; this was where the beat was. We fell in love musically right away. It was like turning on a big light, a big bulb went off in my head. We got along beautifully from the very git, meaning beginning, the beginning of one of the happiest experiences in my life.

We became good friends and I let go of my trio, started playing with Erroll and Doc West. I was entranced with the way he played, loved it. At the time, I had left Emma and had a room on 25th Street at Henry and Marie Coker's house. When Erroll and Doc got a place a few blocks away on 28th Street, I gradually started living there too. I'd come back from a day making the picture and Doc, who was one of the original modern drummers, would cook something to eat. He was a great cook who could take very little and make a fabulous meal. He could make cornbread that would melt in your mouth, he could take a steak and smother it so it was tender, sweet potatoes, rice, chicken, anything. After dinner we'd sit around and drink Pernod, that stuff you put water in and watch it turn green, smoke grass, get high, talk, have a good time. We had a spacious house with a room and a half at the top we called 'the penthouse'. We each had our own room and there was an upright piano in the living-room where we rehearsed.

Often, we'd go around the corner and roam up and down Central Avenue. All the joints were open, like the Last Word, the Chicken Shack, the Turban Room. Jack's Basket Room was one of our favourites; they had chicken in the basket, so we'd either eat, or play and then eat, then go looking for someplace else to play. When Bird was in town we'd find him and jam with him. Too bad none of this was ever recorded; we'd play until it ran over into the next day. I have to say it again – some of the best music has never been recorded. By night all these clubs looked glamorous, though by day, like any nightspot it smelled like beer, had cigarette butts on the floor. The glamour was at night. All these clubs on Central Avenue were really very nice places that served great food and had facilities for musicians. Different groups like Wardell Gray, Dexter Gordon, Teddy Edwards, Carl Perkins, or comedy acts like Jimmy Rogers, or the team of Redd Foxx and Slappy White would be working the different clubs. Sitting in was part of it, even though the union still had its injunction against more musicians on the bandstand than the club-owner was paying for. We'd play until we got caught; we played for the joy of playing.

There used to be Sunday-afternoon jam sessions at the Doll House in Culver City, at Whistling's Hawaii on Sunset and at the Tiki on Western. Erroll played regularly at the Oasis and after hours we'd go to Glenn's Back Room, also on Western. Erroll would go anywhere there was music even though the pianos in some of these places were awful. Someone would say to the owner, 'Why don't you get the piano fixed?' And the owner would say, 'Well, I just had it painted . . .' Really!

Doc West was a real ladies' man, he was in love with the ladies and liked to talk about his prowess with them, the things he'd do to turn them on. He was very proud of his sexual abilities; I can't think of any other way to put it. Erroll, on the other hand, was very secretive about his love life. I knew he had a girlfriend here and there, but he kept all his relationships private. He was very quiet, shy, introverted, real inside. He expressed himself completely through the piano. One on one, he could really rap up a storm. If there was more than one other person, he became kind of tongue-tied. His favourite saying when he was at a loss for words was 'oo-chi-koo'. Mostly we made or talked about music – music is conversation. He thought of the piano (pian-er he called it) as his orchestra and it showed in the way he played. He liked Boyd Raeburn, Duke Ellington, Jimmie Lunceford, Count Basie. Of course he loved Art Tatum and Oscar Peterson. They loved him too.

Erroll was very dapper, kept his hair in place; he was altogether what you see in photos, a very neat, little bitty guy who made the piano scream. I called him a giant elf because he was a small guy who played like a giant. When he sat down at the piano he was a monster. He never did read music. Though he was always composing, he had someone else write it down. He was one person who didn't need to read; it would have slowed him down. His ear was magical.

Playing with Erroll was inexplicable, unexplainable – a complete joy. He was happy and it was catching. I remember it just like it was yesterday . . . the way he'd rhapsodize in his introductions, not even thinking. Then all of a sudden he'd go into something and you'd better be listening. He didn't even know what he was going to play. I always have been a big listener; if you don't hear the music you can't play in tune. One of my pet sayings is that it takes twenty years to learn to hear correctly and that's probably true. With Garner, I'd place myself on the left side of the piano so I could be aware of what his left hand was doing. That was his rhythm section, his whole secret. Hell, he didn't need a bass player, he just enjoyed the luxury, liked the feel.

After you play things together once or twice you know what's going on in the music. Like Ellington never called any tunes, he'd just bring his hand down or tinkle a phrase on the piano and the band would know exactly what to play. I would invent my own lines to fit what Erroll was doing. When you play with piano players who stride you have to play what they play. Modern piano players will lay down a chord and bass players will invent their own lines to complement it. Consequently, you might never play the same thing twice.

Doc West had a very small bass drum; most of the drummers then had a twenty-two-inch bass drum. Doc's was only eighteen inches, maybe smaller. Formerly, guys like Zutty Singleton used to beat the two and the four on the bass drum and you were always conscious of it. But Doc, Max Roach and Kenny Clarke would carry the rhythm on the topside so the bass player is responsible for the beat more or less. You hear that in music now; guys hardly ever bang on the bass drum, it's used only for punctuation. The drum and the bass become a unit; that's where the time comes from, not the bass drum. So Garner's left hand was like a rhythm machine, Doc carried the beat on the sock cymbal and the hi-hat, and I played time until it was my turn to solo. I'm probably still more time-conscious than solo-conscious, even though I like to think of my playing as Leonard Feather once described it – as a counter-melodic line. Bass players think in combinations of chords and scales. The object is to tie things together so that they make sense.

There is no modern pianist who hasn't been affected by Garner. He was a genius if there ever was one. He had a photographic memory. His brother Linton, who lives in Vancouver, told me about their childhood. Linton would be in one room taking a piano lesson. Erroll would be in another room. When the piano lesson was over, Erroll would sit down and play everything he just heard in the lesson. In our pad on 28th Street, I would go over and noodle on the piano, playing a tune I'd written

# DIAL
## R E C O R D S

2-19-47
Contemporary
American Music

    **1016-A**

## TRIO
(Garner)
### ERROLL GARNER TRIO
ERROLL GARNER _____ Piano
RED CALLENDER _____ Bass
HAROLD WEST _____ Drums

(D-1056-B)

---

# DIAL
## R E C O R D S

2-19-47
Contemporary
American Music

    **1016-B**

## PASTEL
(Callender)
### ERROLL GARNER TRIO
ERROLL GARNER _____ Piano
RED CALLENDER _____ Bass
HAROLD WEST _____ Drums

(D-1055-BB)

when I was nineteen. Erroll dug it and after hearing it a few times he had it down. When we recorded with Charlie Parker Erroll says, 'Why don't we do your tune?' It was called 'Please Let Me Forget'; later the title changed to 'Pastel'. Erroll Garner usually gets composer's credit for it, but it was my tune. Though I'd written the melody when I was nineteen, the lyrics came along much later . . . about a guy who had a real case. They were written for Lena Horne and to this day I don't think she knows that.

Lena and I knew each other from working in the MGM picture *I Dood It!* as well as from working together at the Trocadero where she headlined the show. Around that time, 1943, I also recorded together with Phil Moore and Gerald Wilson. In those days I was young and not too unhandsome, and she, she was out of sight then, beautiful, she still is. Lena kind of liked me so I found myself hanging out with her, visiting her at her house on Horn Avenue. Everyone was after her, especially Herb Jeffries, but he couldn't get to first base either. Lena and I had what might be called a heavy flirtation, an infatuation. Everybody thought there was a lot more to it than that. Of course I didn't do too much to change their minds. People would say 'Oh . . . you and Lena . . .' I wouldn't say a thing. We became and remained pretty close friends. We got along because I knew that Lena was an actress even more than a singer; if she'd relax a beat, I'd relax along with her. Some people are rigid with the beat but I had brains enough to know that if she wanted a nuance – just go along with her. She's a brilliant lady, warm, giving, and anyone could see she had magic. I could see that then; she wasn't only pretty, she had the magic that goes along with it.

In 1947 Lena was the featured attraction along with Xavier Cugat's Orchestra at the Flamingo Club in Las Vegas. She took Arnold Ross, Irving Ashby and myself as her trio. The Flamingo was owned by Bugsy Seigel, the kind of guy that when a waiter dropped a plate or made some noise, he'd literally kick him out of the room. That was during the period when blacks in Las Vegas were relegated to a part of town they called the Dust Bowl because of the unpaved streets. We ended up staying in a house owned by a woman who rented rooms, a Miss Harris. Arnold Ross, whom I dearly love, could have stayed anywhere, but he decided to stay with us because we were together. So we all shared one room with three beds in it, that's the best we could do at the time. They gave Lena a cabin, or trailer behind the Flamingo Club. That's when things were really mean. The black musicians had to go in the back door and stay in the back. When you finished playing you couldn't go into the dining-room. I suppose that's the meaning of being invisible. I heard a story which happened in Las Vegas around the same period: Hazel Scott took a dip in the swimming-pool and after she got out, they drained the pool.

Anyhow, one day Lena and I went to see a movie, an Orson Welles picture. They took our money, though when we were ushered into the partially full theatre, they stuck us way over to one side so the picture looked all distorted. We walked out, got our money back and after the engagement was over I vowed I'd never go back to Las Vegas again. I didn't until 1969. By then things were cool. They changed their policies because they didn't want Martin Luther King marching there. The NAACP had 600 people prepared to sit in every lobby of every major hotel. The hotel-owners panicked and came around. Nothing drastic happened; people are people. Everything went on just as usual; they might make a little more money, that's all. But that soured me on Vegas.

I was glad to get back to Los Angeles. Diane was making life very nice for me, Diane Schumann, a millionaire's daughter who lived in a very lush pad over on Sunset Boulevard where all the big movie stars have their mansions. We met a few years earlier when she used to come into the Rite Spot in Glendale where I played with my trio. Diane was there every night listening to the music. She had eyes for me; one thing led to another, she made it known she liked me, made no bones about it. Certainly she wasn't hard to look at. The way I was raised I wasn't prejudiced, and the circles I was thrown into, the jazz clubs, most of the girls happened to be white. For me it was nothing to do with colour. It didn't matter if she was green, although I'm familiar with several black musicians who will choose a white woman simply because she's white. That wasn't my thing.

Erroll and I would hang out over at her Sunset estate. Driving up the incline to the house, we'd see a couple of Cadillacs and a Jaguar parked out front. Inside the mansion there were antiques, paintings worth thousands of dollars and of course the very best piano money can buy, a Bosendorfer grand piano. Diane's sister was a concert pianist. Diane was quite intellectual, read psychology, history and philosophy; she also wrote several children's books. For my birthday one year she gave me *Remembrance of Things Past*.

One night I was up in my room at the Cokers' on 25th Street, which happened to be at the front of the building. Somebody was throwing pebbles at the window. I peered out the window and said, 'Who's there?'

A voice said, 'Paul.'

'Paul who?'

That wonderful voice said, 'Paul Robeson.' He was standing on the street with Diane; they'd come to find me. Robeson had always been my hero; I'd seen him play Othello at the Biltmore Theatre and had been listening to him sing for years. I loved the way he spoke out about society. Not even in my wildest dreams could I have imagined I'd meet him, especially like this. Naturally I was all excited, threw on my jacket and raced downstairs. We went out to have a drink. Robeson was a friend of the Schumann family, a family that was always for the right causes. This was before Paul was branded a Red or whatever they called it. Yet he was always suspect because he'd been to Russia. We spoke about the racism in this country and he mentioned that in Russia he hadn't experienced racism. But I guess every country has its own brand of racism, every country has its scapegoats. We discussed some of the motivations that underlie people's actions. That was another high in my life, meeting Paul Robeson completely by surprise.

Diane wanted to marry me and her family had no objections, though I objected: I just didn't feel as though I could function in a millionaire's circle. I wanted to make it on my own. Besides, although Emma and I hadn't been living together for years, I was still married to her. Part of the reason, I think, was for protection. I keep a big warm spot in my heart for Emma, but the honeymoon was long over. She had her boyfriends; I had my girlfriends. As far as divorce – I just let that one lay. I had never planned to marry again, I liked my freedom.

A record ban was coming up if the union and the record

THE
# RCA VICTOR
## PREDICTOR POINTS TO
# RED CALLENDER

a series of articles
on new stars in jazz by **LEONARD FEATHER**

## VI

THE BASS seems like the least probable instrument on which to achieve either fame or fortune. Both in classical music and in jazz, its possibilities and the achievements of those who have played it have often been overlooked.

In recent years, though, a change has taken place in jazz. The bass, formerly plucked in a monotonous four-to-the-bar style or even slapped in corny old-time jazz groups, has become a vitally important instrument not only for rhythm but often for solos. The late Jimmy Blanton of Duke Ellington's band was the first to show the solo resources of the bass to full advantage; Slam Stewart's original bowed-bass-cum-voice style grew up around the same time.

Red Callender is one of the great men of the bass who have developed the ideas started by Blanton. Born George Callender, and nicknamed for his ginger hair, he first came to jazz fans' attention with the remarkable band headed by brothers Lee and Lester Young, which played at Cafe Society in New York as well as in California.

Since then, Red has been in demand in Los Angeles for almost every important jazz occasion, from jam sessions and jazz concerts to movie studio work. Like so many of the younger jazzmen, he is a schooled musician and fits in perfectly with any kind of combination.

Last year Red had a trio of his own, with Lucky Enois on guitar and Willard McDaniel on piano, which earned wide popularity among musicians at one of Hollywood's after-hours spots.

In September, when Louis Armstrong arrived to make *New Orleans*, Red was selected as one of the small group featured with Satchmo for the bulk of the musical sequences. The youngest man in the group, surrounded by veterans from New Orleans, Red didn't seem at all out of place—on the contrary, he gave the band a terrific lift. You'll see a close-up of him in one of the early scenes.

Red made two RCA Victor record sessions with Louis at this time, one featuring the tunes from the picture, the other being devoted to old favorites and blues.

Later, Red teamed up with pianist Erroll Garner in the latter's trio, completed by drummer Harold West. In addition, he's recorded with innumerable bands, large and small, on virtually every label on the west coast.

Listen to Red and the other modern bass men like him, and you'll realize that the bass can be used to play melodies just like any other instrument. All it takes is technique, ideas and a set of strong fingers. Red Callender has all the qualifications.

## BRIGADOON ALBUM OUT NOW

An album of selections from the new hit musical "Brigadoon" is out now on RCA Victor records.

Recorded by the original cast, the selections are presented the same as in the Broadway production.

Heading up the cast are David Brooks, Marion Bell, Pamela Britton and Lee Sullivan. The orchestral accompaniment is by Franz Allers and the Brigadoon orchestra. Also heard is the Brigadoon chorus.

The romantic, fanciful mood of the show which is playing before packed houses on Broadway is captured in the records. The same top drawer talent that is keeping those houses packed turns in the same kind of performance in the album.

Illustrating the album is a well-written and pictured album liner which explains each number and its place in the story.

The songs recorded are *Once in the Highlands, Brigadoon, Down on MacConnachy Square, Waitin' for My Dearie, I'll Go Home with Bonnie Jean, The Heather on the Hill, Come to Me, Almost Like Being in Love, There But for You Go I, My Mother's Wedding Day,* and *From This Day On.* The album number is P-178 and it is available in RCA Victor record stores throughout the country.

## WHIFFENPOOF COCKTAIL

At a party following the broadcast of the RCA Victor Show on May 18 Robert Merrill was honored for his recording of the *Whiffenpoof Song* by having a "Whiffenpoof Cocktail" devised and introduced. The recipe follows:

2 Parts Coronet Brandy
1 Part Dubonnet
A Dash of Simple Syrup
Twist of Lemon Rind

Mix and serve chilled in either a martini or old fashion glass.

The Whiffenpoof Cocktail may easily be distinguished by its delicate pink color.

**RED**

4

companies couldn't agree by November of 1947. The companies were making records like they were going out of style, which they were, temporarily. That was one of my busiest periods. If I didn't have two record dates in a day, it was a bad day. I recorded with all sorts of people – from Joe Liggins and the Honeydrippers, Al Hibbler, Hadda Brooks and Francis Faye, to Charlie Ventura and Les Paul, who often called himself Paul Leslie because of contract problems. I was even the first musician to play background music for the 'Amos 'n' Andy' radio show. I recorded on Sunset, Victor, Modern, Capitol, Black and White and Aladdin (or Philo as the label was later called, because it was located next to Philharmonic Hall). That's where Eddie Messner recorded Lester Young when he returned from the army, with myself, Vic Dickenson, Dodo Marmarosa and Henry Tucker Green. Lester's tune was 'DB Blues'. That 'DB' stands for Detention Barracks. It was exhilarating to be swinging with all those great people.

I used to count the sides: on any record date of three hours we did at least four tunes. When I got up to 5,000 sides in the early 1950s, I stopped counting. Seems like a lot but when you record every single day it's easy. One day I had five record dates; I managed to get them all in – I'd be in one praying they wouldn't do overtime so I could make the next one on time.

Ted Yertsa, a writer for the *Daily News*, had a column called 'The Lamplighter' in which he featured his favourite musicians – Allan Reuss, Barney Bigard, Zutty Singleton, Barney Kessel and myself. Kay Starr was his number one singer. Whenever we were free, Yertsa would arrange late-night recording sessions for this group, a few times a week for weeks on end. We probably made fifty or seventy-five sides on just one label. This man, Ted Yertsa, loved our music! Quite a few were released, hundreds more never saw the light of day.

I also recorded with Andre Previn on his first date when he was only seventeen. He had the facility then, yet hadn't quite developed his own style. That record was made at 7000 Santa Monica, the same studio where I recorded the fastest record I ever made – with Benny Goodman. It was a sextet with Lee Young, Mel Powell and Red Norvo on vibes, Goodman all alone on the front line, and Johnny Mercer singing. Goodman beat it off, 1, 2, 1, 2 and away we'd go. Prior to this Goodman had recorded one of my songs, which I arranged for his big band when he was working at the Coconut Grove. The song, 'Coconut Grove', was initially called '1,000 Mile Jump' – I wrote it on a 1,000-mile bus ride to Albuquerque. Benny Goodman changed the title and put both his and his brother's name on it as well as mine. He was an aloof man and I found myself never saying a word to him if he didn't say anything to me. Just do my work then split. I knew he was a great clarinet player but I always had reservations about him being the King of Swing. Who made his band swing? The arrangers: guys like Jimmy Mundy, Fletcher Henderson, and musicians like Lionel Hampton, Charlie Christian, Teddy Wilson.

A very special date in late '46, early '47, was with Gerald Wilson's Orchestra. In late 1944 when Gerald came out of the navy, he organized his first band. 'Dissonance in Blues' was a tune he wrote for that group and the solo was originally a baritone solo. When he recorded it he decided to feature me on bass. That was my first recorded bass solo – ever.

It was around this time that Charlie Parker was in Camarillo State Hospital getting his head together. After he came out, the Dial series of recordings was made. Ross Russell was on the scene, he was one of the forward-looking guys on the West Coast who recognized the greatness of Parker and players like Wardell Gray, Joe Albany, Dodo Marmarosa, Chuck Thompson, Dexter Gordon. He set up the sessions at MacGregor's Studio on Western. The tunes are all classics now: 'Stupendous', 'Carvin' the Bird', 'Relaxin' at Camarillo', 'Pastel'. Bird liked the singer Earl Coleman, brought him to the date, insisted that Ross Russell record him. Earl sang on 'Dark Shadows' and 'This is Always'. They both became hit tunes, they sold far more than the instrumentals.

To most people Parker would have seemed a trifle remote because he was always preoccupied with his thing, music. He could sit and write out a chart in a matter of a few minutes. Anything he played he could put on manuscript. Charlie Parker was actually a brilliant man who was unfortunate enough to be into drugs. When he was straight, he was a beautiful person to talk to, he was well versed, even erudite on many topics. Bird would talk Stravinsky or Bartok, he'd talk politics too. Often he'd discuss what was happening with President Truman, who was from his home state, Missouri. He was very articulate, had opinions on everything, especially the structure of the capitalist system and racism in America. Bird wasn't at a loss on any subject, particularly when his head was together. When he was strung out he became another person.

People were misguided about his drug use. Bird would advise people to leave it alone. But they thought that's what made Bird play. That's not what made Bird play; Bird played better when he was straight, like when he came out of Camarillo and we did those Dial sessions, before the hustlers got to him again. He was like Lady Day in that respect, a little weak for it. When Bird was straight he was a demon player. Charlie Parker was so far ahead of his time that now, thirty years after his death, there's still a group called Supersax led by Med Flory playing all his music. By now he would have been doing something entirely different.

Curtis Counce, Johnny Miller, Joe Comfort – they were also the jazz bass players who were making it beautifully on the LA scene, but for whatever reason, Ross Russell called me. I didn't question why, I simply accepted the offer. It felt momentous; I knew I was part of history then. Anyone who worked with Parker knew they were going to do something that hadn't been done before. All of us young ones, we would go anywhere to hear what Bird was putting down because it was so far ahead, he and Dizzy. A whole new period had started. Prior to this I'd worked with Lester, who influenced everybody, but the alto players I'd been listening to were Benny Carter, Russell Procope, Marshall Royal, Luke Jones, Johnny Hodges – alto players out of that school. Charlie Parker lifted the alto saxophone into another era. I knew it was historically different and thought it was great, thought everything we did was outstanding. I was delighted to be a part of it, really delighted – hey, they picked me.

I can remember how Howard McGhee more or less kept Bird in line, just like you lead a small child around and make him behave. See, Bird would do so much and then he'd get a jug. Because he was trying to be straight. However, he drank. I guess when you're trying to kick a habit . . . well, he drank and we'd record all we could until Bird got loaded. Howard McGhee, a guy of short stature, curly light-brown hair, had a very strong influence over Bird. He took care of business. By the time Bird would get loaded the session would be over anyway, though Bird could always play, even if he was loaded. I've never seen him when he couldn't play except when he was so drunk he couldn't stand up.

MacGregor Studio was a big roomy studio and a lot of people would come down and watch the sessions. One guy named Shifty Henry hung out all the time. He was an aspiring bass player who died way before he should have. Many ladies were present also, though during the recordings my mind wasn't on ladies. To me, playing music is utter concentration.

Bird would explain to me how most of the things he wrote at that time were based on standard changes. For instance, 'Stupendous' was based on 'It's Wonderful', and another thing was based on 'Whispering', a jam tune. He'd explain, really break it all down; it wasn't that hard, I understood it, it was pretty obvious. Like he'd call a tune and say, 'Just play "Honeysuckle Rose" and we'll change the bridge.'

Bird was a guy like this – he knew he had something different going but he wasn't an egotist. He knew he had something going but I don't think he knew how great his music was. The new sounds weren't making the heavy bread. Dizzy was much more aware of what was going on in that sense than Bird, and Dizzy was a better businessman. Bird never jammed on and on. He would state what he had to say in three or four choruses and that was it. Bird used to say, 'If you can't say it in two or three choruses, you're not saying anything.' I wholeheartedly agree with him to this day. Playing a million choruses doesn't make you any more eloquent. Course, a guy can get wound up and extend himself sometimes, but most of the time guys just take advantage of a good rhythm section and never stop blowing.

That pisses the rhythm section off, that's why I used to get literally angry. We used to have jam sessions at a place over on Santa Barbara. I remember Lucky Thompson being there, Dexter, Wardell Gray, Teddy Edwards, and some other cats, can't think of their names. We'd play tunes like 'Indiana' way up, fast tempo. One guy took over thirty choruses, then someone would turn to the bassist, which happened to be me and say, 'OK – you got it.' Then they'd light cigarettes, go over in the corner to have a conversation. Well, this would get any bass player pissed.

You want some respect, you've been breaking your butt making them sound good. Then, you don't even get the courtesy of them listening to your solo.

That's one of the things that used to bug me so I would say I'm never going to another jam session. I didn't – for a while. In the rhythm section you're the mule back there carrying the load. The horn players play until they're tired, then say, 'The bass player or the piano or the drums have got it.' By then you've played damn near everything you can think of; and you're already fatigued. When you play bass you can't stop to take a drink of water, you keep going.

Bird never did that, he had great respect for the rhythm section. I loved Bird, I was so sorry he got himself messed up. There are people who have kicked the habit, people who are still around. I never shot anything in a needle in my arm. A trumpet player who shall remain nameless at the YMCA in Dayton, Ohio said to me once, 'Hey – try this . . .'

'No way,' I said. I'd never seen any funny-looking brown stuff before and I wasn't about to shoot it in my vein. I did sniff some of it and was sick for a week. I thought it was cocaine; later I discovered it was heroin. Frequently I've thought about the whole drug thing, but never could understand why anybody would want to feel that way. Personally, I like to be aware of what's happening. I've seen guys nodding and thought, 'How can anybody enjoy life when they don't know what's going on, when they get so far out of it they can't even hold their heads up?' To me, it was ridiculous. How can anybody get hooked unless they want to? That's my opinion. I've been around all kinds of people all my life but I never wanted to get hooked on anything but music.

Some musicians thought it made them play better, got rid of their inhibitions. *Thought* they got rid of their inhibitions. There were a few bass players that got hooked on junk; they didn't live very long either. My contention was, and is, that I need all the energy and awareness I have to play the instrument. Therefore when I go to play I go to play straight-life, like Lester used to say, with no assistance but feeling good inside.

I knew Wardell Gray when he was straight-life. That meant when a cat did nothing – didn't drink or anything. It was after the Dial sessions that Wardell got hung up with some guys in Vegas. So the story came to me – he had an overdose, what they call a hot shot. If the guys he was with had any brains they would have taken him to a hospital, they could have saved him. Instead, he died and they dumped him in the desert. That's what happened. But during the Dial sessions and before when we used to play the clubs on Central Avenue doing things like 'The Chase' with Dexter, Wardell was straight-life and a marvellous tenor player. He couldn't drive a car; I would pick him up and take him to record dates. His mind was always moving, thinking music; he was very involved in the intricacies of harmony. On the way to some record date he'd be humming something, or I'd be humming something like the theme from one of the Paramount newsreels. Then, at the date you'd hear the phrase quoted in what he played; he'd interpolate it right into the tune. He was always thinking of new things to do. Had he lived he would have been one of the truly amazing players of our time. He was anyhow.

Then there was 'Dodo' Marmarosa, he was very inventive, a genius in his own way; and Carl Perkins, who played piano with his left elbow resting on the piano, attacking the keyboard in a crablike fashion. Perkins was certainly an odd one to look at, another one who unfortunately got mixed up in the drug scene and ended his career.

Some of what we played was blues, it didn't have to be written. It all depended on Bird who called the tunes; we played our lines according to that. Hardly any bass parts were written – the music came from one's head. Generally we'd do one, two or three takes. Sometimes the first would be best, sometimes the second. Since then, I've noticed that companies have released all the out takes, the little bits and pieces. There's several editions where they've used all the stuff that we rejected; they've released every scrap, every note we did good or bad. It was enormous fun recording those sessions. We would all walk out of the studio on a cloud, go across the street to Bob's Burgers on Western to get a bite to eat. Then I might go and have a taste of something, but not when I was working. Like I said – straight-life.

Another band I worked with during this period was led by Cee Pee Johnson, a bongo player who also sang. While he worked at a place called the Rhum Boogie, I did a lot of arranging for the group which included Gerald Wilson on trumpet, Ralph Bledsoe trombone, Arthur Dennis and Dexter Gordon on saxes, Warren Bracken on piano and Irving Ashby guitar. We did some recording with this group and garnered enough of a reputation for a contractor to invite Cee Pee on a tour of the Hawaiian Islands. Cee Pee called me around 27 October. The record ban was becoming a reality on 1 November 1947. Since I made my living primarily from making records, the decision was obvious. Besides, I'd heard so many glowing reports about the islands from friends like Henry Coker, the trombonist who later went with Basie, Cecil Carter, and C.L. Burke that my imagination was well stocked with images of paradise. The adventure of it all was probably uppermost in my mind, and the money sounded good too. Of course, I was feeling some pressure due to recent circumstances. The unknown seemed like the perfect antidote.

Diane wasn't making any real demands on me, but her feelings were clear. It was a seemingly impossible situation for me given my independent streak. Emma, I don't think, felt anything about my leaving one way or another. She knew I would always take care of my responsibilities with Sylvia. The urge to go explore someplace new was stronger than anything keeping me in Los Angeles. You always know when you come to the end of any road even if your awareness isn't 100 per cent conscious. My philosophy dictates that I never want to be in any situation I can't tell the truth about – just tell it like it happened and you never have to remember as many details. On all accounts, I decided it was best to leave.

Ironically, during the last few weeks in Los Angeles, I received three tempting offers. One was from Count Basie. Gerald Wilson and I had gone to visit him backstage at the Lincoln Theatre. He was regrouping his band; Walter Page hadn't been feeling well. Basie invited both Gerald and I to join him. Though I was in love with his rhythm section, I passed up the opportunity. Also, I was making more money than they were making at the time. Johnny Miller, the bassist, was leaving the Nat Cole Trio, and Nat asked me to join. Nat was on his way up then, but I felt that way about myself, having had my own trio, so I passed. Nat hired Joe Comfort. Lester Young was forming a quartet or quintet then; we were so tight he just naturally assumed I'd go with him. I loved Lester dearly, yet kept to my own plans. He wasn't the kind of guy to understand that – being so sensitive, he felt bruised. Lester took everything personally. But like I said – no regrets.

It all happened in three weeks: the call from Cee Pee, a few rehearsals, then off to the islands. A day or so before we left, Cee Pee got busted for marijuana. The headline that greeted us in Honolulu was 'FAMOUS BANDLEADER JAILED FOR MARIJUANA . . .'


The flight to Honolulu over 2,500 miles of Pacific Ocean was long and a little frightening. At the halfway point, the point of no return, one of the engines of the Pan Am DC-4 caught fire and they feathered it. As we continued on three engines I thought about Gerald Wilson who had cancelled at the last minute because he didn't like flying over water. He decided he'd rather go on the road in Count Basie's bus.

Arriving in Honolulu was like stepping into a dream. Already dazed from the twelve-hour flight, the air literally shimmered before my eyes. Orchids were placed around my neck. Relief and elation overtook me: heaven . . . man, I'm here in heaven. As soon as we got to our hotel, we threw our bags down, changed clothes and went out to explore the island. The landscape looked like an artist's conception of paradise. This was way before the developers ruined it; in 1947 it *was* paradise. Just to stand in the streets or walk on the beaches was a natural high. I never wanted to leave.

The following evening the Cee Pee Johnson Band played the Honolulu Civic Auditorium. Backstage, the hustlers were waiting for the new mainland musicians, waiting to make that contact. So the band members who were into drugs got their charges and everything was cool for them. The rest of us were pretty square, might have smoked a little pot, but that was largely unavailable, the hustlers couldn't be bothered with that. The personnel had changed somewhat; Arthur Preston had replaced Gerald Wilson on trumpet and Trummy Young was in on trombone rather than Ralph Bledsoe. Other than that it was the same group that had recorded, and it was a hard swinging group. The audience went wild for us. The Hawaiians had never heard the likes of Dexter Gordon or Arthur Dennis play saxophone in person before. During intermission the enthusiasts swarmed backstage to shake our hands, tell us how much they dug it. I was sitting in the dressing-room smoking a cigarette when I looked in the mirror and saw a vision of loveliness walking towards me I could hardly believe.

'You're Red Callender,' this beauty said to me, 'I'm honoured to meet you. I'm Yolanda Mitchell and I manage a record store. We have *all* your recordings.'

Needless to say I was happily stunned. '"Pastel",' she continued, 'all the Dial records are really selling, especially the Erroll Garner Trio's "Pastel".'

The theatre manager came into the dressing-room to give us the five-minute signal. 'What are you doing after the concert?' I asked.

'I'd be delighted . . .' she said.

That evening began my Hawaiian interlude which I thought would last for ever. The tour was suffering because of the marijuana headline; most of the engagements had been cancelled. We played a few more gigs on the big island of Hawaii, Lanai and Maui, but marijuana was a dirty word. Our fabulous tour fizzled out from under us. Fortunately, the disc-jockeys were still interested in interviewing me because of my recent recordings. I envisioned a future there in Hawaii, a future that included my new romance. After our last gig most of the guys in the band returned directly to LA. For our own separate reasons, Trummy Young, Warren Bracken and myself stayed in Honolulu.

Yolanda and I soon became well acquainted. Her background was mixed, like mine. Her father was a Scotsman who had come to the islands, her mother was pure Hawaiian. Yolanda had long black hair, olive skin, beautiful brown eyes. I thought I had been in love before – but this was it, the love of my life. She invited me to stay with her at her place on John Ena Road; she looked after me, made life rather easy for me. After a few months of this relaxed lifestyle, I decided to make Hawaii my home for good, which necessitated a trip to Los Angeles to look in on Sylvia and settle some affairs. I was making payments on a Cadillac, a maroon coupe de ville, that I wanted to have shipped to the islands. It was only a few years since the war had ended; automobiles were still at a premium.

When I arrived back in California I learned that my father had moved to the coast and was living in the house on Newton Street with Emma and her family. Bless Emma! She had and has such a big, warm, open heart. After she spoke with my dad and found out he wasn't in the best of health, she took him in with no second thoughts. Even with two grandfathers around, Sylvia, who was about seven then, still missed her dad. We spent some time together, we were always close. I've always tried my best to be responsible to the people I love. It's made me able to look in the mirror and say, 'Hey Callender, you did the best you could.'

The recording ban was still on; things were pretty much status quo in LA, no reason for me to be there. I made arrangements to have the Cadillac shipped to Honolulu, then hopped the next flight there. Two letters arrived shortly after I did, one from Diane Schumann telling me of her disappointment; the other informing me that although Sylvia wasn't hurt, she'd been hit by a car while riding her bicycle. Believe me, those letters caused a few pangs.

The trio idea had never left me. Once I settled in to John Ena Road, Warren Bracken, the pianist from Cee Pee's band and a Hawaiian drummer named Pepe Bowman and I formed a group to play at a place called Gibson's Bar. It was an upstairs club with the bandstand situated above the long bar. A kind of intimate setting where the local people came to hear jazz. American tourists were far more interested in hearing Hawaiian guitars than jazz. We enjoyed playing for the mixed clientele who truly appreciated our music.

Yolanda had convinced the owner of the record store she managed, a man named Chan Loo, to hire me to work there. That was one of the few non-musical jobs I've held in my life. There I was, waiting on the customers, putting away the stock, taking care of business. Both jazz and pop were big sellers, mostly pop. But everywhere you go there's a hard core of jazz fans, fanatic record-collectors, people who know every date issued, the personnel, the tunes, the years. It's like a worldwide club. We were selling a lot of Lionel Hampton records at that point. Of course the Dial records sold; I was there to push them.

One day as I was unpacking a new shipment I was called to the phone. How on earth he found me, I'll never know; it was Mingus on the line. He tracked me down to tell me about his new record with Lionel Hampton, his tune 'Mingus Fingers'. If Mingus had something to tell me, he'd find me even if I were living in a cave.

His timing was uncanny because the shipment I was unpacking when the phone rang contained the Hampton 78 record. This coincidence took place almost exactly ten years after I'd given him his first bass lesson.

With all that free time in Hawaii to think, I started thinking about having a group larger than a trio again. In the late spring of 1948, Yolanda and I thought we'd give San Francisco a try as the place to launch a new band. After finding a San Francisco apartment on Franklin and Pine, I got on the phone to Los Angeles and called my partner Bill Douglass to be the drummer, Teddy Edwards for tenor saxophone, Jimmy Bunn the pianist, Kenny Bright to play trumpet and Mingus. Everyone was available and I booked the group into the Beige Room of the Barbizon Hotel as the 'Pastel Sextet'. Having two basses in the group was fine, it was a pleasure to play with Mingus then. I'd written him in with the horns on a lot of tunes, and sometimes we'd play in unison or counterpoint. People, however, thought having two basses in a small group was nutty. It was a great-sounding band, but it wasn't what people were used to. Like I heard from Pops – 'You got to play for the people.' The Beige Room lasted a month or so, then we booked two more weeks at a club called Lasio's at Turk and Hyde. When the San Francisco Musicians' Local got wind of this, they called me up before their board for soliciting a job, which wasn't the case at all – the owner of Lasio's had come to me. A Mr Forbes was the SF Local's business agent, a real top sergeant-major type. My being a member of Local 767 in Los Angeles and having just come from Hawaii seemed to irk him, so he sought his own kind of vengeance. Also, the San Francisco Union had rules similar to the ones in LA about being in town for six months before you can work on a steady gig, but someone upstairs in that union must have liked me – I don't think I even got fined.

However, the whole scene was stressful and it began to tell on both Yolanda and me. She was a real tropical flower; the cold summer winds of San Francisco didn't agree with her. She stayed in the apartment most of the time, refused to come out to the clubs with me. Our romance was cooling off with the climate, with the various strains I was under trying to keep the band together, dealing with the union and the strange audience response to our innovative group. She left for Honolulu before the Lasio's gig was finished. We didn't quarrel but a dissonant note had crept into our ideal relationship. When the gig was over at Lasio's I spent some time in LA to check in on Sylvia but Los Angeles didn't appeal to me very much at that point. Hawaii wasn't over yet, not by a long shot.

I returned to Honolulu, to Yolanda on John Ena Road. We reconciled, although I was finding out how different her values and mores were from mine. On the outside I was cool. Nobody knew what was really going on inside of me . . . something was eating away at me. The pace of Honolulu was as slow as Sleepy Hollow. One night we went to a *luau*, one of those parties where they roast a pig in the ground. We were having fun, getting loose. I was drinking my usual, scotch and milk. A waiter came by with a tray of octopus hors d'oeuvres. One bite and suddenly this terrific pain shot through me. I put my drink down, immediately went home. The pain continued all night.

The next day Yolanda took me to her doctor, a Japanese MD. He diagnosed me as having a duodenal ulcer. 'Stop smoking cigarettes,' he told me, 'stop drinking alcohol.' I followed his advice strictly for ten years, though the pain took only three or four months to subside. Maalox and cream and milk were my medicines. Yolanda did all she could to help me, really stuck by me. I was in a kind of shock; I had no idea I was ulcer-prone, no idea how tense I really was. It caused me to do some soul-searching, something I'd rarely had time to do before my body slowed me down.

While I was recuperating, I auditioned for the Honolulu Symphony and got a chair as a bassist. The first-chair bassist was an excellent female player. I also got to play tuba on rare occasions when the music called for it. Being in the Symphony didn't take up too much time – a few rehearsals, four concerts a month. However, symphonic music is complete discipline, you interpret only what you see on the page. The Honolulu Symphony's repertoire reflected the tastes of its supporters, the Dole pineapple family and other European plantation-owners. We played all the familiar classics: Bach; Brahms's D Minor Symphony, which has always been a favourite; Tchaikovsky's 'Romeo and Juliet' with its moving French horns. Beethoven of course, Haydn, Ravel's 'Afternoon of a Faun', and the magnificent 'Concerto Grosso' by Bloch, but not one note of Stravinsky. We also played light classics by Hawaiian composers and some of the more popular things of the day. The Honolulu Civic Auditorium where I had met Yolanda was our primary performance site. The cream of Hawaiian society attended the concerts and it showed me how Hawaii truly is the melting-pot of the world. Both the orchestra and audience were racially mixed.

For years I had wanted to write a symphony, my mind was overflowing with music. Here was a moment to do it. The situation was ideal. Yolanda worked all day at the record store; I was alone in the house with a keyboard, a house sitting so close to the ocean that you could hear the waves crashing on the beach. Outside, flowers bloomed, breezes rustled through the palm trees and birds sang in the fragrant air. Inside the house on the record-player, Bille Holiday sang 'Don't Explain'.

Everyone who starts out to write a symphony has a different idea in mind. Mine started with simple motion. The strings were predominant and the rhythms were many – the rhythms of all the bands I'd listened to my whole life. I used my brass sparsely to highlight, punctuate the moving lines of the full woodwind sections. It developed slowly. Every day for a few months I'd wake up in the morning, turn on the record-player always with the same Billie Holiday side, and begin. Everything went into that symphony. Space and silence as well as motion, everything Basie and Ellington had taught me about how to use space. Oboes, English horns, flutes . . . the themes emerged as the sun rose higher in the sky. Steeped in Debussy, in Stravinsky, I'd orchestrate carefully, writing out every note until it was just what I wanted to hear.

When I got tired, I'd stop, rest, put away the pages until the next morning when the creative energies prodded me out of sleep and back to the keyboard. Nothing else existed in those months, just music, the utter concentration of music coming through me, winding through seven movements. In the last movement the theme from 'Pastel' was incorporated almost as if I'd planned it that way, but I hadn't. So I closed the work with 'Pastel' and for want of a better title called it the 'Pastel Symphony'.

When it was finished I took it to Barati, conductor of the Honolulu Symphony. He studied the score, then said, 'You have

# Honolulu Symphony Orchestra

## ORCHESTRA PERSONNEL

### JAMES SAMPLE, *CONDUCTOR*

**FIRST VIOLINS**
Konrad Liebrecht,
  Concertmaster
Ellery F. Tuck, Jr.
Robin McQuesten
Robert Carbaugh
Paul Schratz
Madeline Childs
Wilhemena Laune
Iwalani Forrest
Walter Robinson
D. C. Parker

**SECOND VIOLINS**
Bill Rusinak
Jack Colburn
John Mark
Jacob Sato
Dan Weller
Gretel Kepner
Jeanette Meheula
Lois Andrews

**VIOLAS**
Nevin Dauer
Russell Cades
Charlotte Liebrecht
Darrell Joachim
Hugo Kortschak

**CELLOS**
Roman Dukson
Ana Drittelle
Belle Shalit
Wendell Mordy
Wah Chiu Chang

**DOUBLE BASSES**
Alda Lee
Richard Warfield
Red Callender
Larry Daggitt
Cy Harris

**FLUTES**
Miri Hargus
George Dietzler

**OBOES**
Moses Sato
Hugh Miller

**ENGLISH HORN**
Bob Fockler

**CLARINETS**
Archie Iwanaga
Michael Callara

**BASS CLARINET**
Ernest McClain

**BASSOONS**
Floyd Uchima
Harry Yoshino

**HORNS**
Mike Wagner
Bill Littlejohn
Richard Choy
Ben Kuraya
Alvin Lamb
Rosalie Roberts
E. J. LeVine

**TRUMPETS**
Richard Thomas
Tiburcia Coria
Bill Sievers

**TROMBONES**
Harvey Shapiro
John Van Patten
Edward Donohue
Floyd Sullivan

**HARP**
James Gallet

**PIANO**
Ruth Orcutt Bacon

**PERCUSSION**
Yan Sau Wong
Al Miller
Richard Furuno

**TUBA**
Floyd Russell

## SECOND PAIR OF CONCERTS

Sunday Afternoon, November 13, 1949
Tuesday Evening, November 15, 1949

JAMES SAMPLE, *Guest Conductor*

BLOCH............................................*CONCERTO GROSSO for*
*STRINGS WITH PIANO OBLIGATO*

1. Prelude
2. Dirge
3. Pastorale and Rustic Dances
4. Fugue

DVORAK............................*CONCERTO for VIOLONCELLO*
*AND ORCHESTRA in B Minor, Opus 104*

1. Allegro
2. Adagio Ma Non Troppo
3. Allegro Moderato

Ana Drittelle, Soloist

### INTERMISSION

DAI-KEONG LEE............*HAWAIIAN FESTIVAL OVERTURE*
GRIFFES................*THE PLEASURE DOME OF KUBLA KHAN*
TSCHAIKOVSKY
*OVERTURE-FANTASY "ROMEO and JULIET"*

KONRAD LIEBRECHT, *Concertmaster*

The Steinway is the Official Piano of the Honolulu Symphony Orchestra enough material in here for three symphonies.'

In retrospect I see that it was rather overloaded, apparently too thick for Barati's taste. At that point in my development I simply hadn't learned enough about the truth, 'less is more'. The manuscript sheets went into a drawer. No thoughts about whether it was great or not crossed my mind; it was simply me, about forty-five minutes of music all down on paper. I can remember it only in terms of sound because after it was performed once by the Humanist Symphony Group in Los Angeles in the early 1950s, both the manuscript and the tape of it were lost.

Though the memory of the music is somewhat vague, I can recall exactly how I felt when I was writing it – like the vividly remembered sensations of a dream. Perhaps creative people do some of their best work when they have conflicts going on in their lives. When I sat down to write, I forgot the pain of the ulcer, forgot how Yolanda and I were losing touch with each other, forgot any and all problems. Problems dissolve when I'm involved in music; I leave them at the door. By the time I'd finished writing the symphony, I knew I was ready to leave John Ena Road.

So I moved out and rented my own little place on Lialokalani which is now part of Don Ho Lane in Wakiki. It was quiet there, peaceful. The temperature was so constant that windows and doors were usually left open, unlocked. The postman could leave a package on your doorstep and no one would touch if it you were gone all day. Lucky, because a dancer friend was smuggling me weed from LA inside ice bags wrapped in a package. No trained dogs, then. I wandered the streets in a kind of daze, met a woman, a schoolteacher on a bustop . . . had a brief assignation until an angry husband started thumping on the door . . . I met a Mormon on another bustop, an old white dude from Utah. That pathetic old man lectured me on how black people used to have tails. He described in detail how blacks were kicked out of heaven because they were devils. My first reaction was fury. Then I thought . . . this man has a problem and I'm not going to join him either way. It's his problem, let him suffer, he's sick. If he thinks I'm any less than he is because my skin is another hue – he's got a big problem. He may never solve it – but it's his, not mine. I know who I am.

Gradually, Hawaiian orchestras and bands started calling me
for arrangements. Eddie Sereno and Duke Heatherly also wanted
arrangements. Writing for these bands was survival. The Symphony didn't pay enough to keep things going. These writing
opportunities led me to form my own little band, a truly
international band, quite an assortment of races and sizes. The
trumpet player was Francis King, a Korean guy about five foot
two. People would see us together and think Mutt and Jeff.
Francis King later made it big in the burglar-alarm business when
Honolulu became a tourist trap. The alto player was Paul Chang,
pure Chinese. On tenor was Pete Peterson, a Chinese-Hawaiian.
The drummer was pure Hawaiian, Pepe Bowman, a real
*poi*-eater, must have weighed about 300 pounds, and the pianist
was Bernie Conception from the Philippines. Tats Matsuo, a
Japanese man who owned a famous Chinese restaurant named
Lai Yi Chai's, hired us for a steady engagement.

Trummy Young was still in Honolulu, playing at a place called
the Brown Derby on Hotel Street where he met Sally, his wife of
thirty-five years. Trummy's band played in a more relaxed setting
than ours, they could wear their *aloha* shirts to work. They were
playing more real jazz, in contrast to my 'jazz' arrangements on
popular tunes. Our band played a little bebop, some of my
originals, some popular Japanese tunes; we were really quite
commercial. In my opinion, Trummy was the father of the
modern trombonists. I'll never forget a thing he did with
Lunceford before he went with Earl Hines – he had a tremendous
solo, very high, he always had an unusually wide range on his
instrument. Trummy was also an entertaining musician, a singer,
a man of great charm who took care of business. It's not easy to
be all those things in one man. Trummy always had my great
respect and admiration.

Our band at Lai Yi Chai's broadcast live every night on radio
station KHON. To keep things fresh I did one new arrangement
every day for the three horns and three rhythm. The guys in the
band used to call me 'Pops'. Larry Grant, the KHON disc-jockey
who did the remotes, became a friend. He invited me down to the
station and before I knew it I was learning how to run the board,
sitting in on his show. Being an apprentice disc-jockey was great
fun – I managed not to throw the station off the air too many
times. Soon I had my own show, playing a mixture of music,

sneaking in the pure jazz now and then. I wasn't all that aware of
my listening public until one day I played a hit record of the tune
'You've Changed', dedicating it to Yolanda. Never did listen
closely to the lyrics, just felt like doing it as the title seemed
appropriate. Yolanda was tuned in that day. She was a literal type
of person who took every word to heart. Well, that doomed
whatever shreds of friendship that remained between us. Since
that . . . slip . . . I've been cognizant of what the lyric says, not
just a title and a melody.

Tats Matsuo at Lai Yi Chai's informed me he thought the band
should have a female singer. That's when I hired Toni Craig, a
mainland '*hauli*' girl. First time I ever heard prejudice in reverse –
*hauli* is what the Hawaiians call white people. Tats said, 'OK, but
I don't know whether it's a good idea or not. You do what you
want to do.' So I hired her. I had heard Toni sing, had met her
briefly when I was writing for Eddie Sereno's band. Sereno had
called her in from Santa Monica to replace his wife Marge who
was visibly pregnant with her first son, Michael, at the time. Toni
had a good sound. At first all she was to me was another pretty
girl whom all the Hawaiian guys were chasing. I had no designs
on her – she was simply another member of the band. Oh, I liked
the way she sang and the way she looked. She dressed in beautiful
gowns, filled them out in all the right places. She was stacked –
that's what the disc-jockeys would talk about, not her singing, her
chest. Typical, and stupid, but a fact of life. We were offered an
opportunity to tour the islands with Katie de la Cruz, a very
prominent Filipino star. J. Akuhead Kapuli (Hal Lewis) was
putting together the show; he was a disc-jockey who later became
the Croesus of disc-jockeys. We had a private Beechcraft
aeroplane for the tour, a special twelve-seater for island-hopping.
Toni and I found ourselves thrown together so often . . . and that
was the beginning of that.

She had a very easy-to-get-along-with personality, low-key.
Some of the big-money guys in Hawaii were pursuing her – if she
had chosen she might have married a millionaire. But she liked
me and it was mutual. We got along fine. Toni loved books, loved
to read, would be absorbed in a book while I was writing out
arrangements. She seemed calm and contented, which is exactly
what I needed from a woman after undergoing all the subtle

wranglings with Yolanda. She accepted me as I was, no questions asked.

In fact, I was getting rock happy, itchy, eager to get back into the swing of things. Island delights were wearing thin; too much calm can be as devastating as too much activity. Once more the 'Callender luck' came my way – this time via the Vido Musso band. Couldn't have been better timing. Vido's band was touring the islands and he asked me to do some arranging for him. Actually, he wanted me to join his band right there in Hawaii, but I still had the Lai Yi Chai obligation. When Vido returned to Los Angeles he mailed me a plane ticket so I could join the band there. The recording ban had been lifted by then. What little money I'd been able to make in Hawaii just wasn't enough to support Sylvia, myself or anyone else in much style. My Cadillac had already been repossessed. A friend hipped me that his father, a credit agent, was after me, looking for my car. It was a cinch he'd find a big coupe de ville parked on the street, half rusted away. Hawaii is murder on automobiles. By then it was smoking, needed a ring job, worn out . . . a wreck. They could have it back.

To someone who has never been bored in his life, Hawaii can be a kind of hell. By the time the ticket arrived I was eager to go. I booked my flight and broke the news to Toni who was also from the LA area, Santa Monica. The day finally arrived for take-off. When I was comfortably situated in the aeroplane, looking around, watching the passengers, I sighted a very familar face. Toni Craig had booked passage on the same flight.

PART FOUR

# Buddy's Eye-view

In Los Angeles from 1947 to 1950 the black-jazz mecca on Central Avenue had begun to close down. During the war and after, some club-owners had temporarily moved into buildings evacuated by the Japanese in the Little Tokyo area near Downtown. On my return from Honolulu in June of 1950, the scene had moved west of Central Avenue and clubs had sprung up all over town. Billy Berg's Capri and Trouville had been in Hollywood; now there were clubs in Glendale, on Slauson, on Crenshaw, reflecting the movement of the black population which had doubled since my arrival in Los Angeles in the mid-1930s. Western Avenue was the new strip and the Oasis Club was the hottest venue for jazz, both black and white. Crestwell's Milamo Club was at 29th and Western. Not far was Whistling's Hawaii Club where the owner got his kicks by staging a miniature electrical storm over the bar every night, complete with thunder rolls and lightning flashes.

I figured it might take a few years to build my career back to where it had been before I left. Playing in and arranging for Vido Musso's band with Bob Harrington on piano and Bobby White on drums at the York Club on Vermont and Florence was good exposure. Then came another stroke of 'Callender luck', positive thinking or whatever you want to call it. The same month I returned, Duke Ellington was playing at the Oasis Club. Duke's bassist Wendell Marshall, a cousin of Jimmy Blanton, wanted some time off, so Duke called me to sit in with the band.

Funny thing about that band, there was no bass book. I'd say to Duke, 'Where's the music?'

He said, 'Oh, you'll hear it.'

There might have been a smattering of a book. You'd think
there would be a bass part to certain things like 'Caravan' or
'Perdido'. No parts. Duke would simply begin – he lit out on
'Caravan', that was the first thing he played. I was standing up
above him on a tier so I could watch and hear what he was doing,
and make up bass lines to go with it. This was still before
amplification; I had really to pull on the strings, Sonny Greer was
in the band. I could see how Blanton wasted himself physically.
When the bass player is predominantly the only guy playing
constant rhythm in a band with full sections, it's hard work. Duke
would start off all the tunes but he never played all the way
through, only a line or two here and there. His thing was reacting
with the audience. Duke Ellington was probably the greatest
salesman who ever lived. And a grossly underrated piano player
. . . a lot of guys said, 'Duke can't play the piano at all.' Which
was ridiculous. Duke was one of the great stride pianists.

I began to understand him better from that experience. Duke is
the source of so much of my feeling about music. He started the
band out but took very few solos himself. Later, when I recorded
the first album of my own tunes, people asked me why I didn't
take more solos. 'Well,' I'd tell them, 'I wrote the music. That's
my solo, my means of expression.'

Once I heard a guy say, 'What did Duke Ellington ever do for
black people?' I got so mad I nearly hit him. Obviously he didn't
know Duke's music . . . 'Black Beauty', 'Black, Brown and
Beige', 'Black and Tan Fantasy', the Harlem compositions . . .
Duke was never unconscious of the plight of black musicians or of
black people. He never described his music as 'jazz', he used the
term 'Negro music' when 'Negro' was the term. He was always
cognizant of his heritage though he didn't make a big deal of it. It
was a natural part of all he did.

Those days at the Oasis were some of the priceless moments of
my life, like working with Bird or Erroll Garner or Lester. I knew
there was magic going on and counted myself very fortunate to be
part of it. Yet when Duke invited me to go on the road with the
band I had to turn it down. I had no desire to go anywhere,
having just returned from a three-year sojourn. My independent
streak was strong too. Musicians who stay in big bands get locked
into the life of the road, the one-nighters, the hotels, living from
suitcases. The players in Duke's band were all stars because Duke

had made them stars. Both Johnny Hodges and Cootie Williams had their own bands for a few years; they eventually came back to Duke. When players stay in a band ten, twelve or more years, their fame is associated with that band. When they decide to settle down somewhere, they have to take their chances like anybody else. Nobody moves in and takes over.

I had also discovered that there was far more money in being a freelance musician than in having a steady job. Things had changed during the record-ban years. Most of the big bands had broken up – even Basie had played the Oasis with a small group. Ellington was one of the very few who kept his band intact. Rhythm 'n' blues was taking over the popular audience. Hit tunes which had been recorded in garage and basement studios during the record ban by groups like the El Dorados were becoming more prevalent. This wasn't jazz – it was blues in a new context, rhythm'n'blues, and laid the foundation for rock'n'roll. There was a big demand for this type of music then. Not the country blues of the South, but the sophisticated, danceable blues of the northern industrial cities; blues played on electric guitars and basses. The millions of black people who had migrated to the North during World War II were thinking of themselves in a far different light than when they were picking cotton down South.

My career as a freelancer really got under way when John Dolphin hired me to be the artist and repertory man for his record label, Dolphin's of Hollywood. Dolphin had a record store on the corner of Vernon and Central Avenue. A disc-jockey sat in the store window spinning records which were broadcast on a local radio station and over a loudspeaker into the street. People driving by in cars would stop, pull up and buy the latest tune. Dolphin had a great set-up for success. He might cut a record in the morning, have an acetate playing on the radio by evening, and by the next day have the records pressed and be selling them in his store. He started with 78s, then switched to 45s when they came into use for jukeboxes.

John Dolphin was a tall, heavy-set, light-skinned black man, dapper in a loud kind of way, kept a cigar in his mouth all the time. He was a bombastic type of guy, an entrepreneur, a supersalesman. Prior to coming to Los Angeles, he had a used-car lot in Detroit. Dolphin had the foresight to choose some of the very best artists in the field. Jesse Belvin was a sensation, had a sound similar to Nat Cole's, but distinctly his. Had he lived – he died in a tragic accident – he would have become a major star. I arranged and played on some of his tunes. Percy Mayfield was another Dolphin discovery. I arranged for him as well as doing Cecil Gant's tune 'I Wonder' with Dan Grissom, another big hit in the 'race records' market. That's what they were calling it before someone picked up on Joe Turner's lyric . . . 'we're gonna rock and roll tonight'. Linda Hopkins was another singer I arranged for who made it big and Fats Domino, another. There were myriads of people I worked with then; so many that I didn't even get to know any of them very well personally because the sessions were so quick. The point was to get their act together, write the music, do the date. No ongoing associations developed; we kept moving on in a hurry to the next thing.

Buck Ram of Mercury Records hired me to write for the Platters. When the Platters moved on to another record company, I was called the day before their date and asked, 'Can you have four arrangements ready by tomorrow?' I developed a short cut. I'd write all my rhythm parts on one sheet and have them photocopied: bass, piano, drums and guitar all on one sheet. Then all the B flat instruments I'd put on another sheet. That way I would just take it from the score, just photocopy the score rather than having all the parts copied out. I'd like to think that I was one of the first to develop this short cut in writing. Previously, you'd write a score and have the copyist copy it. I'd write it out and do my transcription right on the score, photocopy the whole thing, thus eliminating one step. It worked. One of my arrangements for the Platters became a huge hit, 'Smoke Gets in Your Eyes'. I recorded with the Lettermen, the Lamplighters, the Mills Brothers, did numerous dates with Ernie Freeman, a great and prolific arranger for many labels, did Pee Wee Crayton's 'Please Send Me Someone to Love'. Earl Palmer, the drummer, and I worked on so many hits that people started to call us 'the hitmakers'.

The bored, restless feelings I'd experienced in Hawaii became unimaginable. Toni Craig was back in Santa Monica; we got together occasionally for relaxed dates. I was living in an apartment shared with Eddie Beal on 9th Avenue near Western. Gerry Wiggins lived right across the hall, Papa John Creach lived

down the street. I was also working with Buddy Collette and
Nelson Riddle on background music for the Herman McCoy
Choir's performance at the Wilshire Ebell Theatre in 1950, or '51.
One of the singers in the choir caught my eye, a very talented
young woman named Mary Lou Lyons. We met briefly and she
lingered in my mind a while before events swept me up in their
course. Several years passed before we met again.

At Buddy Collette's suggestion, I joined the Humanist
Symphony Orchestra. That's how I first met Jerry Fielding, a man
who became a dear friend, who opened many doors for me,
became a very special person in my life. Jerry Fielding, Buddy
Collette, Bill Douglass, Marl Young, Benny Carter, myself and
many others all became involved with the turmoil leading up to
the amalgamation of the segregated Musicians' Union Locals in
1953. Since I was doing so much freelance work during this period
as well as gigging around town with T Bone Walker and Roy
Milton in Watts and up and down Central Avenue, my
recollection of the union merger is somewhat spotty. So I've
asked Buddy Collette to take over the story here. Buddy was in
on the amalgamation from top to bottom; Buddy Collette's got
the big picture.


BUDDY COLLETTE: In 1949 before Red came back from
Hawaii, Mingus got a job with Billy Eckstine at the Million
Dollar Theatre. Tommy Peterson, the trombone player, led the
band. Mingus was very unhappy when he came back from
rehearsal because he was the only black in the band. He was
always a fighter anyway, civil rights, racial prejudice, things like
that. We used to talk about studio work for black musicians. We
knew that it was going on and that we weren't a part of it. We had
conversations about merging the unions while sitting in my car
after working a club job, had discussed things like that often.

So when he came from that rehearsal he got to me right away:
'Hey man, they're doing the same thing. I'm the only black and
Billy Eckstine is the leader, which is mad!' He wanted to hurt
somebody, that's the way he was.

I said, 'Well, the only thing we can do is – you go ahead and
work the job and don't blow it. Let's see who we can meet there,
maybe we can meet some people we can talk to.'

Mingus continued working there and met Milt Holland, Julie Kessler, a few other people who were receptive to what we were talking about. Although I hadn't gone down to the theatre with him yet, Mingus started telling them about me. He'd say things like, 'God, Buddy Collette should be on this job, he can play better than your flute player.'

Mingus was that kind of guy. I kept saying, 'Mingus – please don't do that!'

The band worked about two weeks and Mingus managed to set up a thing with Julie Kessler, a fine flute player with whom we got to be good friends. This took place in about 1950. I had started on flute in 1948, I was studying then. Mingus set up a duet session between Julie and myself. This is how we got to know these guys, it wasn't just through talking to them. Once they found out we had something, that we wanted to do something, it made it quite nice. Julie liked my playing at the session. He'd also brought in the drummer Milt Holland who was just beautiful. We said to them, 'Hey, we think there should be more blacks in a band like this and we think there should only be one union.'

Milt said, 'Gosh, there's a bunch of guys that I know feel the same way.'

We were surprised. Finding out that some of the guys had similar feelings made it easier. So when we got with Milt, Milt said, 'Let's get together with a bunch of your guys and have a meeting.' I figured a meeting would fall flat and it would have because a lot of people don't like meetings. They want to play music, they want to work.

So I said, 'Why don't we all join this rehearsal symphony orchestra?' Red finally joined it too when he came back. It was a good idea. Several of us were studying at that period. I was studying flute and Mingus, I guess he was still studying, he was kind of in and out. He'd do a little of the classical, but he really didn't want to be there even though he liked the idea. Bill Gain was in a parallel position, he was studying flute, clarinet. We both had the GI Bill. The idea behind the rehearsal symphony, was all about having a proving ground from the teacher to the studio. The rehearsal symphony, which was called the Humanist Symphony Orchestra, was exactly the right kind of thing. If you miss a few notes, it wasn't like missing on a record date.

'What's the matter over there?'

'Well, we haven't quite seen this before . . .'

It was set up not to embarrass anybody. There was a black woman, Thelma Walker, who was a good speaker and knew what the whole thing was about. She'd come to our rehearsals and make a statement every time to the effect . . . 'Now this is a rehearsal group . . . we have a lot of people who haven't done professional studio work yet . . . so if some of the new people want to try a part, please offer them the opportunity . . .' There were several players in the Humanist Symphony from the Los Angeles Symphony, also top studio players. They came because they wanted to be there once they heard it was a minority-type thing, that there were healthy people who wanted training. Some of the musicians there had been playing for over thirty years. After it was established that we were there to learn, one of the more experienced players would say to me, 'You want to play this?' when a wild part came up, maybe a 'Daphnis and Chloë' solo.

I would say, 'Well, it looks hard . . .' They would tell me, 'Why don't you play it, maybe next week or the next time we play.'

The learning process was there and the ones of us who went through this were the first blacks to get into studio work because of the extra training. It was difficult to learn the instrument and just hope to jump in: there are so many different things to learn about blending with instruments, the different timbres of instruments. Things you can't learn from records or tapes – you have to be sitting right there in the orchestra.

The Humanist Symphony continued maybe eight or ten years, but that initial period was the great one for making people aware. Everyone finally got into the act – conductors like Osner Solomon, Peter Cohen, Elmer Bernstein. World-renowned conductors like Joe Aker would be invited to guest conduct when they were visiting Los Angeles. The newspapers would write it up; the publicity was due mainly to the fact it was an inter-racial symphony orchestra.

Percy MacDavid was the first black conductor who conducted us. He should have been with a big symphony; instead he was in the school system. He was an excellent classical pianist. I invited him there because I knew he was qualified. The first night he conducted led to my next step – Jerry Fielding.

I knew who Fielding was, had heard about him and had met

him in 1949 when he attended a concert I was in with the Woodman brothers, Britt and Connie. I knew he conducted the band on the 'Groucho Marx Show' because the newspapers featured him as the twenty-six-year-old whizz who had stepped into the older conductor's shoes. At that time you had to be at least thirty-five or forty to have an opportunity like that. Fielding was of liberal bent, wanted to see mixed groups.

That night was a very important night for me. I had MacDavid as the conductor; it was the first time a black was conducting. MacDavid did a good job, we were playing 'Carmen', he was marvellous. They were tapping the bells and the next thing is a flute and harp part that I had never seen. It wasn't difficult, but the whole orchestra stops at this point and the flute and harp are going it alone. Percy knew the score and he knew the section – there were three, four, maybe five flute players, all fine players. Yet it came as a complete surprise to me when he said, 'Buddy, would you like to try the flute solo?' Everybody's listening. Since I'd been with the orchestra about six months and knew everybody I thought – even if I don't make it, it's OK. I said, 'Yeah, I'll do it.'

So he smiled and started. That was the shocker. Everybody had been playing up to that point, I hadn't realized . . . people always say 'don't play alone' . . . my heart started pounding . . . but I hung on, I couldn't give up. Here was this beautiful idea of training people and saying, yes, these people can play this music. I got through it, I didn't fade out.

At the end of the rehearsal as we're walking out, Jerry Fielding was still there. He walked over and said, 'You sounded quite good.' I was happy about the compliment and said, 'I know you from that Woodman brothers concert. You're a conductor and writer.'

He said, 'Do you know Marshall Royal?'

I said, 'Yes, why?'

'I'm going to have an opening on the show.'

'I know him but he's out of town . . .' Marshall was with Basie then. 'Why . . .'

'Well, I have an opening on the show for saxophone, flute and clarinet.'

'He's out of town and doesn't play flute,' I told him.

'It's too bad you don't play saxophone because I like your flute playing.'

I said, 'I've just been playing flute for two years . . . I do play saxophone . . .'

If Marshall had been here he wouldn't have taken the job anyway. So I took the job. It was flute, piccolo and second-chair alto. There was a lot of playing and you had to be good. Fielding wrote hard and fast, harder than most people wrote. The first day, Fielding tells me there's no time for rehearsal, explains what to do, talking about numbers and cards and four bars here and there . . . it sounded crazy. As much as I knew music, this was a puzzle. But the guys were doing it like clockwork. Number 1. What the hell does Number 1 mean? He told me but it was hard to absorb all of it. We had fifteen minutes, I had to have this routine memorized, in a way the whole thing was resting on my shoulders. I got the opportunity and the word would come out – the black guy couldn't do it. That was the real testing period. Groucho looked over, pointed. 'Hey – we got a new guy in the band!' Everyone was looking and pointing. Now, the main thing is, what can he do? That's the way it happened and it worked out very well. That's how the Fielding thing got started.

As I got to know Jerry we'd go around to the clubs. He liked to listen to jazz and began thinking about having his own jazz band. He wanted me to do it with him. Initially he wasn't quite sure how to have a jazz band. He called his first rehearsal and once I heard his writing I knew it would be difficult for me to write for the band and still have a sense of musical continuity. He was a very unusual sort of writer, quite interesting. He used to talk about Red, wanted to make sure Red would be in the band if he were free, used to say, 'I'd like to get Red in there,' all the time. Finally Red did join us.

It was a good band. We played Monday nights at the Crescendo, played Mission Beach, San Diego. We also did Saturday-afternoon TV spots for a friend of Jerry's named Don Metz who had a show called 'All in the Home'. Metz had invested in tract homes, advertised them on his show and featured the band. By then Fielding had hired Gerry Wiggins as the pianist. Red, Gerry and I were soloing a lot. That was a tricky period when previously the only blacks on television were like Stepin' Fetchit or Willie Best, servant-type roles, not artists. Jerry received much hate mail after we were featured on the show, but he kept very quiet about it. You would hear of things happening and he would say, 'Well, these people are crazy.' He didn't want us to feel that we were any kind of problem.

All the things we were doing with Fielding helped the amalgamation because of the people we were meeting. We'd have parties, food, everybody got to know each other and the whole circle got bigger and bigger. We had the Monday-night concerts with the Humanist Symphony and on Sunday afternoons we'd have the jam sessions at this same Humanist Hall. We thought it would attract different people and it did. We also got the idea to have the big stars help us.

Sweets Edison was with Josephine Baker when she was at the RKO Theatre. Through Sweets, we contacted her to see if she would come to a meeting. She agreed and also let it be publicized.

'Josephine Baker's gonna be WHERE?' Well, you couldn't get them all in the place, the hall was bursting at the seams. It was supposed to hold 1,000 people – there were 2,000 in there on a hot day. Fielding, Benny Carter, Bill Douglass, Marl Young and myself spoke. Officials from both unions were against the idea, they fought the amalgamation tooth and nail. As Red put it then, 'They were afraid for different reasons. The white union figured we would encroach on their jobs, they figured they owned all the jobs, and the black union didn't want to give up their Saturday-night fish frys and pinochle games.'

Josephine Baker's appearance that Sunday was the turning-point. People came whether they were for the amalgamation or not. In all the excitement, with all the people pushing into the hall, with officials from both unions secretly taping things, Josephine simply said, 'I see no reason why you guys have two unions; we're all one people . . .' she went on with her routine which she had been doing everywhere in the world. Civil rights, the unity of peoples, that was her thing. The people applauded her, loved her. She looked down into the audience and there were two little girls near the front. One white girl and one black girl, both about five years old. She had them come stand right in front of her. Remember, the place is packed, 2,000 people all sitting on each other, hanging on to each other, hanging from the ceiling – and she brings the girls over and whispers to them pssssssssssss . . . in their ears. Those two girls began hugging each other and wouldn't let go. The crowd went wild, they really did.

Josephine said, 'They'll teach you. You guys are trying to

*Caricature of Jerry Fielding by Joe Baldwin
in the* Los Angeles Times

figure out how to get there and look at those girls.' She winked
and said, 'They'll teach you.' Then she walked off and went back
to her show.

That was a big boost for us morale-wise and money-wise. We'd
charged a few dollars to get in, so through this we were able to
send out mailings, reach people and express things on paper. Nat
Cole helped us out with a benefit at the Club Alabam. We
reached 3,000 or 4,000 people. We got to Sinatra who said things,
but didn't give us a benefit. We kept right on pursuing it until
people like Marl Young came into it. He had a great deal of legal
ability, later he took the bar and passed. He had all the right
procedures to do things legally for the board of directors,
proposals, etc. If you go that way you have a chance. Marl was

the legal mind we needed and we didn't have to go outside and pay somebody.

We got Benny Carter involved, who was a big help name-wise and talent-wise. We got a team of people who could lay down the steps, what we could and couldn't do. Few officials were really living with the byelaws even though it was the union. Through the quorum, the technicalities – we began to do it. The officials were balky because they had regular salaries. I understood that, but their objections were on a low level. Paul Howard, a dear friend of both Red's and mine, said, 'Why do you want to give up something we can call our own?' It was our own but it wasn't enough. The building was old, the pianos were out of tune, the musicians were making only $30, $40 a week. The officials made more, about $150 steady every week. But they were just looking at their own personal point of view. We pointed out that it was a lot more than just one musician getting over. I happened to be the first to benefit from having a good job. That was due to being in the right place at the right time. It was something I never could have set up.

Florence Cadrez, the Local's recording secretary, thought, 'Hey, don't give up what we've achieved here!' But the fact remained that Local 767 was treated as a subsidiary. All the work came into the white Local. Contractors, who were the ones who formed bands like the band Eckstine led at the Million Dollar Theatre, hired their favourites unless they were specifically requested to put someone on a date. We knew how it worked. If something good came in, a good job for blacks even, they would get on the phone and act almost like an agent for the blacks. The work dues were different. On 'Groucho' I was making $130 a week, big money then, comparable to a grand a week now. Bread was six cents a loaf; you could buy a new car for two or three thousand dollars. When the union officials came by the 'Groucho Marx Show' to collect the work dues, the other guys in the band noticed I was paying only $1.25 when they were paying $2.50. I had to explain, 'Yes, the segregated Local. We have a cheaper thing.'

What our team of people did was try and wrest control. Elections were held once a year. We had a slate set up: I was running for president the first time against Leo Davis, who was strong. Marl Young and Bill Douglass ran for the board of directors. I didn't win, but I lost by only twenty-five votes. I was only about thirty then; Leo was forty-five, fifty, more established. We got a few of us elected to the board. The next election we ran Benny Carter for president. I ran for the board along with Marl Young, Bill Douglass and we all won except Benny Carter. It was difficult to unseat the president. Leo was a nice guy and had friends from way back. Yet five or six people on the board of directors gave us good power. Once we had that power we were in a position to make motions, we could vote a block, we were the majority. We said we wanted to amalgamate. All the legalities were defined in the byelaws. Marl had set it up so we could move from that direction.

Once it was all set up we met with the board of directors of Local 47, the white Local. There had been a case where some of the white musicians tried to join our Local and weren't allowed. We could have gone to court over that. Our position was . . . well, if it's so equal and some white guy wants to join our Local, or some black guy wants to join the white Local and can't do that . . . So we pushed a little further and went to Petrillo, the president of the whole federation. We got him to admit that there was a way to go, and that way was amalgamation. Amalgamation was the term we used which meant Local 767 would merge with Local 47 and all our previous credits like time in the union would count. Nobody lost anything. We pushed to get what we wanted. There was no reason to say no.

Paul Howard, the treasurer and Florence Cadrez, the recording secretary, were both given jobs at Local 47, as was Elmer Fain, the business agent. The only one left out was Leo Davis, the president. We had eliminated all the reasons against amalgamation though we knew we were going to lose jobs. But the main thing was to get it together. Paul Howard was made librarian, actually a demotion. Later, he ran the Local 47's credit union which became a very powerful position.

While all this was going on, Jerry Fielding was having his troubles with the House Un-American Activities Committee. The committee had come through Hollywood in 1946, 1947, chopping quite a few heads. The committee left town after that, but every few years or so they would return to see who else they could frighten. In the early stages of the amalgamation, Red and I went to a party in the Hollywood Hills where the Biberman brothers were there to tell a mixed group of people about their experiences. Everyone was shocked because after all – here are these giants in the motion-picture industry and everything was taken away from them – they couldn't work. I saw the pattern happen three or four years later. By then, Jerry Fielding's swinging, he's got us in the band. People don't like seeing blacks and send a lot of hate mail. In the meantime, the committee comes back to town and they wanted necks!

Fielding was a little fish then, he really was. Conductor of the 'Groucho Marx Show', but nobody knew who he was. Yet the committee knew he was doing something different. They started watching him. One night, guys, biggest guys you've ever seen, about six foot six or seven, came on to the set of 'Groucho'. Jerry's a little guy, five foot seven. They just wanted to rattle him; they walk in with a subpoena for him to appear before the committee. They forced their way in, they wanted to serve him while he was on the bandstand. Ben Barret, the contractor, was able to cool them. Jerry walked off the stand so they could give it to him quietly. Three weeks before he was slated to appear they started calling him up at three and four in the morning. 'HEY FELDMAN,' that's what they called him, 'WE'RE OUT TO GET YOU!' Jerry would say, 'Who is this?' Then, click. He didn't get any sleep, he was getting nervous.

He decided to take the Fifth Amendment because he felt this thing with people losing their jobs and being frightened to death had to end. On the witness stand you'd be questioned, 'Well, do you know Mr Red Callender?' If you say, 'I wish to take the Fifth Amendment,' you can stay put. But once you talk you lose the right to use the Fifth. If you crack even a little . . . 'Now wait a minute,' they'd say, 'you must know so and so . . .' once you said, 'I might have seen him at party . . .'

'Now you've lost the right to the Fifth. Who else were you with?'

They broke quite a few people down this way. The fellows in the band met with Jerry during the hearings. He told us they said, 'If you give us $200,000 you'd be free to go back to what you were doing.' Jerry told them, 'If I had $200,000 I wouldn't care what you guys did or said.' He was that kind of feisty guy.

He was a beautiful man. He met with Groucho and the producers of the show. They told him they'd stick with him only if the papers didn't give it too much publicity and affect the show. They meant if it was on the back page. The committee was vicious, they took advantage of the situation and gave the story headlines . . . CONDUCTOR OF 'GROUCHO MARX SHOW' . . . made a big deal of it. So then the show asked him what he was going to do. Fielding had been requested to repudiate. He stayed with the Fifth. That was a tough period. The entire band thought we were going to go with him, but the band stayed through it all. They brought in a new conductor who was in distinct contrast to Fielding, Jack Meekan. A good guy at heart who had the wrong information. He'd tell stories like, 'this nigger did so and so' – didn't even realize I was there.

Jerry was on the shelf four or five years, couldn't do anything except a little ghosting for Vegas. His records were banned on radio stations the same way that Robeson's had been. The band members donated $15 or $20 a week apiece to help him buy groceries or whatever because he had been so beautiful to us.

It was Betty Hutton who finally got him back in the business. She was a very big star. She waited in her negotiations for a picture until the very right time – when the producers could no longer back out. Then she demanded Fielding, said if she didn't have Fielding, they couldn't have her. We were grateful to her for that because without Jerry Fielding there would have been no amalgamation.                     (*Buddy Collette*)


*Before* I met Jerry Fielding I had been busy, but nothing like *from* the time I met him. Fielding discovered there was nothing I couldn't read and hired me to work on the television series 'The Life of Riley' as well as a stream of picture and recording dates. There were so many through the years that it's virtually impossible to remember them all; hundreds upon hundreds of dates. Even though Fielding's hiring of blacks – myself, Buddy and Gerry Wiggins – caused flak, he stuck to his guns. Jerry Fielding became a real friend, one with whom I've enjoyed myself socially. Of the multitude of people I've worked with, there're very few instances where real friendship developed. Many musicians were buddy-buddy at work, then that would be the last you ever saw of them, until the next date.

Buddy Collette was right out front on the 'Groucho Marx

Show'; the television audience saw the band at least once every show. 'The Life of Riley' band was strictly behind the scenes. We taped the music for each segment of the show – theme, background music, knock-on-the-door-type music. Everything was cued into the story. The music was all prepared for you, put on the stand in the order you were going to perform it. The engineer got a balance, the red light went on, then you just did it. That's the beautiful part of studio work – the challenge of performing music sight unseen. If you can't do it properly, they'll get someone else who can.

Taping 'The Life of Riley' wasn't terribly time-consuming, maybe three hours, two or three days a week. Often we'd tape two or three segments at once, leaving several days free at a stretch. Fielding would also let me take time off if I brought in a good substitute. In 1950, '51, I was still working for John Dolphin, had written the theme song for his radio show, a blues called 'Dolphin Street Boogie'.

My association with John Dolphin came to an abrupt end when he was murdered by a writer to whom he owed money. During the investigation a detective came by to ask me about his character. All I could say about John was that he didn't owe me a nickel. The reason he didn't was that after every date, he'd say, 'Red, I'll pay you tonight.' I'd go stand by the cash register in his store. He sold records like hot cakes; the store was always crowded. It was never long before he'd collect enough cash. I used to charge him about $300 for every date I did and I never left without the money. Nothing bad I can say about John Dolphin. He was the veritable father of rock'n'roll, a man who understood the potential of the disc-jockey to the fullest.

In early 1951, Joe Adams was the leading jazz disc-jockey in Los Angeles, the first black disc-jockey who made it big. He had a television show on KTTV Channel 11 called 'Joe Adams Presents'. Gerald Wilson was the musical director for the eighteen-piece band on the show and Gerald hired me as his musical assistant. The show ran for about thirty-nine weeks; we had to supply new music each week. Gerald and I shared the writing and arranging. There were great guest artists on that show – Lena Horne, Count Basie, Stan Kenton, and many fine singers who were accompanied by the pianist Eddie Beal. I remember how Joe Adams stood in front of the band and conducted while Gerald stood in the wings and did the real conducting.

It didn't take as long as I thought it would to get my momentum back after being out of town. I entered another period where if I didn't have two record dates a day it was a bad day. Exclusive Records signed me on as an artist. The company was owned by Leon Rene. Previously, I'd recorded for Otis Rene when his label was called Excelsior. The Rene brothers were both songwriters who'd had big hits. Leon had written 'When the Swallows Come Back to Capistrano', and Leon, Otis and Clarence Muse had written 'Sleepytime Down South'. Another family operation commissioned me to do arranging for their company, the Biharis: Jules, Saul, Joe and a sister whose name I've forgotten. Jules was the eldest and had to approve everything; Joe was the engineer and A & R man. Saul and the sister dealt with everything else. They had a complete record operation – their own studio, own pressing-plant and their own distribution networks. The Biharis were the ones who came up with the idea of selling LPs in liquor stores, supermarkets, drugstores, all kinds of places, not just record stores. By the mid-1950s they were calling that type of selling 'rack jobbers'. Formerly, only singles had been sold that way. To push LPs into the market like that was a breakthrough. The Bihari brothers had a real love of jazz and didn't forget me when I wanted to do some of my own recordings.

Jack Lauderdale of Imperial Records also hired me to do A & R. The pianist Lloyd Glenn had made a big hit for the label, and Jack was seeking another smash. A date with the great and wonderful Clark Terry, one of my favourite trumpet players, had been arranged for in Chicago. Clark had mentioned a tremendous saxophone player in St Louis, Jimmy Forrest. I convinced Jack Lauderdale to go to St Louis to hear him. We drove out there together, stopping at a cafe in Oklahoma City for food. Now that was an experience . . . the proprietor told us we'd have to eat in the kitchen. This, in 1953. We didn't arrive in St Louis hungry, though; the next place down the road served us in their dining-room with no problems. Lauderdale had more than food on his mind, more than recording artists. There was a special lady in Chicago he was itching to visit; St Louis was just a detour for him. So when we got there to listen to Jimmy Forrest at a private audition, Lauderdale didn't hear a note. Forrest was up there blowing a tune called 'Night Train', a direct note-for-note take-off on Duke Ellington's 'Happy Go Lucky Local'.

On we go to Chicago to record Clark Terry with the guitarist Lonnie Simmons. A good date, but not terribly memorable. After the session, Clark and I hung out together. I returned to the hotel about three in the morning. As I stuck my head out the door of the hotel room to hang up the 'do not disturb' sign, there's Dinah Washington coming out of Jack's room across the hall, dragging a full-length mink coat behind her. I'd had the pleasure of working with Dinah at the Oasis a year or so before and it had turned out that she'd had a row with her old man of that time and developed some eyes for me. I never pursued it because it seemed as though Dinah was always fighting with whomever she was involved with; it always ended in a fight. When she sees me in the hotel hallway she says, 'Hey, Red Callender, see what you missed you motherfucker?'

Two months after our trip to St Louis and Chicago, United Records recorded Jimmy Forrest's 'Night Train' and the record became a best-selling hit. From then on I teased Jack Lauderdale about it by saying, 'See what you missed, you mother?'

As far as Duke Ellington suing Jimmy Forrest or anything like that, Duke was a much bigger man than people realized. He didn't have to let his compositions go so easily. I guess he felt – well, it can't hurt that much. Composers often don't get the credit they deserve. How many people know that Stan Kenton's 'Intermission Riff' is based on Gerald Wilson's 'Yardog Mazurka'? How many people know that it was Barney Bigard who wrote 'Mood Indigo'? Getting that straight took years. There's usually justice in these matters but rarely on time. Many tunes in Duke's book came out of riffs. The guys would set riffs and Duke would write them down. Some of the fellows got bitter because they didn't have enough brains to write those riffs down themselves. Sometimes Duke would credit them. He was the loosest bandleader that ever was. Benny Miller, who played tenor saxophone in the band in 1951, tells a story about how some of the guys would order steaks during a performance. When the steaks were done, the waiter would signal and the guys would leap off the bandstand and sit down and eat. When they were finished, they'd get up and resume playing. Duke would start the

George Callender Sr, *c.* 1920

Hattie Callender, *c.* 1920

Red Callender, aged nine, 1925

Red Callender, aged seventeen, 1933

Buck Clayton Band, 1936. L to r: Kid 'Lips' Hackett, John 'Teddy' Buckner, Arcima Taylor, Ike Bell, RC; top: Bert Johnson, Herschel Evans, Alan Durham; centre: BC, Bumps Meyers, Frank Pasley, Winslow Allan, Caughey Roberts, Eddie Beal

C.L. Burke Band, 1938. L to r: Andrew Blakeney, Herschel Coleman, Caughey Roberts, unknown, RC, Lee Gibson, Puss Wade, CLB

Happy Johnson Orchestra, c. 1939. L to r: Charlie Davis; top: RC, Bill Battles, Rabon Tarrant, unknown, Leroy 'Snake' White, unknown; middle: Bob Dorsey, Leo Trammel, Andy Anderson, unknown, HJ, John 'Streamline' Ewing, Jap Jones, L. Briscoe; front: Rene Cooper, Toni Anthony

Charles Mingus after his first bass lesson, 1938

Walter Page, late thirties

Lester Young, Dickie Wells, late thirties

Lee and Lester Young Band, early forties. L to r: Arthur Twyne, Guydner Paul Campbell, Lester Young, Hubert 'Bumps' Meyers, Louis Gonsales, Lee Young, RC

Jam session, early forties. L to r: Chico Hamilton, Frank Morgan, RC, Dexter Gordon, Gerald Wiggins, John Anderson

Jam session, early forties. L to r: RC, Big Sid Catlett, Garland Finney, Lester Young, Dickie Wells, Harry 'Sweets' Edison, Illinois Jacquet

Three Red Callender Trios. Top: L to r: Louis Gonsales, RC, Sir Charles Thompson, 1944; middle: l to r: Willard McDaniel, RC, Lucky Enois, 1946; bottom: l to r: RC, George Salisbury, Lucky Enois, 1946

Erroll Garner

Spirits of Rhythm, 1944. L to r: Teddy Bunn, Leo Watson, Doug Watkins, Fred Watkins

*New Orleans* cast. RC, Billie Holiday and Louis Armstrong are in the front row

*New Orleans* band. L to r: Zutty Singleton, RC, Kid Ory, Charlie Beale, Budd Scott, Louis Armstrong, Barnie Bigard

RC and Lionel Hampton, Santa Monica,
*c.* 1947

Red Callender in Honolulu, 1949

Band at Lai Yi Chi's, Honolulu, 1949. L to r: RC, Peppy Bourman (d), Johnny Peterson,
Paul Chang, Bernie Conception, Francis King, Toni Craig

Josephine Baker at Humanist Hall, 1950

Vernon Alley's radio programme, San Francisco, 1953. L to r: VA, Curtis Counce, RC

Benny Carter, Eddie Beal, Art Tatum (l to r) at RC and EB's apartment, 1952

Benny Carter, Nat Cole, Craig Huntley (l to r)

'Rosemary Clooney Show', 1956. L to r: RC, Alvin Stoller (d), Ralph Hansell (perc), Bob Bain (g). The contractor is standing by the door

L to r: Emma, Sylvia, Hattie Callender behind RC, 1955

Signing the RCA contract, 1957. L to r: RC, Henry Rene, Eddie Beal, Joe Green

Bill Douglass, mid-sixties

Jerry Fielding, mid-sixties

'Danny Kaye Show', 1956. RC is on the tuba

L to r: Toni, Craig, Sharron, April, RC, 1964

'Flip Wilson Show', 1973

Gerald Wilson's KBCA radio show, 1975. L to r: Charles Mingus, RC, Buddy Collette, GW, Britt Woodman

Mary Lou, RC in Denmark, 1974

'The hat', Denmark, 1974

The Wind Quartet. L to r: James Newton,
John Carter, Charles Owens, RC, John Nunez

Peninsula Jazz Party, July 1984. L to r: Trummy Young, RC, Sir Charles Thompson

At Alton Redd's funeral, late seventies

Buddy Collette, 1980

April and Red Callender, 1984 (Elaine Cohen is in the background)

Sylvia Callender, 1984

Red Callender and Elaine Cohen, 1984

show even if there was only the bass player and the drummer present. Maybe the third alto player or Johnny Hodges would be late. Since the trombone is in the same register, Duke would just change the clef sign and have the trombones play the alto part. Wild sounds came from things like that. Once, Duke called in all the music on a tune while the guys were playing it. He assigned Johnny Hodges or Ben Webster a long solo, then, while the solo was going on, Duke would write a new ending to the tune. Just before the solo was over, he'd pass the music back, and they'd play it – wild sounds. People figured the band sounded like it did on purpose; often it was truly accidental. He explained it once by saying to the audience, 'We are a primitive orchestra . . . we employ the materials at hand.'

# PART FIVE

# Remembering Tatum

In the early 1950s my life was changing into another pattern though I wasn't aware of it at the time. Take it day by day is my philosophy. Toni Craig, who had never really left my life since Hawaii, was now to be the mother of my child. We had been courting, having fun riding around LA going to listen to music. Or she would come and listen while I played. That's the story of my life, me playing and someone listening. When Toni told me she was pregnant, I immediately got a divorce from Emma. Jimmy Tolbert, Lester Young's nephew, accompanied me to the lawyer's office. When he found out how much attorneys make an hour, he began his legal career that day.

We went to Mexico to be married. Though our honeymoon didn't last long, we really loved each other. We moved into a place on Clyde Avenue and our first daughter, Sharron, was born 17 June 1953. As Toni became a real mother, her career as a singer lapsed. After Hawaii we had done some demo tapes; she had a very nice sound. Yet she didn't want to push. The black and white thing, the mixed races, was difficult in those days. We had to be realistic. It's not like it is now, even though die-hards about the racial thing still exist. Billie Holiday could sing with Artie Shaw, but Anita O'Day couldn't sing with Duke Ellington. I can't think of hardly any white singers with black bands at the time. An exception to that would be when Martha Ray or someone of her stature would sit in with bands on Central Avenue. Hawaii was special, it was the true melting-pot of the world. Here was a different story, it wasn't done then, it was just a fact of life. Toni's parents had no hang-ups fortunately. Everyone but one brother-in-law from Alabama accepted me and welcomed me into the family.

My daughter Sylvia was twelve when Sharron was born. She was at the summer camp when I told her she had a new baby sister, she was delighted. Sylvia had been attending Lafayette School where Percy MacDavid, who had conducted the Humanist Symphony, was the music teacher. Sylvia was tall for her age and MacDavid thought she should play the contrabass in the school orchestra. Probably because *I* played bass – which made no sense to me. Sylvia gave it a try. She even taught me that the proper way to rosin the bow was to draw the rosin across the bow in one direction. However, Sylvia's bass career was short-lived. She was far more interested in learning to drive my car and it wasn't long before she was taking me for rides.

In 1953 my mother migrated to Los Angeles. Now both my mother and father were staying at Emma's; my parents had never divorced. My dad was in poor health and he died not long after my mother's arrival in Los Angeles. Mother soon found work caring for an elderly woman who owned a house on 58th Street off Central Avenue. When the woman passed away, I bought the house for my mother. One of her friends from Baltimore, Bertha Burrel, came to visit and they wanted to go out for a night on the town. They had seen an ad in the paper for a great comedian appearing at the Crescendo Club. So I made reservations and Toni and I, my mother and Bertha Burrel, all go to see Lenny Bruce. I knew Lenny as a person but had never seen his act, had heard it was a little rough. Before the show I told him I was with my mother and her friend, very nice ladies, did he think it would be all right for them to see the show?

'Sure,' he says, 'I won't do anything to bruise them . . .'

They ushered us right down in front. I imagine my mother and her friend had heard all those four-letter words before, but not in my presence, you dig. I wanted to crawl out of there, but we were so close to the stage we couldn't just walk out in the middle of the act. If I ever turned redder, it was that night.

Even though Jerry Fielding was blacklisted for a time, he had effectively put the word out about my abilities as a reader. Diverse groups started calling me for dates – even country-and-western groups like Chet Atkins, Joe Mavis and the Sons of the Pioneers. The jazz players didn't know what to make of me.

RECORDED IN

*Hollywood*

Associated Hollywood Pub.          BMI

**8 - YEAR OLD** CAROL KAY
SINGS
**YOU CAN'T DO THE
BOOGIE IN SCHOOL**
(E. Wop)
RED CALLENDER SEXTETTE
42...

RECORDED IN

*Hollywood*

Ico. No
BMI

**I'D RATHER STAY IN THE
HOUSE WITH A MOUSE**
(THAN GO OUT WITH A RAT LIKE YOU)
(Dorsey)

RED CALLENDER SEXTETTE
VOCAL

1065 E. VERNON AVE
LOS ANGELES 11 CALIFORNIA

**168-A+**

Some of them branded me a 'traitor to jazz'. Well, I was making money and my life wasn't strictly jazz. I was involved in all kinds of music, which is what I'd set out to do from the beginning. The truth is, I never made any money to speak of until I disassociated my name from jazz to a degree. When I first started out in the studios, a contractor would call me and ask, 'Do you have a bow? Can you read music?' Those questions could have been insulting, but I took it to mean they were simply ignorant.

Although guys were saying I'd turned my back on jazz, they were wrong. In '53 I went to Chicago to record with Felicia Saunders, one of my favourite singers who'd been with Fielding's band. We recorded a new tune, 'In Other Words'. When the title was changed to 'Fly Me to the Moon' everyone heard it. Felicia had been featured by Fielding along with the singer Ruth Olay. We had a swinging band with Jerry: Hymie Gunkler, Buddy Collette, Ted Romersa and Martin Berman on saxes, Gerry Wiggins piano, Lloyd Ulyate and Joe Howard trombone, Mort Harris and Ralph Fera trumpets, Tommy Romersa drums and myself on bass. A few years later, Felicia wrote lyrics for one of my tunes 'You're Part of Me'.

The Crescendo Club on Sunset, where Fielding's band played, was owned by Gene Norman. Norman, a jazz disc-jockey on KFWB, had got his start as a jazz presenter in the middle forties with his 'Just Jazz' concerts at the Embassy Theatre, the Pasadena Civic and in school auditoriums. Jimmy Tolbert was producing concerts then too and Pat Willard, the great writer on jazz, tells the story of how Jimmy Tolbert would borrow her unemployment cheque on Thursday as down payment to rent Normandy Hall on Saturday night. Only after the concert would she get her rent and grocery money back. Nobody was getting rich then; the wealth was musical. Everyone played those concerts – even Art Tatum.


Art Tatum had been coming to California frequently, dazzling both audiences and musicians. Tatum used to drop by the apartment on Wilton Place that I shared with Eddie Beal before I married. One afternoon, Tatum, Oscar Peterson, Benny Carter and several pianists were there. We had two pianos and everyone sat down to play, even Oscar. Tatum was a listener until all the

piano players got through, then he sat down and played 'Little
Man You've Had a Busy Day'. He effortlessly blew everyone
away. An unforgettable afternoon. Several people tell this story
and have it happening in Chicago or Cleveland or New York. But
it happened here in Los Angeles on Wilton Place.

Horowitz was a fan of Tatum's. Art told me a story about the
time Horowitz had invited him up to his apartment in New York.
Horowitz had just finished working out an elaborate arrangement
on 'Tea for Two'. After he plays it he asks Tatum what he thinks
of it. Tatum says, 'Fine.' Then Art sits down and played *his*
arrangement on 'Tea for Two' embellished by progressions up
and down in thirds.

Horowitz says, 'When did you work that out?'

Tatum says, 'Just now.'

In 1954 Art Tatum moved to California, bought a home in the
Balwin Hills area. At that time I was working with Gerry Wiggins
and Bill Douglass as a trio in the Turban Room, downstairs in the
Dunbar Hotel on Central Avenue. Tatum dropped by almost
every night. Then, he decided he wanted a trio and he hired Bill
and me away from 'Wig'. Who could say no to Tatum? Playing
with him was one of the most joyous, challenging experiences of
my life, a high point that went on for almost three years. People
think it was difficult to play with him but it wasn't, really. Bill and
I would go by his house to rehearse and he would pick a tune
like 'My Ideal' and say, 'I want to use this sequence of chords
here . . .' I'd write them down, play it once and I had it, so it
wasn't really difficult. On all the standards like 'Night and Day'
we used to play the changes and superimpose whatever it was he
wanted over the original changes. No great difficulty, more an
honour to be playing with the world's greatest piano player.

It's hard to say when Bill Douglass and I started working
together. He'd often sit in at the jam sessions Lee Young
organized at the Capri and the Trouville. We worked countless
gigs together, so many that we started thinking of ourselves as a
rhythm-section team. We were the house band at several places.
The singer would bring in his or her accompanist and that was the
band. Working with Tatum was different though, like working
with royalty. One evening last summer, Bill Douglass got to
reminiscing about Art Tatum. Luckily, once Bill starts re-
membering things, there's no stopping him.

BILL DOUGLASS: Our first engagement with Tatum was in Hollywood, the Royal Room. It was a jazz spot at the time, off Hollywood and Las Palmas. That was a very outstanding engagement. We also did several others together – Jazz City, the Suzy Q, Sardi's at Hollywood Boulevard and Vine. We worked several clubs around there, we couldn't wait to get to work with him.

Playing with Tatum there was never a dull moment. No pressure or anything like that, just a matter of musicianship, just a joy to sit there and listen to the man play. Tatum wasn't somebody you thought of as a leader or boss. He was one of the guys, that's the way he felt about it. I've seen statements and heard stories that Tatum sounds better solo, that he doesn't need anybody playing with him. That wasn't the question – whether or not he needed anybody. The fact was, Art enjoyed playing with us, that was the reason for having the trio. He also did his solo thing to break up the set. Then, he'd augment it with the trio.

Tatum was about ninety per cent blind, but he was very independent. He didn't like anything that reflected on his sight problem, and tried to pretend he was perfectly all right and as normal as anyone else. That was tricky because I had the responsibility of picking him up, driving us to work, bringing him back, crossing the street. He kept a big black Cadillac in his garage at home, saw that it was always polished, treated that car like a baby. I guess his wife took him out for drives on Sunday, but I picked him up in my car for work.

We'd get to work, park the car and start walking up the street, walking side by side. Never helped him – you'd better not take his elbow. People who didn't know would always come up and catch him by the elbow. First thing he'd do was snatch it away from them. Well, I understood him. We might be walking down the street, and come to the corner. While I'd be waiting for the light to change, he'd already have stepped off the curb intending to keep right on walking. What I would do is deliberately stumble in front of him, say, 'Uh oh . . . the light almost got us . . .' Then he would step back. When I started crossing the street he'd come with me. When we get to the club we have to weave our way through the crowds of people. Next thing, he's got to learn his way around the club. We're in the back, in the dressing-room. He says, 'Bill, you know where the phone is around here?'

'Oh,' I say, 'it's right here by the men's room. I'm going anyway.' Then I'd start walking there; he's directly behind me, almost stepping on my heels, casing everything as he goes along. When I see the phone I don't say, 'Here's the phone . . .' I say, 'I think the phone is . . . oh, here it is.' Act like I can't see it. Now he's all right, he's on the phone. From there he learns where the rest room is and from there he goes in and out and around, back to the bandstand by himself. No helping him on the bandstand or anything like that.

Imagine the feeling of that club, the Royal Room. Naturally, celebrities, musical and otherwise, are there. Leopold Stokowski was in there one night, Rubinstein, people of that calibre. A hush fell across the audience as we crossed the stage; you could hear a pin drop. And when we played, the same hush, except for applause. They were very careful with the glasses and everything else. It was concert-style every night.

We didn't talk about music, that was just something we did. We were always talking about sport, even on the stand. We're playing all this music and talking about the score of the ballgame. This was before the Dodgers moved to Los Angeles, but we were all avid baseball nuts, all had our idols like Jackie Robinson, Willie Mays, Charlie Neal, Maury Wills, and so forth.

Tatum had several radios, shortwave or whatever and he could tune in any station in the world. Your phone rings at home. It's Tatum calling – 'Hey Bill, Mays just hit two . . .' wherever he is, in or out of town, he'd buzz either Red or me to let us know that Willie Mays hit one.

Tatum never said anything to the audience. Fact is, we never did any announcements at all. The manager of the Royal Room came up to Tatum to ask if he would announce a celebrity in the audience, someone like Frank Sinatra. Art said no, he's part of the audience. Art's letting the manager know that he's the attraction, not who's in the audience. To Tatum, it was the plain, common, ordinary thing that a lot of great people showed up to hear him. We never even announced tunes, we just played. When we finished we got down off the stand. That's all there was to it.

Practically everything we played had been recorded. People knew those tunes, nobody dared say, 'Play so and so . . .' Even Sonny Tufts the movie star was kicked out of the audience one night for talking too loud. The Royal Room was first-class. I enjoyed everything we did but I guess that first one was the best because of the atmosphere. We got used to it after a while I suppose. I haven't experienced anything like it since.

During that first engagement, Red had to be away one evening, tied up in the studio, so Joe Comfort came in to sub for him. Joe was a good friend of ours, a very good bass player. Art liked him a lot, and Art was concerned about our upcoming trip to San Francisco because Red wasn't going to be able to make it. On the first break Art asked Joe about taking the trip with him, asked if he'd be interested in going.

Joe said, 'Yes. I want $500 a week.'

Art said, '$500 a week . . . well, you know Joe, I don't think I can do that.'

Joe said, 'Well then how much were you going to pay?'

Art says, 'I don't see any reason for discussing it since you already told me what you want and I can pay it, our conversation is over.'

That wasn't the end of it. We got up there for the next set. Art can play the most fantastic and rapid tempos. I usually had no problem with them because the three of us worked as a unit. Art got off on such a tempo, I'm telling you, I could hardly make it. And Joe was barely hanging on, really scuffling. That was one of the only times I remember having what's called a rugged set. When we came off I asked Art, 'What the heck kind of tempo was that? What's going on?'

He says, 'Don't worry about it. I wanted to see that cat play $500 worth of bass.'

You learn to think and feel alike as a trio. I'm talking about the way it's supposed to be. I also asked Art later, 'How is it that when the three of us are playing together we can play any kind of tempo, yet we don't overplay. We play just barely above a whisper yet we have no trouble maintaining tempos. Yet with someone else, I might run into problems . . .' He described it like, if you decide to run uphill, you all run uphill together. It's much easier than if you have to carry one of the guys with you. So that explains the Joe Comfort thing, why I was struggling while Art was giving him a bad time. But it never happend with Red, the three of us were always together, no matter what the tempo.

Leroy Vinnegar came on that trip to San Francisco. We played at the Blackhawk, a place where everyone played. Leroy and I stayed next door to the place. It wasn't a ritzy neighbourhood; we got ourselves a nice cheap hotel room. Art was staying downtown at the St Francis Hotel, a whole beautiful suite, television, everything. Of course, he'd always call and invite us to come up and watch the ballgame. He'd sit and look at television. 'Oh man, did you see that?' You wondered all the time how much he really did see, but he knew what was going on. He'd attend ballgames, all sporting events.

Art had a way of tilting his head towards the light and I think somehow, through one eye, he was able to take in enough light for a split second that he might be able to describe your clothes. He might get just enough light for a glance. I never knew because he never said anything about it. I don't think anyone ever knew. Once in a while I'd see him pick up something to read it – hold the paper right up to his eye, then put it down. I've seen him scan sheet music that way. I've seen him play cards, he was a whizz of a card player, almost any kind of card game. You lay a card on the table. He'd pick it up, hold it close to his eye, then pull one from his hand and beat your card.

He always carried all his own money, liked to have crisp new bills. He had a thing about five-dollar bills, always had a lot of them. He carried fifties, twenties and tens all in separate pockets. Maybe the reason for the new money was that perhaps he could feel the imprint on it. He'd pay you or give you money and never make a mistake.

At the club in San Francisco, came pay night. The owner mentioned something about . . . well, we always pay at such and such a time . . . it will be later in the week. Art didn't like that at all. He says, 'Now listen, we don't come late to work, so we do not intend to get paid late.' He was very strong like that. There was nothing for the owner to do but go on and get the money. He counted it out from the cash register and gave Art something like $2,500 or $3,000, most of it in one-dollar bills. I had to take responsibility for this. When I drove Art downtown to the St Francis, I didn't feel good. There were lumps, lumps of these small raggedy one-dollar bills in my pocket.

So I ask him: 'Why can't we put this in the safe?'

Art wants me to take it to the bank in the morning. 'Oh, no . . . the safe is a rip-off.'

Even though I argued, I had to carry this stuff home with me.

Then, lo and behold, we get up the next morning, read the paper, and the news was that the Hotel St Francis safe had been robbed. The morning papers made a big deal of it; it had happened the night before. Big hotel lobby, a safe just like a bank, and all this cash was stolen. The strange thing is, they never found out who did it because of the thief's strategy. The teller was a lady; she conveniently fainted after giving him all the money. People see her on the floor, they pile in around her to see what's wrong. The thief is just walking away with the money. So I always wondered if the teller wasn't in on it.

Norman Granz had a great idea to record Tatum not only solo, but with as many different groups as possible. On the way to work and back each night, Art would tell me about the day's session. The different statements he had to make about musicians were interesting. We discovered what he was talking about when we were called in to do a date with him. It was Buddy De Franco, the clarinet player, with Red and I backing him up. We start playing to get a balance, then say, what should we play? Some tune was decided on and then we'd go ahead and play to the best of our knowledge and ability. I'm listening, thinking about what I'm going to do on the next take.

Except there wasn't any next take. When we finished, Art said, 'That's it. What's next?' This is how it went down, never a second take on anything, never even listen to the playbacks. Buddy De Franco was a bundle of nerves, a basket case. In retrospect it turned out to be his best album. He wanted to play 'Lover Man'; Buddy called a key and Art went into some fantastic introduction, came out somewhere else. Under his breath Art's saying, 'Godammit, you wanted it in such and such a key and this is where you're going to get it.' Art had got himself so far out on a limb that he almost couldn't get back. That's the closest thing to a mistake I ever heard him make. Probably just a result, I think, of him being bothered with Buddy De Franco who was so shaky that day. Art was merciless. It was up to Buddy to find his way through. Before he gets three or four notes out of his horn, Art's playing right along with him, almost second guessing what the man's going to play. Whatever he played, Art would play it again in another inversion. He had total mastery of his instrument. Although Art didn't have big hands, he made tenths from the second and the fifth finger. I don't know how he opened his hand up so wide. While playing tenths, he could play something else with his thumb.

On the way to work that night I asked him about never doing any second takes. He says, 'Man, we don't do it over again in the club, why should we do it over again just because we're in a recording studio? You take what you get,' he says, 'that's musicianship. Hell, if you know how to play you're not going to play bad. Why break your neck trying to create perfection? Whatever you do, that's it, that's the way it is. Today, anyway.'

That was the amazing thing – an hour and you're out of the studio. Give them a good hour, we've done a whole album and that's it.

The day he recorded with Benny Carter they had no bass and used Louis Bellson on drums. It was really a kick when Art told me about the date because Benny is a very dominating character. Red and I both knew him from working with him over the years. Art says, 'Man, that cat was really screwing around with his horn. We cut something and he wanted to do it over again, his solo wasn't right he tells me. Finally I had to tell him – Man, I wish you'd get yourself together because I can't hang around here all day.' That's how big he is – Benny Carter's just a kid having problems as far as Art is concerned. Benny was much older than Art, but not as far as musicianship was concerned. He was the absolute king and that's all there is to it.

Now with Ben Webster – Red was on that date – Ben handled it very well. They were old buddies. It was so beautiful because Ben was playing Ben and Tatum was playing Tatum. That was the idea of the thing. But most people who played with him got all shook up. Red was on a date with Tatum, Buddy Rich and Lionel Hampton. Hamp wanted to sing and Tatum didn't like that very much. If you had any weaknesses, Tatum would expose them. These sessions took place during his last years, from '53 or '54 until 1956 when he died. All during this time we worked with him on and off. If he were still here I'm sure the association would be the same.

He died so young, at forty-six, of uraemic poisoning. He'd had complications, a diabetic condition which was the reason he'd stopped drinking. Before that there was a dramatic weight-loss. One day he was a big, fat jovial fellow and the next thing, he's kind of a little guy; all his clothes are too big for him. Yet it didn't slow him down any on the piano. The weight-loss had happened while he was away on a trip. We had heard that Art wasn't feeling so good. Then, his wife called and asked me to come by; she called all his close friends saying we don't expect him to make it through the night. That was surprising because when we went there, Art was sitting on the edge of the bed smoking a cigarette, talking. 'Oh man, everything's gonna be OK, don't worry about a thing.' Red and I spent most of the afternoon with him. Art was the type of person about whom you felt he'd always be here. When I turned on my radio next morning, they were playing Art Tatum records on AM radio. I didn't have to think twice about that.

Our relationship with him was like a short lifetime. Once, at the club, the Royal Room, he made them rent a brand-new Steinway, then came off the stand grumbling. 'This piano is trying to play me . . . but I'll get it,' talking about the stiff action. 'I'm gonna loosen it up.'

He seemed to know every tune written. He told me he had some originals and at one point he had Dudley Brooks write down bass lines for some arco effect he wanted. This was for things he intended to do at one time or another. He told me the reason he played all the things he did the same way every time was that if he played them differently, no one would know what tune he was playing. He wanted to keep his music identifiable. He never got around to his originals, but he loved the blues. Anytime you play the blues it's original. Listening to all his tunes you realize that no one played like him. The harmonic structures were so complex that every song was a new creation. Cascading from left to right like a waterfall, and if he was ever in trouble you'd never know it. He had ways out of everything. There was really no one qualified to tell him if he made a mistake . . . he rarely knew exactly what he was going to play anyway. His nickname was 'God', all the musicians called him God. Many cats were called King, Count, Sir, Lord, Duke, but to the musicians, Art Tatum was God.

# PART SIX

# Swingin' Suite

Tatum had been a great inspiration, a great light, and he caused me to do a lot of thinking about my own music. The result was the first album of twelve Callender originals, *Swingin' Suite*, recorded on the Bihari brothers' Crown label. I reworked 'Pastel', 'On Again' (the theme song from the Lee and Lester Young band), 'Skyline' from the late thirties, 'You're Part of Me', and wrote a few new ones including 'Bihari' for the brothers. The band was perfect – a complete saxophone section with Buddy Collette doubling on tenor, flute and clarinet, Bill Green on alto and flute, Clyde Dunn on baritone; the rhythm section was myself on bass, Bill Douglass on drums and Eddie Beal piano. John Ewing played trombone, Paur Jones trumpet. Great players all, with experience in both jazz and studio work. We recorded everything in one or two takes.

We had it all on acetate, though presenting an album of one's own work wasn't so simple. I mean, which tune should go first, which should follow? These things were puzzling me when Toni and I decided to take a trip to San Francisco to visit our friend Jimmy Atcheson. It was late in the year 1957 and Toni was noticeably with child then, our second child. Our daughter Sharron had been born the previous June. We left Sharron with her grandmother and started out for San Francisco in our 1953 Buick Roadmaster. When we reached Gilroy, a piston blew. All day was spent in this small town while it was being repaired. Saturday evening we finally reached Jimmy Atcheson's house in San Francisco and started listening to the *Swinging' Suite* tapes. On one hearing, Jimmy knew exactly how to order the tunes. That dilemma solved, we start out for Los Angeles the following day in the midst of a downpour. The main road was washed out; we had to follow a police caravan to safer ground. Right when we reach Palo Alto, about forty miles from San Francisco, the car engine freezes. It's Sunday, everything's closed, the roads are treacherous. I've got a date on Monday I have to make. Everything was shut up tight in that town, everything except the Buick dealership agency. The agent at the Buick place said he couldn't possibly do anything for our car . . . why don't we trade it in for a new one? Wonderful idea, but no pink slip.

'No pink slip? That's all right. Take this floor model . . .' (a shiny black 1956 Buick Roadmaster with maroon upholstery, gold insignia all over) 'send us the pink slip in the mail when you get home. Take the car on trust.'

An hour later we headed to LA in our new car.

Although I had a reputation as a bass player and arranger, very few people knew I played tuba. My big horn had been gathering dust for quite a while. Then one day my inner urge prompted me to take it out again and get my chops back. I began going out to the Hollywood Hills, just me and the tuba, to practise in the open air. Outdoors, there's no resistance, so you really learn to fill the instrument. Once back inside, it's very easy to control. What a pleasure that was, me and the trees and the tuba.

Once I had my facility back, I decided to record an album featuring the tuba. I approached Dick Boch's record company about it. Boch liked the idea, though he thought Bob Brook-meyer should do it since my name wasn't big enough. That didn't sit right with me, so I took it to the Bihari brothers, who went for it right away. 'Speak Low' became the title tune, a Kurt Weill melody. I wrote a song called 'Chris' for my infant son Craig Christopher Callender. The rest of the album was a potpourri of originals and classics like Ellington's 'In a Sentimental Mood' and 'Darn That Dream' which Louis Armstrong had made famous. Buddy Collette contributed 'Nice Day' on which we played a unison duet for clarinet and tuba. The instrumentation was unique for those days. We had Buddy on flute and clarinet, Vince De Rosa playing French horn on all but one cut with Irving Rosenthal, and a rhythm section with Bill Douglass on drums, Red Mitchell on bass, Bob Bain on guitar.

Every last note of that music I copied out myself. The solos were spontaneous except for the French horns; I wrote them out because I wasn't sure if the guys could handle ad lib. There was no rehearsal. We just went into the studio and did it all in one take or two. Sure, there were a few fluffs, a blue note here and there, though listening to it almost thirty years later, even the mistakes sound intended. I've never done anything that I didn't think I could have done better, but you have to settle for something. That's what I consider musicianship – even when you're at your worst, it's still professional. You might rise above that level, but even your worst effort is still acceptable.

Arranging is a fascinating activity. Arranging and composing are synonymous in a way because even working with existing material you're making a new creation; you take any melody and compose around it. What I do when I sit down to write is put my melody line down first. My next line is the bass line because it's like building a house. The bass is the foundation of the whole business of music. One writes differently for different-sized groups; my preference is writing for smaller groups as they stretch my imagination more. Once I have the melody line, the chord progressions and the bass line, I work on the other parts, taking care not to step on vocal lines. Backgrounds for the vocalist or soloist are next, or else you can hand the backgrounds over to the rhythm section.

Once a writer is thoroughly familiar with the keyboard, to see is to hear. Picture what I mean? You hear the music by seeing it on the page, though it's nice to test your theory at times. With experience, it's possible to do it without a piano. A piano makes it more enjoyable and I might also use a piano for a particular voicing I want or a certain inner movement. My theory about writing is to make each part interesting to the person who will play it, as opposed to the old block style of writing where the musicians jump from one chord to another. Studying with Dr Ernest Kanitz helped me lose my fear of departing from the block style. Through the course of much writing, I've found it's possible to invent many different sounds that have nothing to do with chord changes. Like Duke Ellington said, 'Be guided by what sounds good to your ear.'

Unisons sound good to my ear; you can't be afraid of unisons either, whether an octave apart or not. Most symphonies end on a unison note. Billy May, whose music is always full of surprises, taught me a great deal about that. He often uses unisons and they're very strong. For instance, when you're voicing a reed section with five saxophones – two altos, two tenors and a baritone – my inclination was (and still is) to double the lead at the top and the bottom. I'm only now learning about voicing. To learn is to be able to change one's mind.

Leonard Feather was kind enough to give *Callender Speaks Low* three stars. Though the album didn't bust the top of any charts at the time, it worked out beautifully for me. The studios started asking me to double on tuba and bass for picture dates. There was a sudden wave of brass recordings during the late fifties and I was frequently called to play tuba. Jerry Fielding recorded an orchestra featuring me on tuba, *Magnificence in Brass*; Billy May featured the tuba on one of my favourite albums, *Big Fat Brass* and I did several dates with Billy May for Frank Sinatra on the tuba. I even recorded a polka album with Lawrence Welk.

Nat Cole, though at that time a millionaire with his own rhythm section, hired me to play tuba for several of his recordings with large groups. Nat's 1956 top hit 'Straighten Up and Fly Right' had made him a superstar. We were still friends; we just moved in different circles. He became about as big a star as one can get in America and he had to keep up the pace. Being the kind of guy he was, he kept every commitment. It put too much pressure on him, and he eventually developed a lung condition. I'm sure he went to work even when he was in pain. His producers kept grinding records out of him even though they knew he was sick. Even today new Nat Cole records are still being released, records made over twenty years ago. The pressure of being a superstar is unenviable. I'm proud to have known Nat in the early days, but I certainly didn't covet his tremendous success because it killed him.

About a year after *Speaks Low* came out we did another album, this time on MGM, called *The Lowest*. On one side I played bass, on the other, tuba; again a combination of originals and standards. Hymie Gunkler was on alto sax, Marty Berman baritone, Buddy Collette on flute, clarinet and tenor saxophone; Gerry Wiggins on piano, Billy Bean guitar, Bill Douglass drums and Red Mitchell on bass. Gerald Wilson played trumpet on this

*Caricature of Red Callender*
*by Calvin Bailey*

album. Good friends since the forties, Gerald and I rented an office together in Hollywood in 1957 where we each worked on our individual projects. I recorded with Gerald on Mercury during this period and Gerald came to the rescue when it was time for Toni to go to the hospital to deliver our third child, April Callender, born in February of 1958, just as he'd done the preceding year for Craig's birth. That's how tight we were; our families grew up together and we really enjoyed showing off our babies at Sunday dinners.

With a young, growing family to support, I kept up the pace of recording, TV, film work, composing, writing for other people's record dates and generally getting as much work as was available. Never once did I call a contractor for a job, so I must have been doing something right. I was lucky to have often been at the right place at the right time and never had to get involved in the politics of studio hiring. Through Fielding, I'd become a regular with other conductors, especially Nelson Riddle and Greg MacRitchie. There came a point when all the conductors in Hollywood had to show their true colours. That's when I got kicked out of the Musicians' Union.

Local 47, now both black and white, had invoked a quota law which restricted musicians to doing no more than two records and one TV show a week. I had been doing the 'Rosemary Clooney Show', 'You Asked for It' and was doing about two record dates a day. The union asked me to return any money I made over their quota to them. Ridiculous! I wouldn't do it. There were only three of us who refused; Alvin Stoller and Al Hendrickson were the others. The union kicked all of us out. However, it didn't matter; I found out about the Taft–Hartley Act from that episode. The union had no control over anything that involved interstate commerce. Obviously, records, TV shows, and movies were distributed nationally. The union was powerless. Whenever I did a date I simply requested that my cheque be mailed to me at home rather than running it through the union office. I was working on the 'Richard Diamond Show' in addition to the other shows. Bobby Helfer, Pete Rugulo's contractor for Richard Diamond fired me point blank. Couldn't stand up to union pressure. Had I observed the quota I would have worked only one day a week. I was so busy I didn't have time to bother, just thought, 'Some people are chickenshit, so what?' The fearless ones, MacRitchie on 'You Asked for It', Nelson Riddle, Fielding of course, kept right on hiring me because they liked the way I played. And, they had guts.

We didn't stay kicked out for too long, only eight or nine months passed before they kicked us back in. Our union leadership hasn't always been on the side of the musicians. Joseph Weber, President of the American Federation of Musicians, issued an absurd statement in 1929: 'A general danger to employment will not develop as . . . the public accepts Vitaphone merely as a novelty . . . It is the opinion of the federation leadership based on exhaustive study that mechanical music . . . will fail to give satisfaction in any theatre as a substitute for live music.' (*International Musician*, (February 1929). As a result of this short-sightedness, the musicians' contracts with the TV networks were ridiculous. Of all the hundreds of television shows I've played on since the 'Life of Riley', I receive residuals only on shows which were taped in front of a live audience. That's a terrible contract and I hope some day someone is able to do something about it because the musicians get a royal screwing on that. Petrillo, a later AFM president, also negotiated very poorly with the record companies. In the late 1940s and early 1950s, record dates paid about $33.33, eleven dollars an hour with a three-hour minimum, a pathetic amount. Twenty years later they finally got it up to about $150 a date. But even back in the forties, record companies were prepared to pay $100 a date. Petrillo accepted a lesser amount, put the rest in a trust fund. The musicians brought a case against him and we won. I remember receiving about $7,000 from that settlement. The picture contracts are slightly better. Each time a movie is aired at a theatre or on television, the musicians get a little taste, two dollars here and there. Having been on so many picture dates, it all adds up. We had to fight for that, too. Finally, about 1960, Petrillo hung it up and resigned.

Some musicians were still branding me a 'traitor to jazz' and others, mainly critics and uninformed people, were calling me a 'west coast jazz' musician. The labelling started with Gerry Mulligan and Chet Baker's group. Supposedly there were two kinds of jazz during the 1950s – east coast jazz, a hard driving 'funky' sound; and west coast, a non-aggressive, easy-listening kind of sound. I always thought these categories were miserable misnomers. First of all, most of the players who live on the west coast are originally from the east coast. Half the west coast guys made their names back east – like Mingus or Eric Dolphy or Don Byas from Texas – so people think they're eastern musicians. Bob Brookmeyer, Shorty Rogers, Stan Kenton, and the great drummer Shelly Manne, all came to LA much later. There was a fabulous musical scene going on here before they ever arrived. Suddenly, everyone identifies a certain sound with the west coast, and either people liked it or they didn't. I worked with Shorty Rogers and with Marty Paich, who is a very fine arranger, and did countless enjoyable dates with Shelly Manne. Buddy and I were even some of the 'token' blacks in Stan Kenton's Neophonic Orchestra. But never would I identify myself with that certain pallid sound that people think of when they hear the term 'west coast jazz'. That label, perhaps all labels, does a much greater disservice to musicians than the public can imagine.

Regardless of what the critics were writing, great jazz was being made on the west coast. In 1958 I got a call to appear in *St Louis Blues*. Nelson Riddle arranged and conducted the music. The company was excellent: Pearl Bailey, Cab Calloway, Mahalia Jackson, Ella Fitzgerald, Barney Bigard, Lee Young, Teddy Buckner and Nat Cole, who played the role of W.C. Handy. Billy Preston portrayed Handy as a boy and young man. Several film calls followed that one, including two which made it to the top: *Around the World in Eighty Days*, and *Some Like It Hot*. I also did some ghosting for films, yet as far as I'm concerned, that doesn't count because there's no credit. Ghost-writing is a common phenomenon as a composer usually gets a mere six weeks to write an entire score.

During this period I was also the staff bass player at the Gold Star Recording Company, spending so much time there it almost seemed like home. Doing demo tapes was part of my job – I'd get the sheet music and make up bass lines. Wayne Shanklin was the staff writer-composer for whom I'd done several demos, including the hit tune 'Chanson d'Amour'. He was intrigued with my melodic feeling for bass lines and one day suggested we get together to do some writing. We went to his small office studio on Sunset Boulevard, I started playing a line or two; something was happening. I played the line again.

Shanklin says, 'Wait a minute . . . play that again . . . yeah . . . listen . . .' He started singing: 'Primrose Lane . . . life's a holiday on Primrose Lane . . .'

He's singing, I'm playing, we're both making it up as we go along. In forty-five minutes we had the whole tune.

That 'Primrose Lane' became a popular hit was one of the most pleasant surprises of my life. Of the numerous songs I'd written none had touched the pop market. At first I wasn't sure if I wanted to be identified with a pop tune, that's why the sheet music has my real name, George Callender. I was thinking of myself then as a hipster jazz musician. Shanklin took our tune down to the Chappel Music Company to have it published. Everything was a 50/50 split.

The first singer to pick up on it was Jerry Wallace. After that it was sung on many shows – the Mills Brothers, Pearl Bailey, Ella Fitzgerald. Whenever I see Ella or Pearl, they walk up to me, smile and start singing 'Life's a holiday on Primrose Lane . . .' which is quite an honour for me. The tune was so hot for a while that someone even tried to steal it, wrote a tune called 'Life's a Holiday' that sounded damn near our tune. It was so close there was no legal question and now thanks to the very honourable society, ASCAP, we get royalties on both tunes.

The house our growing family had been living in on Clyde Avenue was bursting at the seams. Even before 'Primrose Lane' became big, we had purchased a lot in Baldwin Hills and had hired an architect. 'Primrose Lane' gave us the confidence and clout to build the house the way we wanted. Strange as it may seem, with all the many and various jobs I had had since my return from Hawaii, I still wasn't sure that the prosperity would last. Musicians are hot for a time, somebody new comes along, the old ones cool off, nobody hires them, they fade into obscurity. Although the opposite was happening for me, it still took ten years to convince me that things were going to keep on swinging.

The kids were small then; Sharron was seven, Craig four, and April two and a half. They weren't terribly excited about the move. It was Toni and I who pored over the blueprints and discussed every detail. The lot on Don Milargo Drive in Baldwin Hills was situated on a hilltop overlooking the city. We wanted a spacious split-level: three bedrooms upstairs for the kids, downstairs, the master bedroom, kitchen, family room, living-room with bar, and a two-car garage at the street level. Sliding glass windows panelled the front of the house. At last I had a living-room large enough for my grand piano.

Mixed couples weren't a common sight then, in any neighbourhood. Ironically, it was the only black family in the entire area who took on a snobbish attitude towards us. Couldn't even bear to be in the same square mile and moved away. Only my brother-in-law from Alabama turned out to be a problem. He worked for RCA, thought the idea of his sister-in-law married to a black would hurt his career. He was the kind of redneck who comes to your house with the family on a holiday, gets loaded on your booze, then proceeds to make racist remarks. The kids still remember him.

Shortly after we moved, I had a record date that began at midnight. As I'm driving down the steep, winding road, I notice two guys tailing me in a Plymouth. At the time, I was driving a Buick station wagon, had my bass loaded in the back. I hadn't the faintest notion who these guys were or what they wanted, so when I came out of the hills, I pulled into a gas station with bright lights. I didn't want to be alone when they caught up with me. They pulled into the station and got out of their car, two guys wearing hats. I got out of my car too.

'What do you want?' I asked. There were enough people around to be brave.

'We want to know what you're doing rushing around in Baldwin Hills like you were,' one of them said. They were detectives.

'Hey – I'm on my way to a record date with Billy Eckstine and Sarah Vaughan. I'm driving over to Capitol Studios. See that house up there?' I pointed to the crest of the hill and they peered into the maze of twinkling lights. 'That one, at the top. I built that house, I own it.'

'Oh, we're very sorry sir,' they said. 'See we got a job . . . you know . . . just can't be too sure . . . so we decided to follow you.'

'Well, I'm on my way to work. What about it?'

'No harm intended . . .'

So I continued to my gig, a beautiful session with Sarah and Billy.

Hollywood, as everyone knows, is a 'What Makes Sammy Run' kind of world. Everybody's out striving to get ahead, guys are climbing over one another to get to where they're going, people are thinking strictly of themselves. The casting-couch scenario is real too. There was one woman who wanted to be a starlet, she'd slept with so many producers that people started calling her 'Vagina'. She never made it. That's why I was lucky, whatever happened to me wasn't via the cut-throat route. The conductors respected my work on the big horn and the bass. The calls kept coming.

Thirty years ago I regarded working in the Hollywood studios in a very different light than I do today. The motion-picture industry has changed considerably. Several of those pre-rock'n'roll pictures they made were great. You never knew whether there would be a symphony orchestra in the pit when you arrived, or if you'd be called upon to improvise an introduction. One day it might be *The Marriage of Figaro*, the next it might be a semi-classical modern score with direct lifts from Beethoven and Brahms. Now that I look back on the 1950s and 1960s, I can see that it was a twenty-year grind, though I rarely noticed that aspect of it when I was doing it because most of it was enjoyable.

If a date started at nine o'clock in the morning, I'd be up by seven and out of the house by eight. I always liked to be early, usually forty-five minutes before the date started. If I was doubling, I'd want to get both instruments set up and scan the music for any difficult parts. When the tuba was set up with the brass section, opposite where the bass was positioned, I'd have to tiptoe across the room while the tape was running to join in on the tuba part. When I was just on tuba, I got to play with great bassists like Richard Kelly, who then had the first chair in the LA Symphony.

A day like that might have started with Pete Rugolo conducting the 'Richard Diamond Show' (before Helfer fired me). From that I might go on to another filmed TV show. The musicians never saw the show in sequence, our backs were to the screen. Other than occasional playbacks I never saw any of the shows. The whole point was to get it done as quickly as possible and get the musicians out of there because it was costing money.

After a morning's work, the next call might be one o'clock. I worked at all the different studios: Fox, MGM, Warner Brothers,

Universal, RKO, Paramount, Goldwyn. Republic was still in
business during the late fifties, early sixties and it was there I did
numerous cowboy pictures with the great composing team of Paul
Sawtell and Bud Shefter. Those were musically the most
rewarding. Cowboy pictures are action-packed; behind all that
action is busy music – strings, heavy percussion, brass. If you
were honest enough to tell the conductor you made a mistake,
he'd say, 'Forget it – the horses' hooves will cover it up, don't
worry about it, let's just get all this music done.'

We used to call it making a pound of music a day. Once the
engineer got a balance, it was one scene after another. With the
cowboy movies, we'd hear playbacks only if there was a scene
that went from horses' hooves into dialogue. I'm finally getting to
see some of those movies on the late, late shows.

Very seldom did I make it home for dinner during the week, as
evenings were record dates, sometimes radio commercials.
Usually, I'd have dinner in restaurants with friends from the
rhythm section. Rhythm-section people have a real affinity for
each other, we think alike. The guitarist Al Viola and drummer
Alvin Stoller were frequent dinner partners all through this
period. We used to kid around, calling the string-section people
'The Mice' because of the high-pitched sounds. Naturally,
string-section people congregated together too. We felt their
personalities were different from ours because of the role they
played; music was written for them as a group, and they were
dependent on the concertmaster. Rhythm-section players' roles
are most often more independent. Al Viola and I discussed
everything over dinner: problems our kids were undergoing,
politics, working conditions, finances, our feelings, and the
negotiations taking place around the formation of a studio guild
to strengthen the musician's position. The union, again, was not
making the kind of statements we needed regarding hours and
wages.

Time passed quickly; days were extremely full. Although I was
busy I spent as much time as I could with my family. Toni and I
taught all the kids to read ourselves before they entered
kindergarten. I saw myself become a real family man. Not long
after we moved to Don Milagro, we thought it would be a grand
idea to have a recreational vehicle for taking weekend trips. We
had one custom-built – twenty-six feet long, slept eight people,

had a bathroom, kitchen, air conditioning. Toni designed the entire floor plan. I could have worked seven days a week if I'd wanted to, but that's no way to live. I wanted to have time with the children to watch them grow; time to relax and get away from it all. The RV seemed to be the answer. We took trips to places like Yosemite, the national forests, the wide-open spaces. For April's sixth birthday in February, we drove to the hottest place in the nation, Death Valley. As soon as we arrived it snowed for the first time in thirty years. Never having seen snow before, the kids were elated, ran out to play in it and April's little feet got frostbitten, so we headed home the same day. When the kids were older I'd take them out to the desert and we set up targets. Each of them took turns shooting my .22 rifle and shotgun which had a hell of a kick to it. This was my way of teaching them proper respect for weapons. Craig and Sharron both learned to drive the RV, which was a monster for the road, though I enjoyed driving it through the magnificent California landscapes, listening to the baseball game in one ear, to the family's conversation in the other. All this relaxed me.

Toni wasn't much of an outdoors person. I didn't realize at the time she might have preferred to stay in the comfort of her home or take an entirely different kind of vacation. That's water under the bridge now. I was bringing in the bucks to give everybody a good life and I felt I deserved my own form of recreation. Toni never objected to anything; she was a silent partner in a way. She was a marvellous mother, a real mother-hen type who liked her chicks around her. About other things, she wasn't too talkative. Life was so busy during this time that years passed before I discovered the hidden corners.

We used to throw wild New Year's Eve parties in our house on Don Milagro. Most of my musician friends had gigs till one in the morning. They'd start drifting in about two o'clock, then the jam sessions would get hot. The kids would sneak downstairs until they were noticed and sent scurrying back to bed. The music drew them like a magnet.

April, Craig and Sharron all dig music. Both the girls sing and Sharron played the flute for a time. My son Craig was always the most inquisitive about it. One summer day I drove to work at Goldwyn Studios. Only when I was in the parking-lot did I notice seven-year-old Craig hidden in the back seat. He was burning to know what I did with music all day long. I couldn't take him inside with me that day without prior arrangement, so I called Clarence Daniels, a bass student and friend, to come and take him home. Toni thought he was in the neighbourhood playing as usual. They were just beginning to miss him when Clarence pulled up. Not long afterwards, I took him with me to the studio, took all the kids backstage, behind the scenes. Being my kids, they got to meet everybody. As the girls grew older and more and more good-looking, 'Red's daughters' attracted quite a bit of attention. Craig, persistent Taurus that he is, wanted to start playing the drums. That same year when he was seven he began studying with Bill Douglass. Naturally he had all the best drum sets, got to meet Louis Bellson, Buddy Rich, and other famous drummers. As a teenager he switched to fender bass, began writing songs which he recorded himself in our garage studio.


In 1963 I went on staff at NBC for the simple reason of opening the door for other black musicians. If I hadn't joined the staff, NBC would have hired a white bass player.

It meant less money than freelancing. I could only accept other jobs with the understanding that NBC had my first allegiance. Al Viola was also on staff then and we were both doing other dates together. It was the kind of back-to-back scheduling that keeps you praying there won't be any overtime. Once a United Studio date finished at half past three; we were due at NBC at four – from Hollywood to Burbank in half an hour. I took a short cut and made it on time, sat there on my stool waiting for the conductor to begin. Al walks in about ten minutes late and the conductor goes into a rigmarole about 'staff allegiance'. Meanwhile, I'm reading a paperback, playing Mr Cool. Al still talks about my Oscar performance that day.

Al and I were part of the sixties success formula. Contractors and conductors always got wind of who played on a hit record. We were fortunate enough to have been on many big ones, like 'Strangers in the Night'. So they hired us over and over again. Often, we'd get to the date, scan the music and there would be no written introduction. The conductor would say, 'All right you guys, think of something.' We'd invent the introduction, they'd play it back, look at each other and exclaim, 'Another hit record!'

The conductor, however, always got credit for the music, not us.

When you're on a television-studio staff, the studio throws you anything that's there. NBC was using me for a game show, 'Let's Make a Deal', CBS for the series 'Playhouse 90'. I was walking down the corridor at NBC when Edie Adams comes by and says, 'Hi Red, how come you're not on my show?'

'Nobody asked me,' I replied.

'We'll see about that . . .' The following day Al Lapin called me to join the band on the 'Edie Adams Show'. That lasted about a year until they decided to cut down on staff. I received severance pay and was immediately hired by CBS to work on the 'Danny Kaye Show' along with Buddy Collette.

It seems that in most of the mixed situations I've been in, I've found myself right alongside Buddy. We became partners in non-musical ventures as well. Real estate was an excellent investment at the time and Buddy and I went in on some units in south central Los Angeles. A third partner who negotiated the deals ended up stealing us blind. When the riots happened in Watts during the mid-sixties, many of our buildings were razed by fire. We accepted all our losses and bowed out. My first reaction to the rioters was that they might come and burn my house down too, since we were living high on the hill. Black, white; at that stage of the game no one gave a damn. It was a very disturbing upheaval which provoked serious thought. I was making affluent money but one never stops being a black man in America. On several occasions I donated my services to Horace Tapscott's Pan Afrikan People's Arkestra which played in churches, schools, parks, recreation halls in the black communities, and always played for free. Later, in 1968 when Martin Luther King was shot, both Buddy Collette and myself went on strike for a week from the 'Danny Kaye Show' and the 'Joey Bishop Show'. It was the only way we had of protesting about the tragedy. Joey Bishop took our absence personally, he didn't understand what was happening. Danny Kaye, of course, was completely sympathetic.

Working on the 'Danny Kaye Show' for four years was a true pleasure. Danny always took time to have conversations with me about politics and other matters concerning the realities of America. When a third person came along, he'd break up the serious talk with a joke. Paul Wesson conducted the band, but Danny would frequently come out front and conduct as well.

Once he featured me on 'Slap That Bass'. For me that was quite a big deal, out in front of the cameras with Danny Kaye. He is an astute, expansive, literate and informed man – a beautiful soul. I'll always consider him a friend.

While we were working on the 'Danny Kaye Show', Buddy and I were also hired to work the 'Carol Burnett Show'. Here's another lovely human being. Carol Burnett was a fledgling star then, used to make guest appearances on Danny's show. Gracious, never without a smile for the musicians, she was another person who always remembered you once she'd worked with you. Dinah Shore, Doris Day, Debbie Reynolds, Lucille Ball who hired the first black conductor to work in the studios . . . most of the women in television at that time were far more for real than many of the male stars.

Interspersed with these two shows, I worked on the 'Jonathan Winters Show'. I was in business, too, with Joe Rotondi, a marvellous composer, pianist, arranger and teacher. For about ten years we had a place on Sunset Boulevard, a music production and reproduction centre which had the lingering smell of ammonia from the copying machines. We sold music manu-script and score paper, transparencies, transistor radios and did all kinds of arranging.

When Mingus called me in 1964 to invite me to be in his band for the Monterey Jazz Festival, I accepted gladly, though I wasn't sure what to expect as Mingus was always creating excitement. He asked me to bring both my tuba and my bass. We had a rehearsal, a hodge-podge rehearsal in my estimation, because there was so little written down. He gave me some saxophone parts to play on the tuba. His method was like . . . 'Hey, I'll play the bass out front, then I'll point to certain people – just play anything you want to play.' Along with Ornette Coleman's music, this was the start of free jazz. You might say it was atonal; you'd have a key centre somewhere, that's all. Mostly, Mingus would scream out, 'You do this! You do that! I want YOU to preach on your horn, and YOU, YOU pray to your old lady, YOU pray to those people you owe money to . . . YOU, you're the rabbi overseeing everything . . .' Whether or not anyone in the band even knew what a rabbi did, his exhortations were effective. The whole thing was so inspired and emotional it could never have been repeated. 'Meditations on Integration', which the piece was eventually titled, brought the audience to its feet.

Something had happened to the front mike when Mingus was playing. It was broken, so he borrowed my big bass which he'd always loved, and it cut through the entire orchestra. There was a certain magic in the air. We all loved him very much and played our asses off to make it a success. This was the happy and passionate side of Mingus – no violent scenes or sarcasm like at the Town Hall concert a year or two earlier in New York. All the musicians had minds that grasped everything instantly: Bobby Bryant on trumpet, Jaki Byard piano, Jack Nimitz baritone, Dannie Richmond playing drums, Buddy Collette . . . that concert was a breakthrough. Mingus had far too many wild ideas ever to write them all down on paper, so he'd hum them. I enjoyed it immensely, although that's not the natural way I operate.

Another artist I worked with during this period had something in common with Mingus – Mahalia Jackson. When I recorded with her on Columbia, she hardly ever did anything the same way twice. With Mahalia, you play with your head, your heart, your eyes; you try to catch the nuances. If she felt like extending a bar to five or six beats, she'd just do it. The dates were with bass, organ, drums, guitar and a choir of singers; we all attuned ourselves to her artistry and her whims. Music is emotional for me, but it's much more than being emotional. You have to know exactly what you're doing. If the framework is always changing, it causes a lot of adjustment.

The other extreme would be someone like Peanuts Hucko. A great clarinettist, but Peanuts plays his solo exactly the same every time he plays it. I went on the road with him a few times for short trips with Arnold Ross piano and Jake Hanna drums. We had a little joke about 'working for peanuts . . .' It wasn't true, Peanuts paid very well, he's a thorough businessman. When he says your money will be ready at two o'clock, it's ready at two.

Some performers I worked with weren't really musicians. It was their status in show business that required them to sing. Like playing the background music for Roz Russell in *Gypsy*. She was no singer but actually did sing some of the songs. We would do up to thirty-six takes on one tune. The film editors pieced it together – they do alchemy with the scissors in the studio – and she came out sounding marvellous. The famous 'singer' Eddie Fisher was actually not too musical. While working on his show I observed the conductor standing in the wings to wave him in; he couldn't find his way onstage without someone to cue him. Or a cat like Bobby Darin, who thought he knew more about music than he did. Nervous, always jacked up, he'd often tell people how to play without really being qualified to do that.

It takes all kinds. Carmen Cavalero was a perfectionist. Around 1965 I did a trio date with him on piano and Shelly Manne on drums. Nothing would satisfy Cavalero, we did forty-six whole takes on one tune. Another date then was with Hoagy Carmichael; Ernie Freeman did the arrangements. What struck me as hilarious was that Hoagy couldn't remember the words to 'Stardust', his biggest tune. Had to send his son out to buy the sheet music. Johnny Mercer often would come by different studios when he knew his tunes were being recorded. He was one of the most talented people in the business. Then there was Herb Alpert whose 'Tijuana Brass' had a huge commercial success. I used to do all his demos. Simplicity made for his success, and Herb, though an adequate trumpet player, had enough brains to hire another trumpeter as a featured player in his band. Herbie's a supreme businessman.

My first big orchestra date was with Mario Lanza. The sound stage was large enough for ninety instruments and players. This was my first chance to play with Milton Kesselbaum, one of the great classical bassists who'd played in the NBC Symphony under Toscanini. 'Song of India' sticks in my mind from that experience. The orchestration had one pedal bass note through the whole thing. Kesselbaum simply tuned his A string down a half tone and played it. That was too easy; I played A flat the whole time on the E string, hard work. At that time I wanted to appear 'correct'. This was when I thought everybody was noticing me. Then I discovered that people couldn't care less what I was doing – they were worried about themselves. You learn.

On one occasion people were noticing me – in a very ironic way. Alan Reuss, Leonard Pinario and myself were to be the trio backing Judy Garland for a big CBS TV special. Judy was terrific. At the end of the trio's little bit in the show, she's supposed to kiss everybody, and during the rehearsal, she does. Suddenly the director thinks, 'Now wait a minute . . . this is going to be shown in the South . . . we can't have Judy Garland, a white woman, kissing . . .' So they solved it by placing a big mattress in back of the tier. When the time came for her to kiss everyone, I had to disappear.

Burl Ives is a big man with a strong personality. Working with all these stars, I guess I managed to look cool though actually I've been very excited about it. People thought I was cool, it comes across that way. I was cool enough to have an ulcer at one time, so I'm not that cool. After the TV show with Burl Ives, he comes over to me, takes a pinch of snuff from a little box and offers it to me. I took it and it nearly tore my head off my neck. I'd do it again probably – I'm a Burl Ives fan, like his demeanour, his whole style.

Stan Kenton's Neophonic Orchestra was another of the large groups I worked with during the sixties. He hired Buddy Collette and me together; we were among the very few blacks to work with him. Stan Kenton had a racial problem; he was hyper-conscious of skin-colours. He tried to explain it to us, how everybody had certain hang-ups. However, we were in the band. With Kenton, it felt like tokenism. With most of the other TV and film studio dates, it didn't.

Barney Kessel, Dizzy Gillespie, Nancy Wilson, Paul Horn, Andy Griffith, Neil Hefti, Ry Cooder, Perry Como, Bing Crosby, Frank Sinatra, Taj Mahal, Al Hirt, Ray Charles, the Ames Brothers, Glenn Campbell, Lalo Schifrin, Billy Daniels – all these stars and many many more, I was lucky enough to work with during this period of my life. Though as far as Craig and April Callender were concerned, the best things I did were dates like Sheb Wooley's 'Purple People Eaters'. Later, the reaction was 'WOW!' when I recorded with rock stars like Gregg Allman and James Taylor in the late sixties, early seventies. That was a big deal for the youngsters.

All through the 1960s the pace never slackened. It was up and out of the house every day for one, two or more jobs in the studios. Here's what I was doing in October of 1964, an entry from my ledgers picked at random. It was typical of a decade when less than ten dates a week was considered not too good!

1 OCTOBER: Warner Brothers, date with the arranger Ernie Freeman; date with George Garibejan

**2 AND 3 OCTOBER**: 'Danny Kaye Show', CBS

**6 OCTOBER**: Hollywood Central Studio, record date with pianist Jean Garf; concert with Lalo Schifrin at Plummer Park

**7 OCTOBER**: VeeJays with Jack Elliot; Universal Studio, 'Brooksides' TV show with Jerry Fielding

**8 OCTOBER**: Desilu Studio – 'My Three Sons' TV show; Screen Gems, Liberty High Hatters with Jerry Fielding

**9 OCTOBER**: United Records, date with Hank Levine and the Lancers; 'Danny Kaye Show', CBS

**11, 12 AND 13 OCTOBER**: 'Dinah Shore Show', NBC

**14 OCTOBER**: Motown record date; Bing Crosby TV show

**15 OCTOBER**: Desilu Studio, TV show conducted by Greg MacRitchie

**16 OCTOBER**: Leith Stevens movie, MGM; United Records, date with Sid Sharp, Rene Hall, Ernie Freeman

**19 OCTOBER**: Bing Crosby Productions at Desilu – two dates; United Records, date with Harry Geller

**20 OCTOBER**: Wheat Chex commercial; United Records, date with Frankie Avalon

**21 OCTOBER**: United, date with Martin Berman; record date with Wayne Shanklin 'Rough Riders in the Sky'

**22 OCTOBER**: 'Danny Kaye Show', CBS

**23 OCTOBER**: Hoyd Curtin, Kool Aid ad

**26 OCTOBER**: Johnny Mann Singers

**27 OCTOBER**: Bing Crosby Productions with John Scott Trotter; record date with Rene Hall

**28 OCTOBER**: Capitol Records, Don Costa conducting

**29 OCTOBER**: Desilu, date with Frank DeVol; Desilu, date with Earl Hagen

**30 AND 31 OCTOBER**: 'Danny Kaye Show', CBS

# PART SEVEN

# 'Hip' not 'Hep'

I was still doing the 'Carol Burnett Show', late 1968, when I could feel my marriage was on the rocks. You know it's on the rocks when she starts coming home late, awfully late, dressed up in party clothes. I already knew . . . people told me. Some will make sure and tell you, others will try and hide it from you. I waited up for her one night and confronted her. She could never tell me on her own. It would have been easier if she could. She couldn't deny it, how could she deny it? It was something like the case with Emma years before. Toni couldn't quite make up her mind and the other man was telling her to stay with me because I could do more for her financially. By then I was pissed. I guess if you can talk to each other you can solve those things. If you can communicate.

Toni was passive and she held it in – until the very end and by then it was too late. If we would have fought, the marriage might have lasted. She really felt she was missing out on life. I just couldn't comprehend it then. If the same set of circumstances were to arise now, I'm not sure I would understand it either. Perhaps if I were in her shoes I might have felt the same way. We just couldn't communicate. When something reaches that point, it's over, you know you've reached the end of that road.

I became very depressed for a while and went out looking for solace in other woman. That didn't help, except physically maybe, and that didn't mean a thing – one-night stands don't solve problems. I had to discover that nobody but me could make me happy. If you don't find happiness with yourself, you'll never find it at all. Suffering too long about any kind of wound is useless; you can't live in the past. You live in the moment, look

147

forwards and you can't look backwards. It's a waste of energy just like worrying. If something bugs you – eradicate it. I used to think as I got older that problems would decrease. It's the other way round. There're more, the older you grow. You learn to handle them but they never stop. That's what I had to realize; the problems never stop. You have to deal with things as they come and they're going to come all your life.


My bass has always been my most important love affair. When things didn't work out, I could always pick up my instrument and play; I could literally forget about everything while concentrating on playing my instrument. That's my discipline and my perfect therapy, my avocation and my vocation. A state of depression is only temporary. Down in that deep hole, you know all along that you'll climb out of it. Time solves it. Meanwhile you've never finished perfecting your art and your craft. Perhaps by being shattered is how you grow. Like when Al Morgan was up on the bandstand instead of me when I came to a rehearsal in the late 1930s. I was devastated but the outcome was positive because positive action resulted. I'd been shattered by love affairs before, when I was deeply, madly in love. Once I carried on a romance from a 2,500-mile distance. Totally unrealistic – I was passionately in love with her and she was *fond* of me. I was about twenty-nine or thirty then, and years later when I was married and had three children I ran into this lady at the supermarket. We talked . . . all the feeling had gone by then. Her response was, 'Oh, it was fun while it lasted . . .'

If enough time passes, the pain eases out of your life. When I realized my marriage was on the rocks, I felt that my whole life was falling apart. My mind was slightly befuddled; I was lost, hurt and wondering what was going to happen next. I was living in the house on Don Milagro yet my spirit wasn't there. I put on blinkers for a short time and threw myself into my work. After taping the 'Carol Burnett Show' one day, an old friend, Bob Harrington, stopped by the studio with a woman I'd met years before. She was part of the Herman McCoy Singers when Buddy Collette, Nelson Riddle, June Christie and myself were featured with them at the Wilshire Ebell Theatre. Mary Lou Lyons – I remembered her immediately, never forgot her beautiful sparkling eyes. Bob had to split, and I invited Mary Lou to have coffee with me.

We sat there in some coffee shop in Hollywood and talked for hours. Mary Lou had just returned from two years in Bangkok and Saigon as a nightclub singer. She'd had quite a bit of experience since I'd last seen her. She sang with the Ray Conniff Orchestra and spent two years on the 'Tennessee Ernie Ford Radio Show', working out of New York City with the 'Dave Garroway TV Show' when it was live and everything had to be right the first time. Now she was working for Beechcraft, selling aeroplanes. Mary Lou had a commercial pilot's licence with an instrument rating, and was working on her flight instructor's rating. We discovered that we shared a flying experience. Years before when I had my trio with Duke Brooks and Lucky Enois, the agency had booked us into Elko, Nevada. Had we played country and western, we would have been a hit, but we were playing jazz, singing hip little songs. To relieve the boredom I woke every morning and took a flying lesson. Mary Lou had also worked out of the Elko airport and had been stuck for weeks in that same one-horse town. We sat in that coffee shop for what seemed like days, talking, laughing, renewing our acquaintance. For the first time in months I began to feel that there might be something to live for. The lyrics of an old song popped into my head, a tune I'd first heard in Canada with the Brownskin Models:

> . . . without a word of warning
> my life has begun
> without a word of warning
> two hearts beat as one
> from out of nowhere you came to me
> a breeze passed by, whispering your name to me . . .

A fast friendship between us grew swiftly. Mary Lou lived in an apartment located on my route to the NBC Studio in Burbank and naturally I visited her often. She invited me to come flying with her; at that time she was into aerobatics. Looping and rolling in the sky with Mary Lou was a supreme pleasure. We're both natural birds. The stone in my heart began to dissolve. My relationship with Toni was so far out on the edge that I began hanging out with Mary Lou. Soon, I stopped going home at all. The kids picked up on it, but when I'd mention where I'd been, I said, 'I've been staying at Lou's.' Only later did they find out Lou was a girl, not a guy. By then it didn't matter because I had found a friend who later became a soulmate.

Jerry Fielding was still a moving force in my life, and in 1969 when Mary Lou and I were becoming close, he invited me to join him on a television special he was conducting in New York. I asked Mary Lou to accompany me, and called Mingus who was then in New York, to see if I could borrow a bass for the date rather than hassle transporting my own on the airplane. Mingus readily agreed.

'Tell me about Mingus,' said Mary Lou while we were *en route* to New York.

'No,' I said, 'wait and see for yourself.' Mary Lou knew Mingus only through his Monterey concert. I wanted her to draw her own conclusions. We arrived in New York about four in the morning. Not being sleepy, we checked into our hotel and took a cab down to the Village. The streets were deserted, but for a big round guy in an Australian bush hat, standing on the sidewalk with a giant bow, shooting arrows at the top of a building across the street. It's Mingus. He's shooting, he says, at a guy on the roof who'd been throwing eggs at him.

Then we returned to his loft, knee-deep in papers, books, clothes, music and assorted stuff which he'd paw through to find something he wanted. Mingus had grown much heavier, and it had affected his blood-sugar to the point where he rarely slept. He loved ceremony; when he gave me the bass to borrow, he turned it over to me publicly in Washington Square. Paranoia was an increasing problem for him. Before we departed for LA, he entrusted me with the raw manuscript of *Beneath the Underdog*. The script was in large cardboard boxes, maybe four or five of them. He gave me detailed instructions what to do with it in case 'they' did him in, in case 'they' came to get the boxes. It remained safely with me for a few years until Nell Thompson, the editor designated by the publisher, came to get it.

On the aeroplane back to LA, I asked Mary Lou what she thought of Mingus. 'Well,' she said, 'I certainly learned a lot about him, but in all the time we spent together, he didn't learn one thing about me. Is that genius? He's the most self-involved person I ever met . . .'

I learned to value Mary Lou's perceptions and to love the way she thinks. As we were spending so much time together, it wasn't long before we decided formally to live together. We wanted a place on the outskirts of the town, a place with land around it, breathing space. Mary Lou found the perfect spot – a large house on an acre in the northern end of the San Fernando Valley, near a town called Sylmar. I left Baldwin Hills far behind. By 1970 my double life was over.

That year I was hired to go back on the staff at NBC to do the 'Flip Wilson Show' which was then being prepared. It took them a year to get it together and I drew a cheque for an entire year without doing anything. Other calls took up only one or two days a week. So there was time to dig the excitement of being with Mary Lou at the new place. After months and months of being down, suddenly I was on the up again. My two youngest children, Craig and April, decided to come and live with us. Sharron was eighteen then, an independent young woman who had moved out on her own. Toni and I had divorced by mutual consent and there was no custody question. The kids made their own decision and Toni got the freedom she needed.

It was tricky for Mary Lou, being the stepmother, and she extended herself a great deal. I told the kids that their mother and I had reached the point of no reconciliation and that Mary Lou was my lady, treat her with respect. They were, of course, young teenagers going through their adolescent changes, but they dealt with it. Despite a few flurries, we had loads of fun on that acre. We had a Great Dane called Bozo, as big as a small horse. We bought a couple of Honda dirt bikes, which April, Craig and their friend Gary Walker loved – with our firends Ike Isaacs and Skip Walker we constructed a ninety-foot driveway to the house, did all the cement work ourselves. We built an outdoor hangar for a glider we planned to construct and poured a fourteen-inch cement floor in the garage we were converting to a studio. All these projects went beautifully – therapy plus fun. When our dog Bozo died of pneumonia, we inherited a yellow-eyed Briard called Dawg who was almost human. Dawg shared all our adventures, including a few close calls in and around Mexico where we went to buy tiles and wrought-iron fixtures for the house.

In 1971, Mary Lou and I were married. Creative, articulate, unconventional, fun-loving, loose, brilliant as well as beautiful, Mary Lou was the woman I'd been looking for all my life without ever knowing it. Finally I'd learned to say 'we' instead of 'I'. That's what marriage is all about – commitment. If it's I, me and mine, it's just two people living together with certificates. You have to give up childish ideas.

Mary Lou had become a flight instructor and was working on her instrument instructor's licence. She had taken the motor home down to Redondo Beach for a three-day aircraft symposium. Craig, April and I were alone in the house, each in our separate rooms. About six the next morning I woke to a tremendous rumbling. I was in bed; the bed was shaking and I couldn't get out of it. The Mexican chandeliers are swinging above me, gouging vast holes in the ceiling. I looked out of the window – the ground is rippling like waves in the ocean. Suddenly the house groans and everything shifts to one side. I heard the piano sliding across the living-room floor, and the furniture and china crashing in its wake. Plates tumbled from cupboards; a gallon of honey spilled, gluing the shards together on the kitchen floor. Once I ascertained that April and Craig were all right – April's bed had slid, trapping her inside a closet – I breathed easier. Yet the quake hadn't panicked me; it was simply an amazing new experience.

We had had it all, everything we wanted in that house in Sylmar. Within moments we had nothing. All our plans and dreams for the house were gone. Sylmar was on a fault line very close to the epicentre of the earthquake. All the phone lines, gas lines, water lines, were down. There was no way to contact Mary Lou and no way for her to get in touch with us. Sylmar, the whole area, was a disaster. In spite of the warnings, I drove to Redondo Beach and found Mary Lou getting into the camper to drive back to us. Another few minutes and we'd have missed each other.

The house had to be demolished. Later we learned that it had never been properly bolted down to its foundation. All the cement work we did, however, stood up to the 6.2 quake – we had zealously overbuilt everything. So we had a solid cement driveway leading up to a shambles of a house; a perfect floor for a collapsed studio. We sent April back to stay with her mother and Craig, Mary Lou and I moved into the motor home. Three was definitely a crowd, but that phase soon passed. With government aid, we were relocated in a house in Granada Hills. The disaster aid was only temporary. Luckily I had savings in the record pension fund, and most fortunate of all, 'The Smith Family' television series, thanks to Frank DeVol, had started using 'Primrose Lane' as their theme song in 1970. My ASCAP rating was high enough that when I called them for an advance, a cheque was in the mail the following day. Thank God for hit records; they help.

We didn't like the Granada Hills house well enough to buy it. The backyard had twenty-six orange trees. Lovely, until swarms of flies arrived in the summer. Mary Lou scouted around until she found a suitable place in Encino. There we settled in, had a big swimming-pool, gave parties, had some good times. My daughter Sylvia, from my first marriage with Emma, moved in with us temporarily. It was the first time we'd lived together since she was a pretty little girl.

Soon after the 'Flip Wilson Show' began taping, I received an offer to go to Japan with the Percy Faith Orchestra. Earl Palmer, one of my favourite drummers, Jack Arno, Joe Sample and Lou Morell also took the trip. An interpreter escorted us around Tokyo, which is fortunate because I knew one word of Japanese – *aragoto*, meaning thanks. Being there fascinated me; I could have stayed weeks but for my commitment to Flip's show. No one on staff knew I had left town and somehow I managed to squeak across the international dateline in time to shower, shave and get to the studio. It's a point of honour with me. Very few times was I ever late in my whole career, and there were very few dates I ever missed.

The band on the 'Flip Wilson Show' was a great one, about fifteen, sixteen pieces, full brass, reed and rhythm sections. Buddy Collette played lead alto, William Green third alto; they both doubled on tenor, flute, clarinet, piccolo, and bass clarinet. Bill Green is a marvel though he's not too well known outside the studio scene on the west coast. I have seen William Green playing the bassoon while riding a unicycle! He plays all reeds equally well – alto, saxophone, tenor, baritone, oboe, bassoon, English horn. That's the problem with the studios. Unless you have enough nerve to step outside to let people know what you do, they'll forever be unaware of your talent. Buddy Childers, Conte Condoli and Grover Mitchell were in Flip's band as well. I played tuba, bass and fender bass.

On the show from 1971 to 1975, I had the opportunity to watch Flip grow into being a real singer. When I first began with the show, Flip couldn't carry a tune in a basket. George Wyle, the conductor, used to lead him in, point 'come in – NOW', guide him through the numbers with people like Bing Crosby and Perry Como. At the time he was quite insecure about his singing, yet he pulled it off because he's a hard worker. Since that show Flip really got his act together; improved his voice, got an accompanist and keeps tempo wonderfully. Not too long ago I ran into Flip in the LAX cocktail lounge where Mary Lou and I were waiting with daughter Sylvia, who was returning to Chicago on a standby flight. Flip appeared out of the blue and was looking good. We pass the usual bullshit; Flip then sits down and pulls out a tape-recorder, puts earphones over my ears. I listened to a whole raft of songs he parodied like 'Fry Me Some Liver' for 'Cry Me a River'; some very funny things. When the flight is finally announced he tells Sylvia to forget about her standby status. He escorts her to the plane's first-class cabin and when they arrive, hires a limousine to give her a lift home. He's a prince of a guy and I must say that discipline and hard work made all the difference with him.

It was while I was on the 'Flip Wilson Show' that I became part of a record company. Though short-lived, I considered it a great success. Musicians often gripe about the deals they get from record companies. Al Viola, Buddy Collette, Leroy Vinnegar, Al Aarons, Grover Mitchell and myself all had conversations like that through the years and we decided to do something about it. Thus the Legend Record Company was born in 1971. We felt that by putting our services, ideas and money together, we'd have something tangible in the present and in the future. Legend lasted almost four years; we were on the point of buying our own studio when we discovered we had been defrauded by an unscrupulous and unnamed party. We lost title to the name 'Legend'; Ray Avery of Rare Records has it presently. Buddy, Grover Mitchell and myself formed another company together a few years later, RGB records, and we're still issuing sides.

Bill Douglass and I never lost touch through all the years. So when he called me one day after we'd moved to Encino, it didn't seem extraordinary, not knowing at the time how much that call would ultimately mean to me. 'How about going out to Thousand Oaks to a friend of mine's house,' he said, 'and play a while?' That was my first introduction to John Slais and his charming wife Mary Claire. John is a beautiful pianist and pilot for United Airlines. I started spending Sundays playing and gigging with Bill and John, just to get out and play. Bill's suggestion was right on time as I had been realizing that I needed to get out and play more for people. After years of playing for a microphone, the sense of a live audience fades. It was a joy to begin again and it gave me new confidence. In the studios you're reading all the time, interpreting. I figured my playing had suffered. One needs that reaction and energy you get from people! We played together for about a year and later during the 1970s I joined a trio led by the pianist Ronnell Bright, whom I'd first met when we accompanied Sarah Vaughan in the late 1930s. There were no big bucks involved; I did it for the joy of playing with a great pianist.

In 1973 I received a surprise invitation from Harvey Phillips, one of the world's premier tuba players, to participate in an international tuba symposium at the University of Indiana. Attending were 358 tuba players from Russia, China, Japan, Canada, Australia, every corner of Europe. At one point, they all played together – quite a sound. It was the first gathering of its kind and they wanted me to attend because *Callender Speaks Low* is used in classes worldwide to demonstrate the flexibility of the instrument and how it can be used melodically in jazz. Prior to the recording, the tuba had been used mainly for rhythm, for oompah comedy, or for effects. Like for the Don Knotts movie *Mr Limpet*, I played the part of a dolphin on the tuba for the soundtrack. I felt very honoured to be included with all these top-line symphonic players like Singleton Palmer and Don Harry. Don Harry played a Bach Concerto on the tuba unaccompanied; he's one of the very few people who can do circular breathing on the instrument. I played my little jazz stuff and it was well received.

During 1973 and 1974, there were some interesting picture calls. One was from Twentieth Century-Fox to do the story of the Crickets, a white rock group from Lubboc, Texas. The Crickets had made a record and the Apollo Theatre in Harlem bought the group sight unseen as the Apollo thought that anyone who was playing rock'n'roll in the early fifties had to be black. I played the bandleader of the Apollo and also wrote music for the segments. When the Crickets got to New York, everyone was quite upset because here's a white group . . . that was the gist of the story. Buddy Holly's widow had some legal differences with Fox so the project was dropped until several years later when it came out as *The Buddy Holly Story* produced by another studio. But for three weeks the whole Twentieth Century-Fox entourage filmed in Jackson, Mississippi. That was my first visit to the deep South. They guaranteed me that everything would be cool and it was, mainly because of the Fox money. We stayed at a first-class hotel, I met some nice people, no problems. But the South is still the South, deep down, and they haven't got over the Civil War yet.

Another call was from Marshall Royal who was contracting a band for Warner Brothers' *Blazing Saddles*, the Mel Brooks picture. The band, led by Count Basie, was to appear in a brief shot. They had a bandstand set up in the middle of the Mohave Desert, horses riding away into the distance, kind of a gimmick. The day we filmed the wind was so strong that it almost blew everyone off the bandstand, the sand nearly blinded us. When you see it in the film it looks like fun, but sometimes making pictures can be miserable. You're out there all day long doing nothing for six hours; suddenly, they're ready and you better be ready too. Don't mistake me . . . it's all fun, I love every second of it . . . you can have fun and still be slightly miserable. Fun just being there with all these people you love, capable musicians who can play – that's heaven and you get paid for it too. I might bitch a little, but that's one of the pleasures of being a musician.

Ten years earlier I had worked on the soundtrack for a Sidney Poitier film, *Guess Who's Coming to Dinner*. When I got the call I had no idea what the script was about. I was the only black in a forty-five-piece orchestra and I gave the orchestra members my theory on mixed couples as the plot became evident. 'What's wrong? Is she marrying a horse? No matter what hues, a mixed marriage is a man and a woman.' Nobody was offended when I verbalized this; I just couldn't bite my tongue in these matters.

Finally in 1974 I took my first real vacation. Mary Lou and I, with my daughter Sylvia, who was working for Continental Airlines, went to Europe strictly as tourists. Our first stop was London, which we enjoyed a great deal. On the way from Los Angeles to London, Mary Lou knitted me a hat which became a sensation among the musicians. Ben Webster saw the hat, had to have one; same with Dexter Gordon. From the Montmartre Club to the Tivoli Gardens, that hat was a smash. Dexter told us how the Danish police had arrested him for drunk driving and put him in jail. He happened to have been carrying a piece of hash in his pocket when he was arrested. When his term in jail was up, the police gave him back his hash.

'That's not mine . . .' Dexter told the policeman.

'Yes it is, Mr Gordon; it's legal.'

Denmark was full of exceptionally good bass players who played like they didn't even know it was difficult. Since the amplifier has become standard equipment, all a modern bassist has to concentrate on is his technique. I joined Red Mitchell for a class he was teaching and we had a great session. Red used to be my neighbour in Los Angeles; our families grew up together and were very close. Ironically, he and his wife split up the same time as Toni and I. Twenty-five years ago, Red Mitchell came to me and said, 'I'm going to tune my bass like a cello, an octave lower, but the same tuning.' That might explain Red's unique sound. For a while, Red also used the five-string bass with an alternative tuning. Whatever he uses, he's a great bass player and a dear friend.

Clark Terry was playing at the Montmartre Club when we were there. Ruth Olay happened to be hanging out, Dexter, Ben . . . it was a wonderful reunion. Our ten days passed in an enjoyable hurry. On the return flight we had a fourteen-hour stopover in London due to a strike at Heathrow Airport. We stayed right at the airport hoping to get a flight; I had to be at work on the 'Flip Wilson Show'. There were more delays in Las Vegas for refuelling, then at LAX for customs. I got back just in time to make the gig.

The trip overseas had been so refreshing that Mary Lou and I decided to visit Barbados. I had never seen my father's native land. Sylvia was still working for Continental Airlines and got us another great deal on tickets. She came with us, and once we were there we sent for Sharron. Barbados is only twenty-six miles long and we explored every inch of it. In Bridgetown there is a street called Baxter's Alley where two elderly ladies cooked fish over an open fire on the sidewalk. We'd often stop and eat their food, pass the time of day with them. The savour of their cooking remained with me so strongly that I dedicated a tune called 'Baxter's Alley' to those fine outdoor chefs.

We hadn't been in Barbados ten days when Craig called, informing us that my mother had been taken to the hospital. A fishbone had slipped down her throat, puncturing her lower intestine. We left immediately for LA. Momma pulled through, but while she was in the hospital, her house had been robbed. Luckily the robbers didn't find her cash savings hidden under the mattress. Weakened after being ill, Momma was afraid to live in her house alone. So we found a new senior citizen's residence that was about to open, had the pick of apartments. Momma is still happy there.

My mother is a real broad-shouldered woman. Even now, at eighty-seven, she still gives massages to her friends. She was trained at a Swedish massage school in Chicago and obtained her therapist's licence before coming to Los Angeles in 1953. Many times through the years when the strain of bass playing for many, many hours had put me out of commission, I'd stop by Momma's house. She knew exactly how to release the tension in my aching shoulders. Almost thirty years elapsed between the time I first left home and my mother's move to LA. Since, we've got to know and like each other as people, as well as the love that binds mother and son. Every holiday until her illness, Momma would invite the whole family over to share her Henry VIII type feasts – turkey, ham, mince pie, apple pie, sweet potato pie, etc. She's had her illnesses, but never wanted to go back to the hospital. It's a fact that they experiment on the elderly in hospitals. She stopped seeing her doctor, threw away all the pills he prescribed and she feels better than she's felt in years. Sharron helped her out with this, found a book which lists all the drug effects and systematically went through Momma's medicine cabinet.

All my children have strong personalities. They were never afraid to say 'I love you'. This mutual love that we have sustains us through all the moves, the disappointments, the confusions that come along our paths. Probably I made the mistake which many parents make of giving too many things to my kids out of love, to save them the deprivations I experienced as a child. What I tried to teach them was something I learned from my mother – you can't put anything in a closed fist. I also tried to impart the importance of becoming educated to do something. Sylvia, my eldest, is a warm, proud, generous Leo who adores beauty around her, likes to dress and looks marvellous, is a great soul-food cook. She attended IBM school and now makes her living in the computer field in Chicago. Sharron, also lovely to look at, married a wonderful guy, Bill Craig, and has earned her living as a legal secretary for many years. An intellectually curious Gemini, she's attending night school, always trying to improve herself. Craig lives in Los Angeles too, and was recently married. He's more introverted than the others; growing up the only boy in a bunch of girls most likely had its effect. He's a classic Taurus, and when he makes up his mind to do something, there's no stopping him. Craig got his toes wet in show business when he went to Mexico City with Papa John Creach and played fender bass for 50,000 people. For about a week he was regaled as a star, but now he's come back to earth and is dealing with the problems of everyday life. April is the charismatic Aquarian of our family who attracts friends like a magnet. She's had to learn too – a few years ago she travelled to Japan as a dancer with a show. When she found out the producers had more than dancing in mind for her, she and a girlfriend made a tricky escape. She remained in Tokyo some months and learned the language. Now she's living in the San Francisco Bay Area. Like me, all my kids are still searching: for themselves, for the truth, for the many truths life has to offer.

It was in May of 1974 when Mary Lou and I were on our way to New York to embark on the first Jazz Cruise, that we heard the news of Duke Ellington's death. It affected me profoundly. Only a year before we had seen Duke at Disneyland. An electric current passed through the crowd there; no one wanted to let the Duke and his men go. During the break, Duke saw me; Mary Lou and I were sitting in the front row. He came down off the stand and before I knew it, I was wrapped in his bear-hug embrace. He kissed me twice on both cheeks, then said, 'Well, Red-Man, when are you going on the road with me?'

It was one of the greatest moments of my life.

When we arrived in New York, we attended Duke's funeral at the Cathedral of St John the Divine. All day thousands of people streamed through the church to pay their last respects. The whole city of New York was in mourning as if a world leader had passed. Duke Ellington was indeed royalty, a genius of the rarest kind.

The Jazz Cruise offered some relief and relaxation after this sorrow. Being aboard a big cruise ship surrounded by wonderful musicians was the best thing that could have happened as we went as passengers, not to work. The boat sailed from New York to the Caribbean, stopping at various ports including Nassau, where Ray Charles and his band came aboard. Dakota Staton, Oscar Peterson, Bobby Hackett, Ella Fitzgerald, Dizzy Gillespie were some of the performers who entertained the passengers. Diz was in rare form as a prankster as well as musician. Carl Warwick, generally known as 'Bama', was also on board; we go all the way back to Bordentown School together. Although Duke was no longer with us, everyone on the ship realized that his music was immortal.

Since that first jazz cruise on the *Rotterdam*, numerous shiplines have begun featuring jazz on their cruises, quite successfully. Other outlets for our jazz artists, in this country, are the ever-increasing jazz parties sponsored by wealthy individuals such as Dick and Maddie Gibson in Denver. There are others in Odessa, Texas; Florida, New York, California and other parts of the country, some of which are sponsored by organizations. Most of the affairs last three or four days and the people really party. For the musicians, it's a reunion and some inspired music results. Many who work this party circuit make a large portion of their yearly income from these functions. Jazz festivals, comparable to the well-established European festivals, are also on the increase here in America, and they are successful. There's a general concept that our music is more appreciated in Europe and other foreign countries than it is right here at home, and it's probably true. Fortunately, however, there are many American jazz-lovers who enthusiastically enjoy and support our music in all its varied forms, and keep it alive and growing. I see a lot of young faces in the audiences . . . discovering!

Once back in Los Angeles, I got a phone call from Billy May. He said, 'Jack Webb wants you to stop by his office and talk about something.'

'Yeah? About what?'

'How music was in the 1940s when black musicians, even those who worked in white bands, had to go through the back door. Stuff like that . . . he's working on a new picture.'

I never went through those back-door experiences aside from Vegas, but I knew what he was talking about. Like when Sy Oliver first went with Tommy Dorsey, he couldn't stay at the hotel with the rest of the band. Or when the great trumpet player Red Mack was with the Will Osborn Band in Chicago, the same thing happened. It was traumatic for Red, a guy of my complexion whose real name was McClure Morris. He knew how good he was as a musician, but he wasn't 'good' enough to stay in the white hotels in Chicago. Fortunately, things have changed since the 1940s.

Not knowing what to charge for an interview session like that, I consulted Leonard Feather, who suggested triple scale. But Webb's attorney called Mary Lou and said, 'I don't want to quibble about the money, would a thousand dollars be all right?' That was fine with me. When I arrived at the office, Jack Webb himself made me a cup of coffee. We knew each other from working together in *Pete Kelly's Blues* in the 1950s. The director of the new film entered and they started asking me things like: 'We want to know what a "short" is . . .'

They had heard these terms and needed a translator. They were trying to be as authentic as possible for their projected film, which in the end was never made. But they knew everything they needed to know . . .

'Well, a short is a car, bread means money, a hame means a pad, someplace to live. The term is "hip" not "hep" like the Andrews Sisters sang it. We considered "hep to the jive" as corny as you can get. It was "have you got your hip boots on?" meaning, are you wise to what's happening?'

Black musicians developed a kind of private language. Once the general public caught on to it, they invented new terms. Louis Armstrong was brilliant in this. To him, everybody was a gate, because a gate swings. A box meant square, and with Lester, money was a taste. If you said ten cents soft, that meant a dime, ten cents hard was ten dollars. Vic Dickenson used to say 'ding ding . . . bells are ringing' meaning everything's OK. With Zutty Singleton, everyone was 'face'. Didn't matter if he knew your

name or not – that was his trademark. It was an enjoyable
afternoon telling them a few terms. In my estimation, Jack Webb
was a prince of a person, very aware of what was happening. He
wasn't like deadpan Sgt Friday of 'Dragnet' at all.

After the years of game shows, talk shows, sitcoms, family
dramas, personality shows, specials and 'Gunsmoke', I managed
to limit my television work to 'Hawaii 5-0', 'Policewoman', 'Flip
Wilson Show' and 'Emergency' during the 1970s. I allowed
recording-session work to slacken off, aside from occasional
dates. I was burned out emotionally. Recording just wasn't much
fun any more, the challenge was gone. Thirty-five, forty years ago
when we did it live and most of the time in one take, it was very
exciting. As the technology of recording became more sophisticated, the engineers started building separate compartments for
each musician. All at once the bass and the drums were divorced.
Rather than have an honest feel, recording became mechanical.
The search for perfect separation in sound has its value I suppose,
but the emotion, the feeling is gone. What was once a warm
together experience became isolating and chilly.

With the advent of the multi-track system it takes months to do
an album. Months, instead of the hour-and-a-half sessions we did
with Tatum. It was uncomplicated and great: walk in, get a
balance and play. Come out with a completed album. Now they
use drum machines. Everything is perfect but it doesn't swing
most of the time. Where's the fun? I did many dates by going into
the studio by myself and putting down a bass track one day, a
tuba track the next. Later, it's all mixed together. You didn't
even always see or meet the people with whom you were
recording. Although I did meet Rickie Lee Jones and predicted
she would be a hit. She is.

When an offer to be part of a Louis Armstrong Memorial Tour
arose in 1978, I gladly accepted. The tour featured both a modern
and a New Orleans contingent, Barry Martyn's Legends of Jazz,
the real old-timers. Barry Martyn is a young Englishman who had
discovered gold on a trip to New Orleans. He led and managed
the Legends which included Andrew Blakeney, Joe Garland,
Dolph Morris, Alton Purnell. The last names of the trombonist
and the clarinettist escape me. Ironic, because they were

especially memorable. Louis, the trombone player, would put his teeth in when he went onstage to play. Cornbread, the clarinet player, would take his teeth out. Watching them go on and offstage for their set and switching their dentures around was quite a kick. The youngest member of the group was seventy-five; the oldest, ninety-five.

The group I played with originally had Barney Bigard on clarinet, Cozy Cole on drums, Duke Burrell on piano and myself on bass. At the last minute Barney became ill, so Benny Carter subbed for him. It's always a pleasure to play with Benny Carter and he was cool enough not to remind me of one of the most traumatic moments of my career, which took place in the 1950s. I was on my way to do a nine o'clock record date with him. It was pouring rain and I was running tardy. I jumped from the car, got my bass, started running across the street. Just as I reached the curb on the opposite side, I slipped. Had my bass on a strap over my back, and when I fell the neck broke and the whole thing collapsed. Here I was going to work with the King and my instrument's a wreck. Had to borrow a bass and do the best I could.

On this tour I was again dealing with borrowed basses. The tour supplied an instrument for me, a very difficult instrument to play, strung with gut strings. Our first concert was at the Tivoli in London; it was enthusiastically received, but I was just muddling through. Only on your own instrument can you do your best. When we arrived in Hamburg, this bass had disappeared. Only at the tour's end did we find out that it had been misrouted to Tehran – an excellent mistake. We had to borrow basses all across Europe. Fortunately, I'd brought my rat-tail files which I used to regulate an instrument to suit my taste. I did the best I could with terrible instruments. It wasn't until we got to Berlin and played the Philharmonia where I could choose among fifteen symphony instruments, that I found one or two I could function with nicely.

Leaving Berlin, passing through East Berlin, our tour bus came under heavy scrutiny. The previous vehicle to pass through the Soviet sector was dismantled to the tyres in the search for contraband. We had plenty of room in the bus and Mary Lou and I were stretched out on separate seats. The Russian guards thought this was highly questionable once they had seen our

passports. 'She's your wife? Why aren't you sitting with her?' I
was trying to explain when someone mentioned the fact that this
was a Louis Armstrong Memorial tour. Immediately everything
was cool, like you had mentioned the name of God; say Louis
Armstrong and it's go ahead. I thought that proved something
about what Louis has done for American relations abroad.

In Munich we played a beer hall where Hitler had once spoken.
After the concert, swarms of people came up to me, a few with
books in hand reciting: 'Red Callender, your first record was with
Louis Armstrong on 13 November 1937. You recorded "Sunny
Side of the Street" and "Once in a While". Your next date
was . . .'

I was besieged with dates, personnel, books, discographies,
everything down to the letter. European fans know far more
about American musicians than Americans themselves know. In
Europe, our music is appreciated as a living art form.

The following year we returned to Europe as part of the
Legends of Jazz tour, and our group had Barney Bigard as
originally planned. That year I also travelled to New York City to
pick up the bass which Charles Mingus had willed to me. Mingus
had been ill, paralysed, and he died in Mexico under bizarre and
tragic circumstances. He and his wife were planning to return to
Los Angeles, but the arrangements took time, too much time.
The week they were scheduled to leave Mexico, Mingus left
us all.

We had moved from Encino to Reseda then. The taxes on our
Encino house had doubled, so we bought a small town house in
Reseda. Mary Lou and I continued to have a lot of kicks,
especially with our 1956 Bentley, a veteran of the English
diplomatic corps. For a time we had our own two-seater
Acrobatic Citabria aeroplane. We flew up and down the west
coast in it, and Mary Lou used it to teach aerobatics. By then, she
had logged over 8,000 hours' flight time, had her multi-engine
instructor's licence and was one of the first 300 women in the US
to obtain her air transport rating. We also did spur-of-the-
moment things, like decide to visit the Grand Canyon, by train,
on New Year's Eve. Naturally the train is empty and the waiters
in the dining-car plied us with drinks. We arrived in Flagstaff,
Arizona at 6 a.m., our heads throbbing, and quickly threw on our
light southern California clothes. Outside, there's a blizzard

raging. We had a good laugh, took a bus to Phoenix and got on the next plane bound for LA. To this day I still haven't seen the Grand Canyon.

Mary Lou is also the head of our publishing company, Red Callender Publishing. The Bihari brothers had kept the masters to *Callender Speaks Low*. For whatever reason, they decided to give them to me, so we reissued that long out-of-print album on Red Records, and advertised in tuba journals worldwide. We don't get rich, but we break even and plan on doing several more albums.

Playing tuba in a 1979 Stevie Wonder concert at the Pasadena Civic Auditorium, I had the chance to speak with Charles Owens who was playing tenor and oboe. I had seen Charles around though we had never rapped very much. I had no idea he was the brilliant musician he is until we got a chance to be in close proximity. After the date he said to me, 'How would you like to play tuba in James Newton's Wind Quintet?'

Never having heard of Newton, not knowing what to expect, I went to a rehearsal at his house on 123rd Street with both my large tuba and a smaller one. When I arrived I said to myself, 'What a weird combination . . .' The instrumentation was flute, clarinet, oboe, English horn, bassoon and tuba. When I looked at the music I said to myself, 'Damn! I can't play this – it looks like it's written for clarinet.' Immediately I put the big horn away and used the smaller one. The music was correctly written; I had just never seen anyone write for tuba in that vein. It started with D, second space below the staff, then with an arpeggio movement shot up to A, top line on the staff. An octave and a quarter in one jump. Fortunately I had enough control to do it and the challenge was delightful. James Newton writes passages with a lot of 16th and 32nd notes: groups of six notes on one beat, five notes on the next beat, maybe two notes on the third beat and three notes on the fourth. Moving! The challenge got me right away. I also liked blending with all the soft instruments, that was my thing anyway.

That day turned out to be another eye-opening day of my life, that fateful first meeting with James Newton, flautist, and John Carter, clarinettist. I'd never heard anyone play like either of them. James with his lusty, beautiful tone, and the way he sings and plays a note simultaneously, producing a harmony. John Carter, well, I had never heard anybody with such control on the clarinet and I have heard *many* clarinet players in my lifetime. 'My God,' I said to myself and later to him, 'this man is over-qualified!' His complete mastery of the instrument is astounding. I also met young John Nunez, twenty-three or twenty-four at the time, an equally astounding bassoon player. It was the first time I'd heard Charles Owens on the double reeds and was amazed at his ability. It was an instant musical love affair between all of us. We rehearsed a few times, then recorded *The Mystery School*. We were all quite ecstatic, about the album, about each other.

A European tour for the Wind Quintet materialized in the summer of 1981. It began at the Bracknell Festival south of London. All the things we played were original James Newton compositions except for two things I arranged. One was 'Lush Life' featuring tuba and bassoon, the other 'Chelsea Bridge', a tuba solo. The reception there was so overwhelmingly positive that it made me cry, and I'm no cry-baby. To have one's music appreciated so much by so many people moved me immeasurably. We played dates in Karlsruhe and Munich in Germany, then took the long train ride to Nimes in the south of France. There we were billed along with rock'n'roll groups and Ornette Coleman's disciple, the electric guitarist James Blood Ulmer. The gig was at an ancient Roman amphitheatre and I imagine the audience was somewhat kinder to us than in former times they were to the Christians. We bombed in Nimes; it was a drunken crowd geared up for loud electronics. However, the producers loved what we did and apologized for the lack of respect. The North Sea Jazz Festival made up for Nimes. Again, standing ovations, again, the tears.

During the tour, John Carter, whom I call 'Gentleman John', came up with the idea of forming a music school, calling it the Wind College. When we returned to LA, John scouted out a location near the Culver City–Los Angeles city line and we opened our doors to the public in late 1982. After spending over twenty-five years in the Texas and California public-school systems, John Carter's dream of an alternative jazz-learning environment is beginning to be fulfilled. John realistically sees that the age of the jazz club and the jam session is on its way out;

# The Wind College Presents ♪♪♪

# The
# Mini Jazz ♪♪ Festival

## November 11, 1983 ♪♪

## Featuring

**James Newton**
Flute

**Red Callender**
Bass & Tuba

**John Carter**
Clarinet

**Gerald Wiggins**
Piano

**Danilo Lozano**
Flute

**Valarie King**
Flute

**William Jeffery**
Drums

**Theresa Grenot**
Flute

**Karl Vincent**
Bass

**Richard Simon**
Bass

## 8:30 p.m.
## Steinway Hall
## 3330 Wilshire Blvd.
(Upstairs in the Sherman Clay Bldg.)
(Enter on Catalina)

**Free**
**Refreshments**

Vermont | Wilshire | Catalina | X

**559-2290**
**Information**

## Admission $7.50

he's a visionary with his feet on the ground. The Wind College has turned out to be a learning experience for all of us, me especially. After so many years of performing, arranging and recording, staying a few jumps ahead of my students keeps me on my toes. Although I have a few tuba students, I primarily teach bass. In addition to private lessons, John, James, Charles and myself also teach scoring and arranging classes, theory and improvisation and composition.

It seems that all the significant events in my life are due to being in the right place at the right time. Meeting Charles Owens at the Stevie Wonder concert couldn't have been planned. Associating with James Newton, Charles Owens and John Carter has brought me alive musically. It's inspired me to get back into writing music, things for the Wind Quintet as well as themes which have been floating in my head for quite some time. James and John have opened up many new thoughts about the complete freedom of music.

PART EIGHT

# Be Happy Pappy

The other night I had a dream about Coleman Hawkins. I could see him standing there . . . that nightclub in the Majestic Hotel in Cleveland . . . I was a kid . . . he talked to me kindly. Enthralled with his words . . . his sound . . . standing two feet from the bandstand . . . letting his words, his sound pour into my ears. Later the same kid was still hanging around, soaking it up . . . letting the music permeate everything until it began to flow outward . . . People, all kinds of people . . . black, white . . . every shade and hue in between . . . were listening . . . were making the music . . . accents, language blended in harmonies.

The dream was a dream but it's real. I grew up thinking about music as a contribution of both black and white. Music is something one learns to do and colour has nothing to do with it. When I recorded with Joe Mavis and the Sons of the Pioneers, I put no less energy into that than I put into recording with Charlie Parker. I simply played in the style they did and tried to add something to it. Same as with interpreting symphonic music written hundreds of years ago. As far as jazz is concerned, it doesn't matter who you are. If you can swing, you can swing.

Anything Louis Armstrong did, any pop tune played by him was considered jazz. Louis started the whole ball rolling by bringing jazz into international prominence. Before Louis there was Freddie Keppard, Joe Oliver, all the New Orleans guys. The thing was, play for the people. Play with a beat so the people could dance. Entertain them; showmanship, like spinning the bass, catching drumsticks in mid-air. That's where I came into the music scene. People called the bass a dog house and made jokes about it. My main thing was, and is, to get people to listen to the

169

real sound of the instrument. The bands I listened to as a kid: Don Redman, Benny Carter, Fletcher Henderson, Claude Hopkins, Luis Russell, Eddie 'the dark angel of the violin' South, Willie 'the Lion' Smith, Bix Beiderbecke, Albert Ammons, Meade Lux Lewis, the Santa Domingans, Goodman . . . so many great bands . . . Basie. Count Basie was the one who freed up the rhythm sections to explore the lines they wanted to explore. And Ellington. Ellington took the music a step further than dance music. He evolved a concert form for sheer listening pleasure when he went into Carnegie Hall with 'Black, Brown and Beige'.

Louis Armstrong was the man with the name who'd been to Europe and made history as a young man. Too, there was Red Allen, another great stylist who played nothing like Louis. Buck Clayton, Jabbo Smith, Fats Navarro, Sweets Edison. Along comes Roy Eldridge and the music takes another stylistic leap. Louis remained on the top of the heap for a long time until Dizzy Gillespie showed up, a real musical clown whose trumpet playing was more articulate than anyone imagined trumpet playing could be. When Louis first heard Dizzy, he put him down hard. Roy Eldridge resented Diz as well. They thought this guy was doing tricks. The respect came later.

Dizzy and Bird took standard tunes, played them in a completely different way, and they called that jazz. By then it was no longer dancing music; it was listening music for those who could understand it. Most musicians and the general public couldn't dig what Bird and Diz were doing because they had turned the music and the whole music business around 180 degrees. Although Parker didn't live to see how pervasive his influence was, Diz has lived to witness all the changes.

Clifford Brown emerged, and Miles. Miles Davis was able to turn his back on the audience and get away with it. Other leaders always faced the people, made sure they were happy, but Miles walked off the bandstand and the people loved him anyway. They still do. The emergence of Miles Davis in the 1950s was the beginning of the cult element in jazz.

By the fifties, the music was firmly into the analytical stage begun by Parker, Diz and Charlie Christian a decade earlier. I've been talking mainly about trumpet players, yet the evolution of this music has to do with all instruments and all players, whether they were known to the public or not. Coleman Hawkins *made*

the tenor saxophone. Ben Webster, Illinois Jacquet, Arnett
Cobb, Budd Johnson, Paul Gonsalves, Don Byas, Benny Carter,
Hilton Jefferson and so many others perpetuated the heavy-toned
style. Then along came Lester Young who had been listening to
Frankie Trumbauer's pure, light tone. Lester analysed the music
thoroughly, created a new style and a new generation of tenor
players. Lester laid the foundation for Bird as well, and Bird laid
the cornerstones for Ornette Coleman, the next major stylistic
leap. Coleman's style, which I don't consider melodic, confirmed
the cult element that has cropped up in modern jazz; meaning
that the general public doesn't accept it, only a hard core of fans.
Then Coltrane came along.

Mingus, Eric Dolphy, Coltrane, Archie Shepp, Albert Ayler,
Cecil Taylor – a whole next generation of innovators started using
the outer extensions of a chord to play on – or no chords at all,
just scales and lines. People who are used to listening to the basic
three-tone triad, the root, 3rd and 5th of a chord, had difficulty
hearing this music based on the 7th, 9th, 11th and 13th tones of
the chord, the outside tones. Some ears still aren't ready for it,
the ear must be attuned. Solos no longer have to have any chord
centre, progressions or form except for what the player makes up
in his or her head. Regular-type jazz used to follow the
twelve-bar blues form or thirty-two bars, but no more.

Coltrane knew exactly what he was doing musically. Many of
his numerous emulators don't really know what's happening.
They play from the top to the bottom of their horns with no
regard for the musical interchanges. They just run a lot of notes,
like reading from a dictionary. In my opinion, music is conversation. Reading from a dictionary doesn't necessarily make a good
sentence or paragraph. What I feel is that music should tell a
story; cut out the fat and present what you have to say in the
simplest form.

Thirty years later people are now beginning to understand
Charlie Parker. The horizons in music are unlimited. Music can
be written with a computer – not that it has any soul or depth –
but it's adequate because the average musical mind in America
hasn't progressed much beyond twelve years of age. They say
that's the average mind. Yet in the right hands, like those of
Herbie Hancock, electronic music can be unbelievably good.
Music is a lifelong study; after more than fifty years I know I'm

just beginning to learn about it. If I'm still around in the year 2000, what I'm doing now will undoubtedly seem like corn. There's no such thing as a finished musician.

People still want to dance and that's where the rock'n'roll thing came in to play, when jazz became more of a listening music. They want a beat they can dance to – a rather monotonous beat, I might add. That's what made rock'n'roll so popular. That, and the American concept of instant money. The media blare it constantly; jazz is relegated to twelve speciality stations for the entire US. I don't want to put the whole rock thing down, there's also some great stuff that came out of it. The Beatles wrote beautiful tunes: 'Yesterday', 'Michele' . . . but I've often heard one four-word phrase repeated over and over and that inanity becomes a hit record. Today there are rock musicians who know about music, yet when it first got under way during the record ban, and even now, all some famous hit recording stars know is five or six chords on the guitar. That's all you need to make a hit.

The rock phenomenon has to do with the way the music is presented. Elvis Presley started something when he copied the style of T Bone Walker and other entertainers in the black community. The gyrations and sexual innuendoes were nothing new for black audiences, that's what the chittlin' circuit is all about. Yet when Elvis, a white man, took that style into the mainstream, it made history, and things have never been the same since. Ray Charles is another musician who moved the music into another era. He was criticized for bringing sanctified church music into the marketplace. A great pianist, bandleader, singer, composer, arranger who plays all kinds of music, Ray Charles laid the foundation for the Motown sound. He's a great jazz player playing what's called commercial music. It's commercial because you can dance to it.

Jazz is now solidly in the concert realm. Some young people today have never heard of Art Tatum, Fats Waller, Ben Webster, Coleman Hawkins or Charlie Parker. Rock'n'rollers have lifted little pieces of the music and never become involved in the true essence of it. Yet when the wheel turns, it always comes back to the true creators of this music. Millions of dollars don't necessarily mean good music. Jazz will never die. A true jazz musician is a bottomless well of invention.

The American jazz musician today is much more respected

than he or she used to be. I'm discovering that daily. My longevity has given me the respect I didn't command years ago. In general however, the jazz musician in this society is still considered to be a dope fiend. I'd like to point out that that's false. There was a period when many musicians thought they had to be junkies or drink a lot of booze in order to play. In recent years, that idea is outmoded, discarded, even though a musician who gets busted for dope will still make headlines, while lawyers, doctors and all the other affluent people who have the bread for drugs rarely seem newsworthy to the press. As far as drugs are concerned, musicians are in the minority – very few jazz musicians can afford them, and most subscribe to the kind of clean-living philosophy that has to do with the fact that one's body is one's instrument as well as one's horn.

You need freedom to create, freedom to be alone when the creative energy starts to flow. Your partner in life must understand that because you don't really compose when there's a whole lot happening. Perhaps the TV or radio is on – that I can shut out easily. It's like being in a music school where someone is playing clarinet in one room, saxophone in another, and I'm teaching bass in the third room. I tell the students, 'This is what you have to get used to – shut everything else from your mind and concentrate on what you're doing.' The background slips into the subconscious, like Billie's 'Don't Explain' when I was writing my symphony.

Sometimes my best ideas come when I'm sitting around doing nothing. I heard a story years ago about David Rose. He'd get into a boat, float around on the water all day thinking. When he went home, he sat down and started writing because it was all mapped out in his mind. I might lie down, sleep a little, wake up and an idea has come. I used to get up in the middle of the night and write down ideas, but now I figure if I can't remember it, it wasn't any good anyway. There are two suites now all mapped out in my mind. One is possibly a concerto with 'Pastel' as the main theme. Since the symphony I wrote incorporating 'Pastel' is lost, I'll write another one, a better one. The Inglewood Symphony recently requested my original symphony, but this new one, written with thirty more years' knowledge about music, will be freer, less stilted, probably a lot simpler. The other suite, entitled 'Jazz Travels' has several recent songs in it including

'Baxter's Alley', 'Birds on the Wing', 'See You Later, So Long' (originally 'Dolphin Street Boogie') with dynamite new lyrics by Mary Lou Callender, and 'Merry Go Round', a tune which began by hearing certain outside intervals. That's what turns me on, that's what comes from being steeped in Ellington, Strayhorn and Stravinsky.

Those three composers all broke away from traditional forms, and along with Gerald Wilson and Billy May, they are among my favourites. It's a matter of personal taste what appeals to the ear. If I were to list all my favourite bass players, piano players, singers, *et cetera*, it would fill another volume. I still enjoy listening to all the people who came before Charlie Parker. Without them, there wouldn't have been a Charlie Parker – he wouldn't have had anything to improve on or to explore against. What's being done now will be a basic foundation for the new things in the wind. No one can pin it down, it's unlimited, music is always in transition.

I've been very happy in doing what I want to do; if I want to work, I do, if I don't, I don't. I'm not rich, but in the sense of experience, I'm Rockefeller. Writing, bass and tuba playing are my triumvirate of love. I'm one of the most fortunate people in the world, I've never even worked in my life because I've been doing what I love. Though there have been some dumb record dates when the music got so loud I had to tell myself, 'In a few hours this will be all over.' Small dues, really.

When you spend the earlier years of your life getting up every morning before dawn to practise for hours it never leaves you. Now I feel I'm playing better than ever, I've got out of the safe mould. In studio work you play only what you know will work, you learn to play the microphone, to judge what you're doing by the needle (not the one you put in your arm), by the pot (not marijuana) on the dials they turn in the control room. When I first began in the studios I would stand up and play. After working many fifteen-hour days I learned to conserve my energy and function within a small radius of the mike by sitting down, anchoring the bass so it would never vary more than an inch or two from the area that was picking up my sound. In the early days of recording you weren't allowed to play long notes because the equipment couldn't handle them – you had to stop a note at a certain length, cut it off to separate the sound. Now with thirty-two different channels, you can play whatever you want to play. The techniques have changed so much that one could write a separate book about recording.

One of the most important things I've learned is that you can't do it by yourself. Anyone who always speaks in terms of I, I, I, gets on my nerves. It's the we, or you, or them or us. One can't do it by oneself, nobody can. Yet in a lifetime of knowing thousands of people I can count the number of real friends on my hands. Real friends, not acquaintances, people whom I would go to if I were in dire trouble. Friends who would come to my rescue, those who are there when you need a favour. A friend is a person whom you trust with your life. And Mary Lou – I happen to be married to her, but first of all we're friends. With Mary Lou I met my match; you can't keep running all your life so you settle down and figure it out. Communicate – without that, nothing. Love is an attitude like music is an attitude. When two guys meet at a lodge meeting they hug each other – that's supposed to signify friendship. When I see Buddy or Wig or Gerald Wilson or John or James or Charles, there's that sincere hug. That's what love is, friendship is. With Benny Carter or Diz or the Duke and the guys in all the bands that I've known twenty, thirty years, that feeling of love and respect exists.

The same thing goes for the student–teacher relationship. I'm as much of a student as they and they're teaching me new things about the bass every day. My main thing is teaching people how to play their instrument in tune, how to approach making a note. Usually I teach one on one, though there are days when three or four bass players will be at the school and I have them play duets which is excellent practice for intonation. A guitar has frets, but on a violin or double bass you need to memorize where your hands should be. Some bassists slide up to a note because they don't really know where that note should be. Only when you've played the instrument long enough can you hit any note right on the head. You should be able to play in tune in a dark room. It's no big thing that twenty years can't cure.

Like a proud poppa, I must say all my students are doing extremely well. Richard Simon is now playing with Teddy Edwards, one of the world's boss tenor players. Leslie Baker auditioned for a symphony playing a Vivaldi bass solo and she got the job. Karl Vincent, already an accomplished fender bassist, is

learning to be a marvellous double bass player. While Karl was
studying at UCLA he befriended a young composer-
percussionist-pianist, Chris Young. Chris has been writing for the
movies and Karl has played on several of his dates. It reminds me
of another relationship between a young composer and a young
bass player – myself and Jerry Fielding.

I've also done a few lectures at the University of California at
Santa Barbara for a black-history class of about twenty students.
When I asked who had ever heard of Charlie Parker, nobody
raised a hand except for one high-school kid who happened to be
sitting in on the class that day. None of them had heard of Art
Tatum. I thought this was pathetic. Thanks to Norman Granz, I
saw to it that they all received Art Tatum records. Among the
thank-you letters was a request for a Benny Carter album. So
those few kids got to hear something, which was nice, but the fact
that people can live in this country in this century and not have
heard of the genius of Art Tatum or Charlie Parker is
devastating. That's one of my jobs, to tell people about the
history of this music from the point of view of someone who has
been and still is a part of it. At another class at Santa Monica
College, I asked the students who Louis Armstrong was and the
answer was 'the first man on the moon'.

Most of the jazz clubs of Los Angeles are gone. You might have
to drive thirty miles in any direction to listen to jazz. Recently, we
took a drive down Central Avenue. It's still there, a shadow, a
skeleton of what was. At 103rd and Central, almost where Watts
begins, a Bank of America stands on the former site of the
Plantation Club. Further down Central at around 64th or Gage,
closer to the stretch where all the action was, junkyards, slag
heaps and light industry have replaced the bungalow houses with
palm trees in their front yards. At 56th Street, the Torrence Hotel
still stands, condemned, boarded up; my first residence in LA,
the place where I met Buck Clayton and Eddie Beal, the place
where it all began for me here. We crossed 47th and Central
where I mistook Bumps Meyers's mother for my own; passed
Lovejoys, the after-hours spot where Tatum presided until dawn.
Now the area is predominantly Mexican, *carnicerias* and Mexican
groceries occupy the storefronts once so familiar – the drugstore

where anything you wanted was available over the counter, the five-cent hot-dog stand, the cleaners where I had my suits pressed. On the site of the Club Alabam is an empty lot. Next door, the Dunbar Hotel still boasts a faded sign, as does the Rosebud Theatre where Mingus and I went to see the latest picture show after his bass lesson. The once proud Florence Mills Theatre now houses a TV and stereo store, though the apartment building next door where trombonist Tyree Glenn lived is still occupied by tenants. Graffiti marks the walls of the Last Word. The U Car tracks have long been torn up on this winding street of memories. Muslims inhabit the former Elks Lodge, the Lodge that sponsored such opulent parades. At 12th Street where Lionel Hampton lived is a wholesale produce palace with signs in Spanish. Across the street, the Clark Hotel Annex still stands, Billie Holiday's home away from home. The former Dolphin's Record Store is currently doing a brisk business in wigs. And the Santa Monica Freeway stretches across the lot where the Musicians' Union Local 767 once stood, in leaping distance from the roof of Lester Young's house.

The past is gone. Looking back through my life while driving down Central Avenue or reading the pages of this book, I see that the 'good old days' are *now*. Life is an adventure. A few years ago, Mary Lou and I were driving east on Highway 14 when we passed an interesting road sign, investigated, saw property for sale and went into the nearest town to find a real-estate agent. With a partner, Marge Robinson, a friend from Hawaii days, we bought five acres at an altitude of 3,258 feet with a panoramic view of snow-capped mountains. You can hear the wind talking there. We let the land sit for a while, then Mary Lou and I got out our pickaxes, our hoes and rakes and cut a road through the yucca bushes and juniper trees. Once the access road was finished, we laid a foundation and build a storage shed all by ourselves. Then we dug a well 260 feet deep, found water, twenty gallons a minute, good clear water. We planted fruit, nut and eucalyptus trees. Soon we'll be living there in a double mobile home which we put on the property. We'll see how we like it. If we don't like it, we'll go somewhere else.

The past few years have been crowded with wonderful things: Gerry Wiggins, one of my all-time favourite pianists and friends, returned to LA after many years on the road. He now lives here with his lovely wife Lynn, also a long-time friend. His son, J.J. Wiggins, now one of my favourite young bass players, used to stand on a chair so he could play my bass while my young son Craig played drums. Gerry and I have worked together, off and on, over the last forty years, and each time I feel extremely fortunate to be there. We recently spent a year working together two nights a week at the Money Tree in Toluca Lake. I recorded the soundtrack of *A Soldier's Story* with music by Herbie Hancock; appeared on 'This is Your Life' with Scatman Crothers; on 'Fantasy Island' with Sammy Davis Jr; recorded again with the Wind Quintet, Gerald Wilson, Gerry Wiggins and Jeannie and Jimmy Cheatham; performed a very happy concert of new compositions at Santa Monica College where my whole family got into the musical act; worked with Buddy Collette and many other great musicians I've known for years . . . life is beautifully full. Finishing this book means another new beginning. Unfortunately, I've had to attend too many funerals lately, but there's a tune I wrote when I had my trio in the forties called 'Be Happy, Pappy'. The other day I remembered the words to the bridge:

> Socrates said there was no gloom
> Who are we moderns to defy him so soon?
> The world is a lamp, so light it and see
> Open, sesame . . .

I never started out to set the world on fire. One of the greatest blessings I've had is to be able to learn from the mistakes of others, like Charlie Parker, or Herschel Coleman, who thought if he hadn't made it by the time he was thirty-five, he'd never make it. Things happen in their own time. I want to keep going and learning, even if it's only one new thing, one new word a day. I'm a patient person. I've seen too many quick blazes for that to be my style . . . it never occurred to me to be the greatest this or that. No matter how great you are, there's always someone who can wipe you out. I'll keep on learning as long as I'm on this earth. Then when I go, just burn me up, toss me away and my sound will still be out there.

Until then, I'll take a day at a time and keep asking, 'What's next?'

# Musical Examples

**"BARBAROSSA"**
Air Varie - Solo for Tuba.

1ˢᵗ E♭ BASS.

C. L. BARNHOUSE.

First tuba solo learned at the age of twelve under Alexander
Valentine at Bordentown.

# SEE YOU LATER, SO LONG

Words by
MARY LOU CALLENDER

Music by
RED CALLENDER

# MERRY GO ROUND

WORDS BY **MARY LOU CALLENDER**

MUSIC BY **RED CALLENDER**

# Primrose Lane

By
WAYNE SHANKLIN
GEORGE CALLENDER

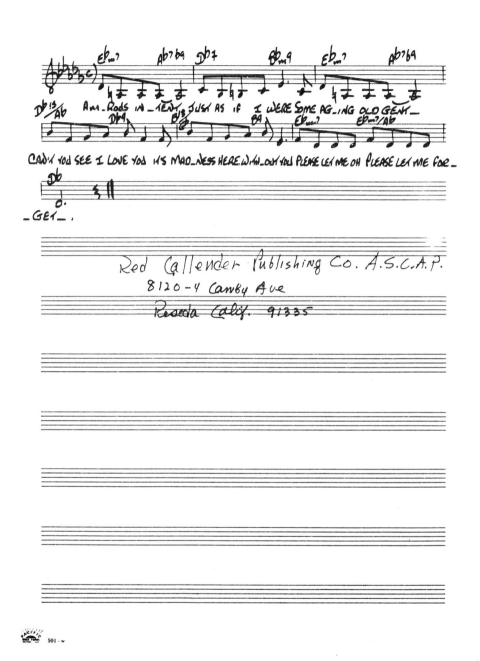

BABY I'M GONE

# Select Discography

*Recordings 1937–1984*
*Compiled by Elaine Cohen*

This discography includes listings from *Sixty Years of Recorded Jazz 1917–1977*, collated and compiled by Walter Bruyninckx, Mechelen, Belgium and could not have been produced without the assistance of Bill Schweitzer and Sharron Callender.

## LOUIS ARMSTRONG
Louis Armstrong (tp, vcl), J.C. Higginbotham (tb), Charlie Holmes (as), Bingie Madison (ts), Luis Russell (p), Lee Blair (g), Red Callender (b), Paul Barbarin (d)
*Los Angeles, 15 November 1937*

| | |
|---|---|
| **Once in a While** | Decca 1560 |
| **Sunny Side of the Street** | – |

## LOUIS ARMSTRONG AND HIS ORCHESTRA
Louis Armstrong (tp, vcl), Charlie Holmes (as), Bingie Madison (ts), Luis Russell (p), Lee Blair (g), Red Callender (b), Paul Barbarin (d)
*Los Angeles, 12 January 1938*

| | |
|---|---|
| **I Double Dare You** | Decca 1636 |
| **Let That Be a Lesson to You** | Decca 1661 |
| **Sweet as a Song** | Decca 1653 |

## MAXINE SULLIVAN
Maxine Sullivan (vcl), vcl acc by Lloyd Reese (tp), Leo Trammel (cl), Floyd Turnham (as), Ulysses Banks (ts), Eddie Beale (p), Red Callender (b), Oscar Bradley (d)
*Hollywood, 20 March 1939*

| | |
|---|---|
| **I Dream of Jeannie with the Light Brown Hair** | Victor 26260 |
| **I'm Happy About the Whole Thing** | Victor 26237 |
| **Drink to Me Only with Thine Eyes** | Victor 26260 |
| **Corn Pickin'** | Victor 26237 |

193

LESTER YOUNG – NAT COLE – RED CALLENDER TRIO
Lester Young (ts), Nat Cole (p), Red Callender (b)
*Los Angeles, 15 July 1942*

| | | |
|---|---|---|
| **Indiana** | Philo 1000, | Crown CLP5305 |
| **I Can't Get Started** | Philo 1001 | – |
| **Tea for Two** | Philo 1001 | – |
| **Body and Soul** | Philo 1000 | – |

NAT COLE
Nat Cole (vcl), Oscar Moore (g), Red Callender (b)
*Los Angeles, 1943*

| | |
|---|---|
| **Vom Vim Veedle** | Capitol 139 |
| **All for You** | – |

JAZZ AT THE PHILHARMONIC
Joe Guy, Howard McGhee (tp), Willie Smith (as), Illinois Jacquet, Charlie Ventura (ts),
Garland Finney (p), Ulysses Livingston (g), Red Callender (b), Gene Krupa (d)
*Los Angeles, 1944*

| | | |
|---|---|---|
| **How High the Moon pt. 1** | Asch 4531, | Stinson LP 23 |
| **How High the Moon pt. 2** | – | |
| **How High the Moon pt. 3** | Asch 4532 | |
| **Lady Be Good pt. 1** | – | |
| **Lady Be Good pt. 2** | Asch 4533 | |
| **Lady Be Good pt. 3** | – | |

RED CALLENDER
Red Callender (b), Louis Gonsales (g), Emmanuel 'Duke' Brooks (p), Leon Rene (vcl)
*Los Angeles, 28 October 1944*

| | |
|---|---|
| **Everything About You Appeals to Me** | Exclusive 201 |
| **How Come** | – |

RED CALLENDER
Red Callender (b), Duke Brooks (p), Louis Gonsales (g), Dan Grissom, Leon Rene (vcl)
*Los Angeles, 11 November 1944*

| | |
|---|---|
| **I Wonder** | Exclusive 202 |
| **Skyline** | – |

JAMMIN' THE BLUES
Warner Bros. film produced by Norman Granz and Gjon Mili, personnel includes: Harry
Edison (tp), Lester Young, Illinois Jacquet (ts), Marie Bryant (vcl), Red Callender (b),
Sidney Catlett, Jo Jones (d), Dickie Wells (tb), Garland Finney, Marlowe Morris (p),
Barney Kessel (g), John Simmons (b)
*Los Angeles, 1944*

| | |
|---|---|
| **The Midnight Symphony** | Palm Club PALM 451, Jazz Archives 18 |
| **On the Sunny Side of the Street** | |
| **Jammin' the Blues** | |
| **Blues for Marvin** | |

**If I Could Be with You (One Hour)**
**Sweet Georgia Brown**


JAZZ AT THE PHILHARMONIC
Shorty Sherock (tp), Illinois Jacquet, Jack McVea (ts), Nat King Cole (p), Les Paul (g),
Johnny Miller (b), Lee Young (d), Red Callender (b)
*Philharmonic Hall, Los Angeles, 2 July 1944*

| | | |
|---|---|---|
| **Bugle Call Rag pt. 1** | Mercury MG35006, | Verve MG Vol 13 |
| **Bugle Call Rag pt 2.** | – | – |
| **I've Found a New Baby pt. 1** | Clef 106 | Verve MG Vol 15 |
| **I've Found a New Baby pt. 2** | – | – |


BUNK JOHNSON's V-DISC VETERANS
Bunk Johnson (tp), Floyd O'Brien (tb), Wade Whaley (cl), Fred Washington (p), Frank
Pasley (g), Red Callender (b), Lee Young (d)
*Radio broadcast, San Francisco, 11 July 1944*

| | | |
|---|---|---|
| **Spicy Advice** | Purist LPP101, | Nola LP6 |
| **Arkansas Blues** | | |
| **Ballin' the Jack** | | |
| **I Ain't Gonna Give Nobody** | | |
| **Careless Love** | | |
| **Panama** | | |
| **Mama's Gone Goodbye** | | |
| **Alexander's Ragtime Band** (unissued) | | |


LESTER YOUNG AND HIS BAND
Vic Dickenson (tb), Lester Young (ts), Dodo Marmarosa (p), Red Callender (b), Henry
Tucker Green (d)
*Los Angeles, October 1945*

| | | |
|---|---|---|
| **D.B. Blues** | Aladdin AL801, | Ember (E) CJS814 |
| **Lester Blows Again** | also on Blue Note LA456–H2, Score LP4028 | |
| **These Foolish Things** | | |
| **Jumpin' at Messner's** | | |


SONNY GREER AND THE DUKE'S MEN
Taft Jordan (tp), Barney Bigard (cl), Otto Hardwicke (as), Dudley Duke Brooks (p),
Fred Guy (g), Red Callender (b), Sonny Greer (d)
*Hollywood, 24 February 1945*

| | | |
|---|---|---|
| **Mood Indigo** | Capitol 10028, | (E) LC6650 |
| **Bug in a Rug** | Capitol 48013 | – |
| **The Mooche** | Capitol 10028 | (E) LC6656 |
| **The Mooche** | Capitol  H240 | (E) LC6507 |
| **Kandy Lamb** | Capitol 1128 | (E) LC6650 |


ERNIE ANDREWS
Ernie Andrews (vc), Red Callender (b), Lucky Enois (g), Clare Lewis (d)
*Los Angeles, 1945*

| | |
|---|---|
| **Green Gin** | Gem 2 |
| **Dream Awhile** | – |

## FOUR STAR FOUR OR FIVE
Gus Bivona (cl), Charlie Davis (p), Red Callender (b), Zutty Singleton (d), Slim Coates (vcl)
*Los Angeles, 1945*

| | |
|---|---|
| **Jay Walker's Blues** (SC vcl) | Four Star 1024 |
| **Hot Fudge** | Four Star 1023 |
| **Some Guy** (Lucky Enois (g), | Four Star 1029 |

Gloria Woods (vcl) added Los Angeles, 1946

| | |
|---|---|
| **Blow Joe Blow** (SC vcl) | Four Star 1024 |
| **Toy Boy** (GW vcl) | Four Star 1029 |
| **Dopus Opus** | Four Star 1023 |
| **Butter My Roll** | Four Star 1031 |
| **Sweet Lorraine** | – |
| **Cotton Tail** | Four Star 1032 |
| **Zu-ra-bo-do-la-do** | – |

## RED CALLENDER SIX
Red Callender (b), Harry Edison (tp), Herbie Haymer (as, ts), Arnold Ross (p), Les Paul (g), Shadow Wilson (d)
*Los Angeles, 12 September 1945*

| | | |
|---|---|---|
| **These Foolish Things** | Swing 395, | Sunset Records |
| **Ode to a Giant** | Swing 394 | SRC105 |
| **Get Happy** | Swing 395 | |
| **I Cover the Waterfront** (RC, AR only) | Swing 394 | |

## JOE ALEXANDER
E. Colburt (d), Joe Luther (as), Willard McDaniel (p), Red Callender (b), Lucky Enois (g)
*Los Angeles, c. 1945*

| | |
|---|---|
| **Donkey Serenade** | Excelsior 172 |
| **I Woke up with a Teardrop** | – |
| **Without a Song** | Excelsior 177 |
| **I Won't Have to Dream on You** | – |
| **Baby I'm Gone** | Excelsior 179 |
| **I'll Have to Put You Down** | – |

## SPIRITS OF RHYTHM*
Leonard Feather (p), Teddy Bunn (g, vcl), Ulysses Livingston (g), Red Callender (b), George Vann (d, vcl), Leo Watson (vcl)
*Los Angeles, 24 January 1945*

| | |
|---|---|
| **Honeysuckle Rose** | Black & White 22 |
| **Scattin' the Blues** | Black & White 23 |
| **Suspicious Blues** | Black & White 21 |
| **She Ain't No Saint** | Black & White 23 |
| **Last Call Blues** | Black & White 23 |

**Coquette** Black & White 21
*This group was inspired by the original Spirits of Rhythm and contains Bunn and Watson, two of the original members.

## CLARA LEWIS
Clara Lewis (p), Lucky Enois (g), Red Callender (b)
*Los Angeles, 1945*

**Sunday** Gem 3
**Clara's Boogie** –

## LAMPLIGHTER ALL STARS
Ray Linn (tp), Vic Dickenson (tb), Barney Bigard (cl), Willie Smith (as), Calvin Jackson (p), Allan Reuss (g), Red Callender (b), Zutty Singleton (d)
*Los Angeles, 12 December 1945*

**My Melancholy Baby** Lamplighter 104
**Sweet Georgia Brown** –

## KAY STARR AND HER ALL STARS
Vcl acc by Ray Linn (tp), Vic Dickenson (tb), Barney Bigard (cl), Willie Smith (as), Calvin Jackson (p), Allan Reuss (g), Red Callender (b), Zutty Singleton (d)
*Los Angeles, 12 December 1945*

**Love Me or Leave Me** Liberty LRP9001
**Sweet Lorraine**
**Stormy Weather**
**Who's Fooling Who?**
**All of Me**
**Honeysuckle Rose**
**I'm Confessin'**
**Cried for You**
**Baby Won't You Please Come Home**

## LOUIS ARMSTRONG AND HIS HOT SEVEN
Louis Armstrong (tp, vcl), Vic Dickenson (tb), Barney Bigard (cl), Allan Reuss (g), Red Callender (b), Charlie Beal (p), Zutty Singleton (d)
*Los Angeles, 6 October 1946*

**I Want a Little Girl** (LA vcl) Swing 223
**Sugar** –
**Blues for Yesterday** (LA vcl)* Swing 251
**Blues in the South*** –
*Leonard Feather replaces Beal

## LOUIS ARMSTRONG – BILLIE HOLIDAY (Soundtrack from *New Orleans*)
Louis Armstrong (tp, vcl), Billie Holiday (vcl), Charlie Beal (p), Kid Ory (tb), Barney Bigard (cl), Bud Scott (g), Red Callender (b), Zutty Singleton (d)
*Los Angeles, September–October 1946*

**Farewell to Storyville** Victor 20–2087, Saga (E) ER09014, 6918 reissue
**Do You Know What It Means to** (1982) Legend Records – Giants of Jazz 1025

**Miss New Orleans?**
**Dippermouth Blues**


LOUIS ARMSTRONG AND HIS DIXIELAND SEVEN
Louis Armstrong (tp, vcl), Kid Ory (tb), Charlie Beal (p), Barney Bigard (cl), Bud Scott
(g), Red Callender (b), Minor Hall (d)
*Los Angeles, 17 October 1946*
**Where the Blues Were Born**                          Victor 20–2088
**Mahoney Hall Stomp**                                 –


IRVING ASHBY
Ernie Royal (tp), Bumps Meyers (ts), Willard McDaniel (p), Irving Ashby (g), Red
Callender (b), Ed Hall (d), Jesse Cryor, Edith Wilson (vcl)
*Los Angeles, 1946*
**My Oh My**                                           Enterprise 285
**If You Can't Control Your Man**                      –
**Chop Chop**                                          Enterprise 283
**Sweet and Easy Blues**                               –


JUNIOR JAZZ AT THE AUDITORIUM
Howard McGhee (tp), Lucky Thompson, Jack McVea (ts), Jimmy Bunn (p), Irving
Ashby (g), Red Callender (b), Jackie Mills (d), Ralph Bass (announcer)
*Hollywood, August 1946*
**Oodie Coo Bop pt. 1 (Harlem Bop)**                   Black & White 150
**Oodie Coo Bop pt. 2 (Harlem Bop)**                   –
**Boppin' Bop pt. 1 (What is This Thing**
    **Called Love?)**                                  Black & White 151
**Boppin' Bop pt 2. (What is This Thing**
    **Called Love?)**                                  –
    Les Robinson (as) added
**Big Noise pt. 1 (Lover)**                            Black & White 1223
**Big Noise pt. 2 (Lover)**                            Black & White 1224
**Big Noise pt. 3 (Lover)**                            –
    Les Robinson (as) + same p, g, b & d
**Body and Soul**                                      Black & White 1223


LUCKY THOMPSON QUARTET
Lucky Thompson (ts), Dodo Marmarosa (p), Red Callender (b), Jack Mills (d)
*Los Angeles, 13 September 1946*
**Dodo's Bounce**                                      Downbeat 100
**Dodo's Lament**                                      –
**Slam's Mishap**                                      105
**Scuffle That Ruff**                                  –
**Smooth Sailing**                                     107
**Commercial Eyes**                                    –

HELEN HUMES
Helen Humes (vcl), vcl acc by unknown (tp), W. Woodman (tb or ts), Wild Bill Moore

(ts), Ed Hall (as), Meade Lux Lewis (p), Irving Ashby (g), Red Callender (b), Chico Hamilton (d)
*Los Angeles, 1946*

| | |
|---|---|
| **Be Ba Ba La Ba Boogie** | Black & White 109, 798, |
| Eddie Beal (p) replaced Lewis | |
| **Married Man Blues** | Black & White 109, 798, |
| **Be Bop Bounce** | Black & White 114 |


## RED CALLENDER TRIO
Red Callender (b), Willard McDaniel (p), Lucky Enois (g)
*Los Angeles, 1946*

| | |
|---|---|
| **Red Light** | Black & White 781 |
| **By the River St Marie** | Black & White 782 |
| **Be Happy Pappy** | Black & White 781 |
| **Red Boogie** | Black & White 782 |


## WARDELL GRAY
Wardell Gray (ts), Dodo Marmarosa (p), Red Callender (b), Harold Doc West (d)
*Los Angeles, 23 November 1946*

| | | |
|---|---|---|
| **Dell's Bells** | Font (Dan) 883907JCY, | Vogue (E)V2105 |
| **How High the Moon** | | V2262 |
| **The Man I Love** | | – |
| **Steeplechase** | | V2105 |
| Chuck Thompson replaces West (d) same date | | |
| **The Great Lie** | | V2105 |


## ERROLL GARNER TRIO
Erroll Garner (p), Red Callender (b), Nick Fatool (d)
*Los Angeles, April–May 1946*

| | |
|---|---|
| **Full Moon and Empty Arms** | Mercury MG25157, MG20009 |
| **Frantonality** | Ember EP–1–607 |
| **Frantonality** | Merc/Spinx M6 (Belgian) |
| **If I Loved You** | Merc 1034, MG25157 |
| **For You** | – MG20009 |


## ERROLL GARNER
Erroll Garner (p), Red Callender (b), Lou Singer (d)
*Los Angeles, 14 July 1946*

| | |
|---|---|
| **Memories of You** | Mercury MG25117, MG20009 |
| **Blue Skies** | |
| **Don't Blame Me** | |
| **Where or When** | |


## LENA HORNE
Vcl acc by Phil Moore Orchestra: Gerald Wilson (tp), Murray McEachern (tb), Willie Smith (cl, as), Marshall Royal (cl, ts), Phil Moore (p), Irving Ashby (g), Red Callender (b), Lee Young (d)

*Los Angeles, autumn 1946*

| | | |
|---|---|---|
| **Whispering** | Black & White 815 | |
| **Squeeze Me** | Black & White 819 | |
| **You Go to My Head** | – | |
| **Glad to Be Unhappy** | Black & White 817, | Gala GLP 330 |
| **Old Fashioned Love** | Black & White 816 | |
| **I Don't Want To** | Black & White 815 | |
| **Little Girl Blue** | Black & White 816 | |
| **At Long Last Love** | Black & White 815, | Tops 9761 |
| **More than You Know** | Black & White 817 | |
| **Blue Prelude** | Black & White 818 | |

JULIE LEE
Karl George (tp), Dave Cavanaugh (ts), Julie Lee (p, vcl), Lucky Enois (g), Red Callender (b), Sam 'Baby' Lovett (d)
*Los Angeles, September 1946*

| | |
|---|---|
| **Oh Marie** | Capitol 340 |
| **I'll Get Along Somehow** | Capitol 379, 830 |
| **A Porter's Love Song** | Capitol 40008 |
| **Have You Ever Been Lonely?** (unissued) | |

ANDRE PREVIN
Andre Previn (p), Irving Ashby (g), Red Callender (b)
*Los Angeles, 25 March 1946*

| | |
|---|---|
| **Take the 'A' Train** | Sunset 7563 |
| **Subtle Slough (Just Squeeze Me)** | Sunset 7565 |
| **I Got It Bad and That Ain't Good** | Sunset 7563 |
| **Warm Valley** | Sunset 7565 |
| **Main Stem** | Sunset 7564 |
| **Something to Live For** (p solo) | – |

CLAUDE TREINER
Vcl acc by Barney Bigard (cl), Eddie Beal (p), Allan Reuss (g), Red Callender (b), Zutty Singleton (d)
*Los Angeles, 29 January 1946*

| | |
|---|---|
| **Young Man's Blues pt. 1** | Lamplighter 102 |
| **Young Man's Blues pt. 2** | – |

FRANTIC FAY THOMAS
Frantic Fay Thomas (p, vcl), Red Callender (b), Lee Young (d)
*Los Angeles, 1946*

| | |
|---|---|
| **Lover Man** | Exclusive 126X |
| **I'm in Town** | – |

KAY STARR AND THE LAMPLIGHTER FIVE
Vcl acc by Barney Bigard (cl), Milt Raskin (p), Allan Reuss (g), Red Callender (b), Zutty

Singleton (d)
*Los Angeles, 15 June 1946*
**After You've Gone**                    Liberty LRP9001
**St Louis Blues**
**Stardust**
**Where or When**


DEXTER GORDON
Dexter Gordon (ts), Melba Liston (tb), Charles Fox (p), Red Callender (b), Chuck
Thompson (d)
*Hollywood, 5 June 1947*
**Mischievous Lady**                    Dial 1018, Jazztone
**Mischievous Lady**                    J1005, Spotlite 130
**Lullaby in Rhythm**                   also Polydor 582735


TEDDY EDWARDS
Teddy Edwards, Dexter Gordon (ts), Jimmy Rowles (p), Red Callender (b), Roy Porter
(d)
*Los Angeles, 4 December 1947*
**Blues in Teddy's Flat**               Pablo 2310 324
**The Duel**                            –
**Hornin' In**                          –


HADDA BROOKS
Hadda Brooks (p, vcl), Teddy Bunn (g), Red Callender (b), Al Wichard (d)
*Los Angeles, 1947*
**Hungary Rhapsody #2**                 Modern 153, M2007
**Variety Bounce**                      –
**That's Where I Came In**              Modern 155
**Don't You Think I Ought to Know**     –
**It All Depends on You**               Modern 156
**Minuet in G Boogie**                  –
**Shanty in Old Shanty Town**           Modern 157
**The Best Things in Life Are Free**    –


WARDELL GRAY
Wardell Gray (ts), Erroll Garner (p), Red Callender (b), Jackie Mills (d)
*Hollywood, February 1947*
**Blue Lou**                            Font 883907JCY


DEXTER GORDON
Dexter Gordon, Wardell Gray (ts), Jimmy Bunn (p), Red Callender (b), Chuck
Thompson (d)
*Hollywood, 12 June 1947*
**The Chase pt. 1** (1)                 Dial LP211, Jazztone J1005
**The Chase pt. 1** (2)
**The Chase pt. 2**                     also on Spotlite 130, Polydor 58273

(only DG on ts) rest same
**Chromatic Aberration**    Dial LP204, Spotlite 130, Jazztone J1005
**Iridescene**
**On the Town**
**It's the Talk of the Town**
**Bikini** (1) or **Blues Bikini**


DEXTER GORDON
Dexter Gordon (ts), Jimmy Rowles (p), Red Callender (b), Roy Porter (d)
*Los Angeles, 4 December 1947*
**Ghost of a Chance**                    Dial LP204, Jazztone J1005,
**Sweet and Lovely**                     Polydor 852735 and Spotlite 130
  add Teddy Edwards (ts)
**The Duel pt. 1**
**The Duel pt. 2**


DEXTER GORDON – THE HUNT 'LIVE AT THE ELK'S CLUB'
Dexter Gordon (ts), Howard McGhee (tp), Trummy Young (tb), Sonny Criss (as), Wardell
Gray (ts), Hampton Hawes (p), Barney Kessel (g), Harry Babison or Red Callender (b), Ken Kennedy, Connie Kay (d)
*Los Angeles, 6 July 1947*
**Disorder at the Border**                Savoy SJL2222,        BYG (F) 529608
**Cherokee**                              –
**Byas-a-Drink**                          –
**The Hunt**                              –
**After Hours Bop**                       SJL2211


PHIL MOORE ORCHESTRA
Snooky Young, Ray Linn, Gerald Wilson (tp), Henry Coker, Murray McEachern, Ben Benson (tb), Harry Klee (fl), Harry Schumann (fhr), Marshall Royal (cl, as), Lucky Thompson (ts), Calvin Jackson (p), Al Hendrikson (g), Red Callender/Art Shapiro (b), Lee Young (d) + strings
*Los Angeles, 1947*
**Concerto for Trombone**                 Verve MGV2005
**125th St Prophet**
**Cornucopia**
**Fugue for Barroom Piano**
**Misty Moon Blues**
**Concerto for Piano and Orchestra**
**Day Dreams**
**Mood for You**


CHARLIE PARKER'S NEW STARS
Howard McGhee (tp), Charlie Parker (as), Wardell Gray (ts), Dodo Marmarosa (p), Barney Kessel (g), Red Callender (b), Don Lamond (d)
*Hollywood, February 1947*
**Relaxin' at Camarillo**        Dial 1030, LP901, Saga (E) ER08052

|                        |                                        |
|------------------------|----------------------------------------|
|                        | Esq (E) 10–79, Spotlite (E) LP 103     |
| **Cheers**             | Dial LP202, Saga (E) ER08007           |
|                        | Spotlite (E) LP103                     |
| **Carvin' the Bird**   | Dial LP901, Soc (E)1026                |
|                        | Saga (E) ER08052, Spotlite (E) LP103   |
| **Stupendous**         | Dial 1022, 1030, Par (E) R3142         |
|                        | Dial LP202, Spotlite (E) LP103         |

CHARLIE PARKER QUARTET
Charlie Parker (as), Erroll Garner (p), Red Callender (b), Harold Doc West (d), Earl
Colman (vcl)
*Hollywood, 19 February 1947*

|                               |                                      |
|-------------------------------|--------------------------------------|
| **This Is Always** (EC vcl)   | Dial 1015, 1019, LP905,              |
| Vogue (E) LDEO16, Spotlite (E) LP102, Saga (E) ER080005 |   |
| **Dark Shadows** (EC vcl)     | Dial LP202, LP901, Saga (E) ER080005 |
| **Bird's Nest**               | Dial 1014, LP901, Saga (E) ER08052   |
| **Hot Blues (Cool Blues)**    | Dial LP202, LP901, Saga (E) ER080005 |
| **Blowtop Blues**             | Dial LP901, Vogue (E) LDE004         |
| **Cool Blues**                | Dial 1015, LP202, Saga (E) ER08052   |

GENE NORMAN PRESENTS
Howard McGhee (tp), Vic Dickenson (tb), Benny Carter (as), Wardell Gray (ts), Erroll
Garner (p), Irving Ashby (g), Red Callender (b), Jackie Mills (d)
*Concert, Pasadena, April 1947*

|                          |                  |
|--------------------------|------------------|
| **Blue Lou pt. 1 & 2**   | Modern LP1203    |
| **One o'Clock Jump**     | Modern LP1207    |
| **Two o'Clock Jump**     | –                |
| **Three o'Clock Jump**   | –                |
| **Four o'Clock Jump**    | –                |

GERALD WILSON ORCHESTRA
pers. inc. Gerald Wilson (tp), Melba Liston, Henry Coker, Robert Wagner, Trummy
Young (tb), Willie Smith (as), Gerald Wiggins (p), Red Callender (b), Lee Young (d),
Dan
Grissom (vcl), Ernie Royal, Walter Williams (tp)
*Los Angeles, 1946–47*

|                                   |                      |
|-----------------------------------|----------------------|
| **Dissonance in Blues** feat. RC (b) | United Artists 509 |
| **My Last Affair**                | –                    |
| **What a Fool I Was**             | United Artists 510   |
| **Vance**                         | –                    |

ERROLL GARNER TRIO
Erroll Garner (p), Red Callender (b), Harold Doc West (d)
*Los Angeles, 17 February 1947*

|           |                                              |
|-----------|----------------------------------------------|
| **Pastel** | Dial 1016, Roulette RE0110, Vogue DP28      |
| **Trio**   | Esq (E) 10–176, Mode (F) MDR9168, Blue Star 6814 |

LUCKY THOMPSON AND HIS LUCKY SEVEN
Lucky Thompson (ts), Neal Hefti (tp), Benny Carter (as), Bob Lawson (bar), Dodo
Marmarosa (p), Barney Kessel (g–1), Red Callender (b), Lee Young (d)
*Los Angeles, April 1947*
**Just One More Chance**          Victor 20–2504, RCA (F) 741106
**From Dixieland to Bop** (1)
**Boulevard Bounce**
**Boppin' the Blues** (1)


RED NORVO SEPTET
Ray Linn (tp), Jimmy Guiffre (as, ts), Dexter Gordon (ts), Red Norvo (vib, p), Barney
Kessel (g), Red Callender (b), Jackie Mills (d)
*Los Angeles, 28 November 1947*
**I'll Follow You**               Capitol 15233
  (add Dodo Marmarosa (p))
**Bop**                               –


BENNY GOODMAN AND HIS ALL STARS
Benny Goodman (cl), Charlie Shavers (tp), Benny Carter (as), Dave Cavanaugh (ts), Joe
Koch (bar), Red Norvo (xyl, vib), Jimmy Rowles (p), Irving Ashby (g), Red Callender
(b), Lee Young (d)
*Los Angeles, 1947*
**Them There Eyes**            Cap (F) OCO54–82005M


HOLLYWOOD JAZZ CONCERT
Howard McGhee (tp), Trummy Young (tb), Sonny Criss (as), Dexter Gordon, Wardell
Gray (ts), Hampton Hawes (p), Red Callender (b), Roy Porter (d)
*Hollywood, July 1947*

| | | |
|---|---|---|
| **Bopland I–II** | Savoy 962, | MG9020 |
| **Bopland III–IV** | Savoy 63 | – |
| **Bopland V–VI** | Savoy 64 | – |
| **Jeronimo I–II** | Bop 111, | Regent MG6049 |
| **Jeronimo III–IV** | Bop 112 | – |
| **Jeronimo V–VI** | Bop 113 | – |
| **Jeronimo VII–VIII** | Bop 114 | – |
| **Bop After Hours I–II** | Bop 115 | – |
| **Bop After Hours III–IV** | Bop 116 | – |
| **Bop After Hours V–VI** | Bop 117 | – |


AL HIBBLER
Al Hibbler (vcl), acc by Harry Carney's All Stars: Taft Jordon, Harold Baker (tp), Russell
Procope (as), Jack McVea (ts), Harry Carney (bar), Lady Will Carr (p), Ralph Hamilton
(g), Red Callender (b), Harold Doc West (d)
*Los Angeles, 1945*

| | | |
|---|---|---|
| **How Long** | Aladdin 154, | Score LP4013 |
| **Don't Take Your Love from Me** | Aladdin 155 | – |
| **I Got It Bad** | Aladdin 154 | – |
| **S'posin'** | Aladdin 155 | – |

| | | |
|---|---|---|
| **I Surrender Dear** | Aladdin 156 | – |
| **Fat and Forty** | Aladdin – | – |

## MEL POWELL QUINTET
Jake Porter (tp), Bumps Meyers (ts), Mel Powell (p), Red Callender (b), Lee Young (d)
*Los Angeles, 10 December 1947*

| | |
|---|---|
| **Anything Goes** | CAP 15056 |
| **Way Down Yonder in New Orleans** | CAP 10135 |
| **You Go to My Head** | CAP 10136 |
| **There's a Small Hotel** | – |
| **Hallelujah** | CAP 10135 |

Los Angeles, 31 December 1947 Frank Beach (tp) replaces Porter and Chuck Gentry (bar) added

| | |
|---|---|
| **Cuban Pete** | CAP 15842 |
| **Cookin' One Up** | CAP 10137 |
| **That Old Black Magic** | CAP 10156 |
| **When a Woman Loves a Man** | CAP 10137 |

## WILLIE SMITH QUINTET
Willie Smith (as), Dodo Marmarosa (p), Barney Kessel (g), Red Callender (b), Jo Jones (d)
*Los Angeles, November 1947*

| | |
|---|---|
| **Not So Bop Blues** | Verve MGV8126 |
| **Tea for Two** | – |
| **Sophisticated Lady** | Verve MGV8060 |

## HOLLYWOOD HUCKSTERS
Charlie Shavers (tp), Benny Goodman (cl, vcl), Benny Carter (as), Dave Cavanaugh (ts), Joe Kock (bar), Red Norvo (vib, xyl), Jimmy Rowles (p), Irving Ashby (g), Red Callender (b), Lee Young (d), Stan Kenton (vcl)
*Los Angeles, 29 May 1947*

| | |
|---|---|
| **I Apologise** | CAP T441, Swag (Aus) S1381 |
| **Them There Eyes** | (E) UMP1002, Cap 4022 H322 |
| **Happy Blues** (BG, SK sk vcl) | |

## CEE PEE JOHNSON AND HIS BAND
Gerald Wilson (tp), Ralph Bledsoe (tb), Arthur Dennis, Dexter Gordon (saxes), Warren Bracken (p), Irving Ashby (g), Red Callender (b), Cee Pee Johnson (d, vcl)
*Los Angeles, 1947*

| | |
|---|---|
| **Rainin' Blues** | ATOMIC 265 |
| **Liza** | – |

## JUNIOR JAZZ AT THE AUDITORIUM
Red Callender (b), Jimmy Bunn (p), Jackie Mills (d), Howard McGhee (tp), Jack McVea (ts), Lucky Thompson (ts), Irving Ashby (g)
*Los Angeles, 1947*

| | |
|---|---|
| **Sunny Side of the Street** | Tops – Masterpiece Records L928 |

**Lover**
**Body and Soul**
**What Is This Thing Called Love**


BENNY GOODMAN SEXTET
Benny Goodman (cl), Red Norvo (vib), Mel Powell (vib), Red Callender (b), Lee Young (d),
Johnny Mercer (vcl)
*Los Angeles, January 1947*

| | |
|---|---|
| **After You've Gone** | AFRS 271 |
| **Sent for You Yesterday, Here You Come Today** | – |
| **Air Mail Special** | AFRS 299 |
| **Rose Room** | – |
| **The World Is Waiting for the Sunrise** | – |
| **Flying Home** | – |

add Ernie Royal (tp), Wardell Gray, Vido Musso (ts)

| | |
|---|---|
| **Jungle Bells** | AFRS H83 |
| **Sugar Blues** | – |
| **I Never Knew** | – |


PERCY MAYFIELD
Maxwell Davis, Richard Wells (ts), Charles Waller (bar), Eddie Beal (p), Floyd Phillips (g), Red Callender (b), Lee Young (d), Percy Mayfield (vcl)
*Hollywood, 16 August 1950*

| | | |
|---|---|---|
| **Strange Things Happening** | Speciality 390, | SPS2126 |
| **Please Send Me Someone to Love** | – | |
| **Lost Love** | Speciality 400 | |
| **Life Is Suicide** | – | |
| **Nightless Lover** | Speciality 408 | |
| **What a Fool I Was** | – | |
| **My Blues** | Speciality 416 | |
| **Prayin' for Your Return** | – | |
| **Cry Baby** | Speciality 425 | |
| **Nappin' the Nickles** | – | |
| **The Big Question** | Speciality 432 | |
| **The Hunt Is On** | – | |
| **Louisiana** | Speciality 439 | |
| **Two Hearts Are Greater than One** | – | |
| **Lonesome Highway** | Speciality 460 | |
| **Lonely One** | – | |


HELEN HUMES
Vcl acc by Dexter Gordon's Orchestra: Vernon Smith (tp), Dexter Gordon (ts), Maurice Simon (bar), Ernie Freeman (p), Red Callender (b), J.C. Heard (d)
*Los Angeles, 20 November 1950*

| | |
|---|---|
| **Ain't Gonna Quit You Baby** | Savoy SJL2215, |
| **Helen's Advice** | Discovery 535 |
| **Knockin' Myself Out** | |
| **Airplane Blues** | |

## RED CALLENDER
Red Callender (b), Marshall Royal (as), Maxwell Davis (ts), Floyd Turnham (bar), Chico Hamilton (d), Al Calderone (timb), Mauri Lynn (vcl)
*Los Angeles, 5 August 1951*

| | |
|---|---|
| **Fooled Again** | Victor 20/47–4266 |
| **Perdido** | |
| **Chico's Boogie** | |

*Lost Angeles, 21 September 1951*

| | |
|---|---|
| **Midnight with Sampson** | Victor 20/47–4368 |
| **Number Three** | Victor 20/47–4525 |
| **Carvin's Company** | – – |
| **Pastel** | Victor 20/47–4368 |

## LINDA HOPKINS
Vcl acc by Red Callender's Orchestra: no details except Red Callender (b), Linda Hopkins (vcl)
*Los Angeles, November 1951*

| | |
|---|---|
| **Is This Goodbye?** | Grand Prix LP 405 |
| **Get Off My Wagon** | |
| **Two Time Loser** | |
| **Tears of Joy** | |

## JIMMY WITHERSPOON
Jimmy Witherspoon (vcl), vcl acc by Jewel Grant (as), Maxwell David (ts), Clyde Dunn (bar), Earl Jackson (p), Mitchel 'Tiny' Webb (g), Red Callender (b), Bill Douglass (d)
*Los Angeles, 30 September 1952*

| | |
|---|---|
| **One Fine Gal** | King LP 634 |
| **Don't Tell Me Now** | also Federal 12128, Pol. Int 623256 |
| **Corn Whiskey** | |
| **The Day Is Dawning** | |

## INEZ JONES
Vcl acc by Howard Biggs (p), Red Callender (b), Chico Hamilton (d)
*New York, 17 July 1952*

| | |
|---|---|
| **I Want a Man to Gimme Some Luck** | Victor 20–4989 |
| **Take a Back Seat Mr Johnson** | Victor 20–5135 |
| **They Say** | – |
| **Proud of You** | Victor 20–4989 |

## HAZEL SCOTT
Hazel Scott (p), Red Callender (b), Lee Young (d)
*Los Angeles, 1952*

| | |
|---|---|
| **The Girl Friend** | Capitol H 364 |
| **The Way You Look Tonight** | |
| **Thou Swell** | |

JESSE BELVIN
Vcl acc by Que Martyn Orchestra, Red Callender (arr)
*Hollywood, 1952*
**Dream Girl**                                    Modern 1005
**Let Me Love You Tonight**                       –
**Goodnight My Love**                             –
**Hang Your Tears Out**                           –


JOHNNY HODGES
Johnny Hodges (as), Emmett Berry (tp), Lawrence Brown (tb), Flip Phillips (ts), Leroy
Lovett, Teddy Brannon (p), Red Callender (b), J.C. Heard (d), Al Hibbler (vcl)
*Los Angeles, 22 July 1952*
**Rosanne**                            Norgran MGN1061, Clef MGC128
**This Love of Mine** (AH vcl)
**Hodge Podge**
**Jappa**


ROCKHEART JOHNSON
Rockheart Johnson (vcl), unknown (hmca), Jeanne Jamerson (p), Red Callender (b), E.J.
'Buddy' Harper (d)
*Los Angeles, 22 July 1952*
**Black Spider**                                  Victor 20–5136
**Evilest Woman in Town**                         Victor 20–4967
**Midnight Rambler**                              Victor 20–5136
**Rockheart's Blues**                             Victor 20–4967


RED CALLENDER
Red Callender (b), Chuck Norris (g), Marshall Royal (as), Maxwell Davis (ts), Floyd
Turnham (sax), Chico Hamilton (d), Eddie Beal (p), Albert Colderone (timb)
*Los Angeles, 17 July 1952*
**Hollywood Drive**                               Victor 20/42–5172
**Early Times**                                   –
*Los Angeles, 18 July 1952*
**Lonesome Rebecca**                              Victor 20/47–4908
**Mississippi Blues** (unissued)                  –
**Empty Ice Box**                                 –
**Blues for J.T.**                                –
**Loose Pork Chops**                              –
**Blow Mr Norris**                                –


RED CALLENDER SEXTETTE
Pers. incl Maxwell Davis or Bumps Meyers (ts), Chico Hamilton (d), Red Callender (b),
Imogene Myers (vcl), Eddie Beal (p)
*Los Angeles, 1952–54*
**Basin Street Blues**                            Hollywood Records 139
**Glow Worm**                                     –
**C Jam Blues**                                   Hollywood Records 140
**The One I Love**                                –

| | |
|---|---|
| **Dolphin Street Boogie** | Hollywood Records 141 |
| **Poinciana** | – |
| **How Come Baby** | Hollywood Records 142B |
| **Tonight of All Nights** | Hollywood Records 142A |
| **You're a Part of Me** | Hollywood Records 237 |
| **Here Is a Letter** | – |
| **Voodoo** | Hollywood Records 1008 |
| **September in the Rain** | Hollywood Records 166B |
| **Tabor-Inn** (N. Wilson, Boo Williams vcl) | |
| | Hollywood Records 166A |
| **I Like Your Mother Better** (Scat Man Crothers vcl) | |
| | Hollywood Records 168A |
| **Papa (Jacques)** (Scat Man Crothers vcl) | |
| | Hollywood Records 142A |
| **Til I Waltz Again with You** | Hollywood Records 142A |

RED CALLENDER SEXTETTE
Red Callender (b), Duke Upshaw (vcl), remaining personnel same as above
*Los Angeles, 1952–54*

| | |
|---|---|
| **Soldier's Blues** | Bayou 002 |
| **In the Meantime** | – |
| **The Honey Jump, pt. 1** | Bayou 001 |
| **The Honey Jump, pt. 2** | – |
| **In the Meantime (I'll be Blue)** | Bayou 002B |

PEE WEE CRAYTON
Vcl acc by Red Callender Sextette, Bumps Meyers (ts), Red Callender (b), Chico
Hamilton (d), Maxwell Davis (ts), Eddie Beal (p)
*Los Angeles, 1954*

| | |
|---|---|
| **Pappy's Blues** | Hollywood Records 408 |
| **Crying and Walking** | – |
| **Baby Pat the Floor** | – |
| **I'm Your Prisoner** | – |
| **Steppin' Out** | – |
| **Hey Little Dreamboat** | – |
| **Please Send Me Someone to Love** | |
| | – |

CLARENCE 'BON TON' GARLOW
Clarence Garlow (g, vcl), acc by Maxwell Davis (ts), Willard McDaniel (p), Red
Callender (b), Peppy Prince (d)
*Culver City, CA 1954*

| | |
|---|---|
| **Crawfishin'** | Flair 1021, Modern 971 |
| **Route 90** | |

BILLIE HOLIDAY AND HER ORCHESTRA
Vcl acc by Harry Edison (tp), Willie Smith (as), Bobby Tucker (p), Barney Kessel (g),
Red Callender (b), Billie Holiday (vcl)

*Los Angeles, 3 September 1954*
**Too Marvelous for Words**                    Verve VE2–2515,            Clef MGC721
**P.S. I Love You**                                                        –
**Softly**                                                                 –
**I Thought About You**                                                    –
**Love Me or Leave Me**                                                    –
**Willow Weep for Me**                                                     –
**Stormy Blues**                                                           –


SUGAR PIE DESANTO
Sugar Pie Desanto (vcl), acc by Donald Johnson (tp), Preston Love (as), Plas Johnson
(ts), Floyd Turnham (bar), Ernie Freeman (p), Pete 'Guitar' Lewis (g), Red Callender
(b), Leard Bell (d)
*Los Angeles, 17 March 1955*
**Please Be True**                             Federal 12217
**I'm So Lonely**                                           –


MEADE LUX LEWIS – CAT HOUSE PIANO – MEADE LUX LEWIS TRIO
Meade Lux Lewis (p), Red Callender (b), Jo Jones (d)
*Los Angeles, 16 January, 1955*
**The Pittsburgh Flyer**       Verve MGV1006, Col. (E) 33CX10094
**Jabouti**
**Torpedo Juice**
**Joe Prein's Blues**
**San Francisco Shuffle**
**629 Boogie**
**Dragon Blues**
**Meade's Mambo**


PRESTON LOVE
Donald Johnson (tp), Preston Love (as), Plas Johnson (ts), Floyd Turnham (bar, ts),
Ernie
Freeman (p), Pete Lewis (g), Red Callender (b), Leard Bell (d)
*Los Angeles, 17 March 1955*
**Boom Diddy Wa Wa**                           Federal 12216
**A Man Goin' Crazy**


ART TATUM TRIO
Art Tatum (p), Red Callender (b), Jo Jones (d)
*Los Angeles, 27 January 1956*
**Blue Lou**                                   Verve MGV 8118
**I'll Have to Change My Plans**
**Isn't It Romantic**
**Just One of Those Things**
**Love for Sale**
**More than You Know**
**I'll Never Be the Same**
**If**

**Trio Blues**
**Some Other Spring**


ART TATUM QUARTET
Art Tatum (p), Buddy De Franco (cl), Red Callender (b), Bill Douglass (d)
*Los Angeles, 6 February 1956*
**A Foggy Day**                                  Verve MGV 8229 ·
**Makin' Whoopee**
**Deep Night**
**Memories of You**
**This Can't Be Love**
**Once in a While**
**You're Mine You**
**Lover Man**


ART TATUM – BEN WEBSTER QUARTET
Ben Webster (ts), Art Tatum (p), Red Callender (b), Bill Douglass (d)
*Los Angeles, 11 September 1956*
**All the Things You Are**                       Verve MGV 8220
**My One and Only Love**
**My Ideal**
**Gone with the Wind**
**Have You Met Miss Jones?**
**Night and Day**
**Where or When**


JERRY FIELDING – SWINGIN' IN HI-FI
Ralph Fera, Maurice Harris, Frank Beach, John Audino, Buddy Maynard (tp), Joe
Howard, Bernie Hart (tb), Hymie Gunkler (as), Buddy Collette, Pete Terry (ts), Martin
Berman (bar), Marty Paitch (p), Red Callender (b), Jerry Fielding (d)
*Los Angeles, 1956*
**Smack Dab in the Middle**                      De DL9371
**If I May**
**Razzle Dazzle**
**Fish Roll**
**The Boss Is Home**
**Ooo Wee**
**Burn That Candle**
**Look Out**
**Turkish Torture**
**Heavy Henry's First Flirtation**
**Doll Face**
**Southwind**


BUDDY COLLETTE
Gerald Wilson (tp), Dave Wells (b tp), Buddy Collette (fl, as, ts), Bill Green (as), Jewell
Grant (bar), Ernie Freeman (p), Red Callender (b), Max Albright (d)
*Los Angeles, 13 February 1956*

**Cycle**                                        Contemporary C3522
**Ruby**
**Santa Monica**
**Slappy's Tune**


JUNE CHRISTY
John Cave (fhr), Bud Shank (fl), Howard Roberts (g), Red Callender (b), Irv Cottler (d)
+ strings
*Los Angeles, 18 June 1957*
**Lazy Afternoon**                              Capitol T902
**It's So Peaceful in the Country**
**Interlude**
**Lost on a Summer Night**


BUDDY COLLETTE
Buddy Collette (fl, cl, as, ts), Gerald Wiggins (p), Pete Jolly (accord), Jim Hall (g), Red
Callender (tu), Louis Bellson (d)
*Los Angeles, 1957*
**Bess You Is My Woman Now**                    Interlude M0505
**Bess Oh Where's My Bess**
**My Man's Gone Now**
**Summertime**
**It Ain't Necessarily So**
**I Got Plenty of Nuttin'**
**There's a Boat Leaving for New York**
**A Woman Is a Sometime Thing**


ART PEPPER
Don Fagerquist (tp), Stu Williamson (tb), Red Callender (tu), Art Pepper (as), Bill
Holman (ts), Bud Shark (bar), Russ Freeman (p), Monty Budwig (b), Shelly Manne (d),
Shorty Rogers (arr)
*Los Angeles, 12 August 1957*
**Bunny**            World Pacific WP1257, Pacific Jazz PJLA896–H
**Popo**
**Powder Stuff**
**Didi**
**Diablo's Dance**


STUFF SMITH
Stuff Smith (vln), Carl Perkins (p), Curtis Counce/Red Callender (b), Frank Butler/Oscar
Bradley (d)
*Los Angeles, 1957*
**It's Wonderful**                              Verve MGV8282
**Ja-da**
**Comin' Through the Rye**
**Indiana**
**Oh But It Is**
**Stop Look**

ERNIE ANDREWS
Vcl acc by Lucky Thompson (ts), Eddie Beal (p), Barney Kessel (g), Irving Ashby (g), Edward Hall (d), Red Callender (b)
*Los Angeles, 17 June 1957*

| | |
|---|---|
| **Being in Love** | Columbia 30187 |
| **You'd Better Be Satisfied** | – |
| **Hickory Dickory Dock** | Columbia 37975 |
| **South Me** | – |

JACK SHELDON
Jack Sheldon, Conte Candoli (tp), Stu Williamson (v-tb), Vince de Rosa (fhr), Red Callender (tu), Lennie Niehaus (as), Bill Root (ts, bar), Pete Jolly (p), Buddy Clark (b), Mel Lewis (d)
*Los Angeles, 1957*

| | |
|---|---|
| **Brown Cow** | GNP GNP60 |
| **On Green Dolphin Street** | |
| **I'm Also a Person** | |

CARMEN McCRAE – AFTER GLOW
Carmen McCrae (vcl), feat Red Callender (b)
*Los Angeles, 1957*

| | |
|---|---|
| **Dream of Life** | Decca DL 8583 |
| **Perdido** | |
| **Between the Devil and the Deep Blue Sea** | |
| **All My Life** | |
| **Guess Who I Saw Today** | |
| **Nice Work if You Can Get It** | |
| **I'm Through with Love** | |
| **I Can't Escape from You** | |
| **The Little Things That Mean So Much** | |
| **Exactly Like You** | |
| **East of the Sun** | |
| **My Funny Valentine** | |

BOB SCOBEY ORCHESTRA
Bob Scobey, Dick Cathcart (tp), Jack Buck, Abe Lincoln, Warren Smith (tb), Matty Matlock (cl), Ralph Sutton (p), Clancy Hayes (bj, g, vcl), Bob Short (tu), Red Callender (b), Sammy Goldstein (d)
*Los Angeles, 21 January 1957*

| | |
|---|---|
| **New Orleans** | Victor LPM1448 |
| **Carolina in the Morning** | |
| **Snag It** | |
| **Waiting for the Robert E. Lee** | |

BING CROSBY WITH BOB SCOBEY
Vcl acc Bob Scobey, Frank Beach (tp), Abe Lincoln (tb), Matty Matlock (cl), Dave Harris (ts), Ralph Sutton (p), Clancy Hayes (g), Red Callender (b), Nick Fatool (d)
*Los Angeles, 1957*

**Dream a Little Dream of Me**                    RCA DP27032
**Some Sunny Day**
**I'm Gonna Sit Right Down**
**Tell Me**
**Exactly Like You**
**Let a Smile Be Your Umbrella**
**Mama Loves Papa**
**Down Among the Sheltering Palms**
**Last Night on the Back Porch**
**Along the Way and Wikiki**
**Whispering**
**Mack the Knife**


RED CALLENDER SPEAKS LOW
Red Callender (b, tu), Buddy Collette (fl, cl), Vince de Rosa, Irving Rosenthal (fhr),
Bob Bain (g), Red Mitchell (b), Bill Douglass (d)
*Los Angeles, 1957*
**Speak Low**                         Crown CLP5012, Reissue RED Records
**Nice Day**                             Collector's Item RRLP–0269
**In a Sentimental Mood**
**Foggy Day**
**Darn That Dream**
**Gone with the Wind**
**Chris**


RED CALLENDER – SWINGIN' SUITE – Twelve Callender Originals
Red Callender (b), Parr Jones (tp), John Ewing (tb), Buddy Collette (cl, ts), William
Green (as), Clyde Dunn (bar), Eddie Beal (p), Bill Douglass (d), Frank Bode (bgo)
*Los Angeles, October–November 1957*
**On Again**                          Crown CLP5025
**Greenery**
**Pastel**
**October Blue**
**Dancers**
**Bihari**
**Skyline**
**Sleigh Ride**
**All for You**
**Outlines**
**Walking on Air**
**You're Part of Me**


RED CALLENDER – THE LOWEST
Red Callender (b, tu), Gerald Wilson (tp), John Ewing (tb), Buddy Collette (cl, ts, fl),
Hymie Gunkler (as), Marty Berman (bar), Gerald Wiggins or Eddie Beal (p), Billy Bean
or Bill Pittman (g), Red Mitchell (b), Bill Douglass (d)
*Los Angeles, 1958*
**Autumn in New York**                MGM E1007, Metrojazz E1007
**Pickin', Pluckin', Whistlin' and Walkin'**

**The Lowest**
**Of Thee I Sing**
**Dedicated to the Blues**
**They Can't Take That Away from Me**
**Five-Four Blues**
**Tea for Two**
**Another Blues**
**I'll Be Around**
**Volume Two**


JERRY FIELDING – MAGNIFICENCE IN BRASS
Jerry Fielding arr, cond, & his orchestra, feat Red Callender (tu, b)
*Los Angeles, 1958*
**City of Brass**                    Time Records S2042
**Moonlight in Vermont**
**Cheek to Cheek**
**When the Saints Go Marching In**
**Isn't It Romantic**
**Frenesi**
**Prologue from West Side Story**
**The Magic Circle**
**Ritual Fire Dance**
**Skyliner** (Red Callender comp)
**Shadow Waltz**


JOHN EWING AND THE STREAMLINERS
Joe Graves, Mel Moore (tp), John Ewing (tb), Bill Green (bar), Buddy Collette (ts),
Eddie Beal (p), Rene Hall (g), Red Callender (b), Bill Douglass (d)
*Los Angeles, 1958*
**Tavern in Town**                    Lark LS459
**Caroline**


ALTON PURNELL QUARTET
Plas Johnson (ts), Alton Purnell (p, vcl), Red Callender (b), Earl Palmer (d)
*Los Angeles, June 1958*
**Yancy Special**                    Warner Bros
**Stockolee**                    WB(WS)1228
**Pinetop's Boogie**
**Yellow Dog Blues**
**Sentimental Journey**
**Slow Goin' Fast Comin' Back**
**Buster Anderson's Blues**
**I Want You, I Need You**
**Alberta**
**C.C. Rider**
**Someday You'll Be Sorry**
**St Louis Blues**

BELAFONTE SINGS THE BLUES
Harry Belafonte (vcl), feat Red Callender (b)
*Los Angeles, 1958*
**Cotton Fields**                                RCA LPM–1972
**God Bless the Child**
**Mary Ann**
**Hallelujah I Love Her So**
**Fare Thee Well**
**One for My Baby**


ERROLL GARNER – A NEW KIND OF LOVE
Leith Stevens, cond, Erroll Garner (p), Red Callender (b)
*Los Angeles, 1950s*
**You Brought a New Kind of Love to Me**          Mercury SR60859
**Louise**
**Steve's Song**
**Paris Mist – Bossa Nova**
**Mimi**
**The Tease**
**In the Park in Paree**
**Paris Mist – Waltz Swing**
**Fashion Interlude**


NAT KING COLE – JUST ONE OF THOSE THINGS
Billy May Orchestra feat Red Callender (tu), Sweets Edison (tp solos), Willie Smith (lead
as), Conrad Gozzo (lead tp), John Collins (g), Lee Young (d)
*Los Angeles, 1950s*
**When Your Lover Has Gone**                      Capital W 903
**A Cottage for Sale**
**Once in a While** – (tu feat)
**Who's Sorry Now?**
**These Foolish Things**
**Just for the Fun of It**
**Don't Get Around Much Anymore**
**I Understand**
**The Song Is Ended**
**The Party's Over**
**Just One of Those Things**


BIG FAT BRASS
Billy May Orchestra feat Red Callender (tu), Vince De Rosa (frh), Pete Condoli, Sweets
Edison (tp), Conrad Gozzo (tp), Joe Howard (tb)
*Los Angeles, 1958*
**Autumn Leaves**                                 Capitol
**Love Is the Thing**
**Big Fat Brass**
**Moonlight Becomes You**
**Brass Fat Tuba**
**The Continental**
**Singapore**

## HARRY BELAFONTE
Vcl acc by Don Fagerquist (tp), Milt Bernhart (tb), Plas Johnson (ts), Jimmy Rowles (p)
Millard Thomas (g), Howard Roberts (el-b), Red Callender (b), Jack Sperling (d)
*Hollywood, 5 June 1958*

| | |
|---|---|
| **Los Hands** | RCA (E) RD27095 |
| **Cotton Fields** | – |
| **God Bless the Child** | – |
| **Summer's Prayer** | – |

## BILLY ECKSTINE
Billy Eckstine (vcl), vcl acc by Pete Candoli, Don Fagerquist (tp), Bud Shank (as), Gerald
Wiggins (p), Red Callender (b), Larry Bunker (d) + others
*Los Angeles, 1958*

| | |
|---|---|
| **Love Is Just Around the Corner** | EmArcy MG36129 |

**Ghost of a Chance**
**Imagination**
**What a Little Moonlight Can Do**
**I Cover the Waterfront**
**That's All**
**I'm Gonna Sit Right Down and Write Myself a Letter**
**It Was So Beautiful**
**A Faded Summer Love**
**Lullaby of the Leaves**
**I Wished on the Moon**

## SHORTY ROGERS
Shorty Rogers (tp), Bud Shank (as), Plas Johnson (ts), Jimmy Rowles (p), Al Hendrik-
son, Bill Pittman (g), Red Callender (b), Mel Lewis (d), Jack Sperling (perc)
*Los Angeles, 2 February 1958*

| | |
|---|---|
| **Juicy** | Victor 20–7269 |

**Midnight Stroll** (unissued)
**Cerveza**
**Papuana**
**Corrido Rock**

## ANN RICHARDS
Vcl acc by Jack Sheldon (tp), Barney Kessel (g), Red Callender (b), Larry Bunker (d),
Ann Richards (vcl)
*Los Angeles, c. 1959*

| | |
|---|---|
| **Is You Is or Is You Ain't My Baby** | Atco LP 33–136 |

**The Masquerade Is Over**
**Yes Sir! That's My Baby**
**An Occasional Man**
**I Couldn't Sleep a Wink Last Night**
**And That's All**
**Love Is a Word for the Blues**
**Evil Gal Blues**
**There's a Lull in My Life**
**How Do I Look in Blue**

**Bewitched**
**You Go to My Head**


GOOGIE RENE
Conrad Guzzo (tp), Buddy Collette (saxes), Red Callender (b), Larry Bunker (d) +
unknown vibes and others
*Los Angeles, 1959*
**Serenade in the Night**                    Class 262, LP33–136
**Caesar's Pad**
**Cool It at the Coliseum**
**Cafe Roman Candles**
**Romesville**
**Flippin at the Pizza**
**Come Back to Sorrento**
**Cherry Ferrari**
**Farewell to Rome**


ART AND DOTTY TODD – CHANSON D'AMOUR
Feat Red Callender (b)
*Los Angeles, 1959*
**Chanson d'Amour**                          Dot CLP5129
**The Bodie Tree**
**Sunrise, Sunset**
**On a Clear Day You Can See Forever**
**I'll Take Care of Your Cares**
**It's the Talk of the Town**
**Mood Indigo**
**Spanish Eyes**
**So Beats My Heart for You**
**Vaya Con Dios**
**A Taste of Honey**


KINGS OF DIXIELAND
Dick Cathcart (tp), Elmer 'Moe' Schneider (tb), Heinie Beau (cl), Eddie Miller (ts), Ray
Sherman (p), George Van Eps (g), Red Callender (b, tu), Nick Fatool (d)
*Los Angeles, 25 July 1959*
**Royal Garden Blues**                       Crown CLP5129
**New Washington and Lee Swing**
**Somebody Stole My Gal**
**Lassus Trombone**
**When the Saints Go Marching In**
**South Rampart Street Parade**
**Careless Love**
**Wait Til the Sun Shines**
**High Society**
**Dixieland Blues**

BILLY ECKSTINE – ONCE MORE WITH FEELING
Billy May (cond, arr), feat Red Callender (b, tu)
*Los Angeles, 1960s*
**I'm Beginning to See the Light**                    Roulette R25104
**I Apologize**
**Blues in the Night**
**Secret Love**
**Every Breath I Take**
**I Hear a Rhapsody**
**That Old Black Magic**
**Once More with Feeling**
**Cottage for Sale**
**Stormy Weather**
**I Love You**
**As Time Goes By**


CAL TJADER – WEST SIDE STORY
Cal Tjader, acc by Clare Fisher's Orchestra feat Red Callender (tu)
*Los Angeles, November 1960*
**Cool**                    Fantasy LP3310
**Maria**
**America**
**Prologue**
**Jet Song**
**Tonight**
**Dance at the Gym**
**Something's Comin'**
**I Feel Pretty**
**Somewhere**
**One Hand One Heart**
**Maria Interlude**


MEL TORME
Vcl acc by Al Porcino, Stu Williamson (tp), Frank Rosolino (tb), Vince De Rosa (fhr),
Red Callender (tu), Art Pepper (as), Bill Perkins (ts), Bill Hood (bar), Marty Paitch (p),
Joe Mondragon (b), Mel Lewis (d)
*Los Angeles, 1959–1960*
**Too Close for Comfort**                    Verve MGV(S6)2132
**Once in Love with Amy**
**A Sleepin' Bee**
**On the Street where You Live**
**All I Need Is a Girl**
**Just in Time**
**Hello Young Lovers** .
**The Surrey with the Fringe on Top**
**Old Devil Moon**
**Whatever Lola Wants, Lola Gets**
**Too Darn Hot**
**Lonely Town**

THE MILLS BROTHERS TODAY
Vcl acc by the Sy Oliver Orchestra, Red Callender (b)
*Los Angeles, 1960s*
**Honeysuckle Rose**                                           Dot 25766
**Blues Bossa Nova**
**Confess**
**Moonlight and Roses**
**One Dozen Roses**
**Highways Are Happy Ways**
**You Didn't Want Me When You Had Me**
**Mexicali Rose**
**Smack Dab in the Middle**
**Go in and out the Window**
**Since We Fell out of Love**


NAT KING COLE – WILD IS LOVE
Nelson Riddle cond, Red Callender (tu)
*Los Angeles, March 1960*
**Wild Is Love**                                               Capitol 10637
**Hundreds and Thousands of Girls**
**It's a Beautiful Eve**
**Tell Her in the Morning**
**Are You Disenchanted**
**Pick Up** (tuba solo)
**Beggar for the Blues**
**World of No Return**
**In Love Again**
**Stay with It**
**Wouldn't You Know**
**He Who Hesitates**


MAXWELL DAVIS – COMPOSITIONS OF DUKE ELLINGTON
Conte Candoli, Ray Linn, Al Porcino, Jake Porter (tp), Juan Tizol (vtb), Lloyd Elliot,
Jimmy Henderson, Dick Noel, Tommy Pederson (tb), Mahlon Clark, Jewell Grant (as,
cl), Al Hendrickson (g), Red Callender, Curtis Counce (b), Mel Lewis, Jackie Mills (d),
Blues Boy King (vcl)
*Los Angeles, 13–14 January 1960*
**Cottontail**                                                 Crown CLP5153
**Don't Get Around Much Anymore**
**East Side, West Side**
**Jack the Bear**
**Jeeps Blues**
**Main Stem**
**Mood Indigo**
**Solitude**
**Sophisticated Lady**
**Take the 'A' Train**

PLAS JOHNSON
Plas Johnson (ts), Ernie Freeman (org), Ray Johnson (p), Rene Hall, Bill Pittman (g),
Red Callender (b), Earl Palmer (d) + unknown strings
*Los Angeles, 1960*
**Since I Fell for You**                        Capitol T1503
**Tanya**
**Chole**
**Mood for the Blues**
**Don't Let the Sun Catch You Crying**
**One Mint Julep**
**Fool That I Am**
**Blues in My Heart**
**How Long Has This Been Going On**
**I've Got a Right to Cry**
**Please Send Me Someone to Love**
**I Wanna Be Loved**

DINAH WASHINGTON
Vcl acc by Ernie Freeman (p), Barney Kessel, Rene Hall (g), Red Callender (b), Earl
Palmer (d) + strings, Belford Hendricks (arr, cond)
*Los Angeles, January 1961*
**Love Is a Many Splendid Thing**      Mercury MG211119, MVL309
**An Affair to Remember**
**Cabin in the Sky**
**Pagan Love Song**
**Blue Skies**
**Three Coins in the Fountain**
**Stormy Weather**
**Love Letters**
**On Green Dolphin Street**
**Six Bridges to Cross**

PEARL BAILEY
John Audino, Jimmy Zito, Conte Candoli, Frank Giggins, Ray Triscari, Van Rasey, Al
Porcino (tp), Dick Damario, Mike Barone, Ernie Falk (tb), Arthur Maebe (fhr), Red
Callender (tu), Joe Maine, Bill Green (as), Garrington Visor, Bill Perkins (ts), Teddy Lee
(bar), Lou Levy (p), Tony Rizzi (g), Jimmy Bond (b), Louis Bellson (d), Gene Estes
(vibe)
*New York, 1962*
**Just Me, Just You**                           Roulette R25167
**That Certain Feeling**
**I'm Glad There's You**
**Easy to Love**
**Gee Baby**
**Let There Be Love**

LOUIS BELLSON BIG BAND – THE SUMMIT
Louis Bellson cond, arr, feat Red Callender (tu)
*Los Angeles, 1962*

Who's Who                                    Roulette R52087
Cool
Ambrosia
Prelude
Gumshoe
Blitzen
St Louis
Doozy
The Moon Is Low
Lou's Blues
With Bells On
The Diplomat Speaks


DIZZY GILLESPIE AND HIS ORCHESTRA
Dizzy Gillespie, Al Porcino, Ray Triscari, Stu Williamson, Conte Candoli (tp), Frank
Rosolino, Mike Baron, Bob Edmondson, Kenny Shroyer (tb), Ches Thompson, Steward
Rensey, Luis Kent (fhr), Red Callender (tu), Phil Woods, Charlie Kennedy (as), James
Moody, Bill Perkins (ts), Bill Hood (bar), Lalo Schifrin (p), Al Hendrickson (g), Buddy
Clarke, Chris White (b), Mel Lewis, Rudy Collins (d), Emil Richards, Larry Bunker,
Francisco Aquabella (perc), Benny Carter (cond)
The Conquerors                        Limelight LM82022,            Trip TLP5584
The Swords
The Chains
Chorale
The Legend of Atlantis
The Empire


MAVIS RIVERS
Vcl acc by Shorty Rogers and His Giants: pers incl Shorty Rogers (tp), Dick Grove (p),
Red Callender (tu), Chuck Sagle (arr)
*Los Angeles, 1962*
I'll Remember You                            Reprise R(9)6074
I'm Gonna Live Til I Die
I Feel So Smoochie
The Best Thing Is Yet to Come
Nothing But the Best
My Shining Hour
Get Out of Town
You Brought a New Kind of Love to Me
Desafinado
By Myself
When Sunny Gets Blue


STAN KENTON WITH THE RALPH CARMICHAEL ORCHESTRA AND CHOIR
Stan Kenton (p, narration), Robert Miller (org), Allan Reuss, Robert Gibbons (g), Red
Callender, Hy Lesnick (b), Frank Carlson (d) + choir, Ralph Caramichael (arr, cond)
*Hollywood, 6 September 1962*
Mama Song a Song (SK, choir vol) (1)              Capitol F4847
Whispering Hope (choir vol) (2)

THE SENSATIONAL PETE JOLLY GASSES EVERYBODY
Buddy Collette (saxes, fl, b-cl), Pete Jolly (accor), Jim Hall (g), Gerald Wilson (org), Red
Callender (b), Louis Bellson (d), Buddy Collette (arr)
*Los Angeles, 1963*
**Where's My Bess**            Charlie Parker Records PLP825
**My Man's Gone Now**
**Summertime**
**It Ain't Necessarily So**
**I Got Plenty Of Nuttin'**
**There's a Boat That's Leaving for New York**
**Bess You Is My Woman**
**A Woman Is a Sometime Thing**

BUDDY COLLETTE – POLYNESIA
Buddy Collette (saxes), Gene Cipriano (reeds), Earl Palmer (perc), Red Callender (b,
tu), Gerald Wilson (tp), Ed Lustagarten (cello), Marni Nixon (sop), Al Viola (g)
*Los Angeles, 1960s*
**Singapore Sling**            Music & Sound S–1001
**Taboo**
**Flight**
**Gaugin**
**Polynesian Suite**
**Japanese Suite**

FIFTY VELVET BRASS
Pete King, con, arr, feat Red Callender (tu)
*Los Angeles, 1963*
**Shangri-la**            Liberty 14029
**Star Eyes**
**The Way You Look Tonight**
**Midnight Sun**
**Day by Day**
**Almost Paradise**
**The Party's Over**
**Till**
**If Ever I Would Leave You**
**Where Are You**
**The End of a Love Affair**

BUDDY COLLETTE – NOW AND THEN
Al Aarons (tp), Red Callender (b, tu), Al Viola (g), Frank Severino, Frank Chavez (d),
Buddy Collette (as, ts)
*Los Angeles, 1960s*
**Fun City**            Legend LGS1004
**Veda**
**Safari West**
**J. Power Buzzard**
**Now and Then**
**Shatara**
**Andre**

CHARLES MINGUS – MINGUS AT MONTEREY
Bobby Bryant, Lonnie Hillyer, Melvin Moore (tp), Lou Blackburn (tb), Buddy Collette
(fl, pic, as), Charles McPherson (as), Jack Nimitz (b-cl), Red Callender (tu), Jaki Byard
(p), Charles Mingus (b, p), Dannie Richmond (d)
*Monterey Jazz Festival, Monterey, 20 September 1964*
*Callender featured on:*
**Meditations on Integration pt. 1**                    C.M.E. JWS002
**Meditations on Integration pt. 2**


PAUL HORN – JAZZ SUITE ON THE MASS TEXTS
Paul Horn Quintet acc by Lalo Schifrin's Orchestra, Paul Horn (as, cl, alto flute, fl), feat
Red Callender (tu)
*Hollywood, 5–6 November 1964*
**Kyrie**                                  RCA Vic LPM(S)3414
**Angus Dei**
**Gloria**
**Interludium**
**Offertory**
**Sanctus**
**Credo**
**Prayer**


DIZZY GILLESPIE WITH THE NEOPHONIC ORCHESTRA
Dizzy Gillespie, Conte Candoli, Ollie Mitchell, Al Porcino, Dalton Smith, Marvin Brown
(ts), Bob Fitzpatrick, Frank Rosolino, Lyod Ulyate (tb), Jim Amlott (b-tb), Jack Cave,
Vince DeRosa, William Hinshaw, Arthur Maebe, Richard Perissi (fhr), Red Callender
(tu), Buddy Collette, Chuck Gentry, Bill Hood, Bill Perkins, Bud Shank (reeds), Mike
Lang (p), Al Viola (g), John Worster (b), Shelly Manne (d), Fran Carlson, Emil Richards
(perc), Stan Kenton (cond)
*Concert, Music Center, Los Angeles, 1 February 1965*
**Jambo**                                                Limelight
**Fiesta Mo-jo**
**And Then She Stopped**
**Things Are Here**


HARRY 'SWEETS' EDISON
Harry Edison (tp) acc by strings, Don Abney/Gerald Wiggins (p), Red Callender/Leroy
Vinnegar (b), Jackie Mills/Alvin Stoller (d)
*Los Angeles, June 1965*
**What Is There to Say**        Vee-Jay VLP1104, Vee-Jay Int. 3065
**I Wish You Love**                   also Font 3L5312, Sue LP1030
**Call Me Irresponsible**
**Willow Weep for Me**
**But Beautiful**
**Blues for Christmas**
**On Green Dolphin Street**
**Everything Happens to Me**
**The Days of Wine and Roses**

**Carpetbaggers**
**Sweets for the Sweet**

JOHNNY HODGES ACCOMPANIED BY THE LAWRENCE WELK ORCHESTRA
Francis Howard, Lloyd Ulyate, Richard Nash, George Roberts (tb), James Decker,
David Duke, Alan Robinson (fhr), Johnny Hodges (as), Lou Singe (vb, marimba, xyl),
Frank Scott (p, harpsichord), Neil Levang, Les Behunin (g), Red Callender (b), Earl
Palmer (d) + string section, George Gates (dir)
*Los Angeles, 20 December 1965*
**Misty**                         Dot DLP3682, (F) CUD1710
**Fantastic – That's You**
**In a Sentimental Mood**
**Canadian Sunset**
**Someone to Watch Over Me**
**I'm Beginning to See the Light**

IKE ISAACS – AT THE PIED PIPER
Prod. Red Callender, Ike Isaacs (b), Jack Wilson (p), Jimmy Smith (d)
*Los Angeles, 1966*
**Impressions (Coltrane)**          R.G.B. Records 2000
**Mercy, Mercy, Mercy**
**I'll Drown in My Own Tears**
**Soulin'**
**Walk on By**
**Red 'I'** (Callender & Isaacs)

OLIVER NELSON + BILLY BYRES ARR.
John Audino, Bobby Bryant, Conte Candoli, Ollie Mitchell, Al Porcino (tp), Mike Bar-
one, Richard Leith, Billy Byres, Dick Noel, Ernie Tack (tb), Bill Hinshaw, Richard
Perissi (fhr), Red Callender (tu), Plas Johnson, Bill Green, Bill Perkins, Gabe Baltazar,
Jack Nimitz, Oliver Jackson (reeds), Mike Melvoin (p), Ray Brown (b), Shelly Manne (d)
*Los Angeles, 27–28 September 1966*
**Sound Pieces for Jazz Orchestra**      Impulse A(S)9129
**Flute Salad**
**The Lady from Girl Talk**

PERCY FAITH – BLACK MAGIC WOMAN
Percy Faith cond and Orchestra, Earl Palmer, Jack Arnold, Milt Holland (perc), Bill
Tole (tb), Lou Morell, Al Hendrickson (g), Red Callender (b, tu)
*Los Angeles, 1970*
**Viva Tirado**                     Columbia AL 30800
**Wave**                            C  –
Black Magic Woman
The Sun King
If
Reza
The Wailing of the Willow

Oye Como Va
Never Can Say Goodbye
Très


B.B. KING – L.A. MIDNIGHT
B.B. King (vcl, g), acc by Red Callender (tu), Paul Harris (p), Taj Mahal, Randy Wolfe,
Jesse Edwin David (g), Brian Garofalo (el-b), Bob Morin (d), personnel changes on some
selections
*Los Angeles, 22 March 1971*
**(I Believe) I've Been Blue Too Long**                    ABCX–743
**I Got Some Help I Don't Need**
**Lucille's Grany**
**Can't You Hear Me Talking to You?**
**Midnight**
**Sweet Sixteen**
**Help the Poor**


LADY SINGS THE BLUES
Diana Ross (vcl) acc by Gil Askey Orchestra, feat Red Callender (b, tu)
*Los Angeles, 1972*
**Lady Sings the Blues**                    Motown M7580
**'Tain't Nobody's Business If I Do**
**C.C. Rider**
**All of Me**
**The Man I Love**
**Them There Eyes**
**I Cried for You**
**Don't Explain**
**Mean to Me**
**Fine and Mellow**
**What a Little Moonlight Can Do**
**Love Is Here to Stay**
**My Man**
**Strange Fruit**
**God Bless the Child**
**Good Mornin' Heartache**


RED CALLENDER – BASIN STREET BRASS
Red Callender (b, tu), Al Aarons (tp), Grover Mitchell (tb), Buddy Collette (fl, cl, as, ts),
Harold Jones (d), Walt Sage (d), Al Viola (g, banjo), Leroy Vinnegar (b on Fat Cat),
Patrick Boyle (tam)
*Los Angeles, 1973*
**Basin Street Blues**                    Legend LGS–1003
**Primrose Lane**
**When the Saints Go Marching In**
**Just a Closer Walk with Thee**
**Sophisticated Lady**
**Dedicated to the Blues**
**I Want a Little Girl**

**Magna**
**Fat Cat**
**Lush Life**


ODESSA SOUND OF JAZZ, VOL. 1
All Star Texas Jazz Party: Ashley Alexander (tb, euph), Mousey Alexander (d), John
Best (d), Red Callender (b), Kenny Davern (sop s), Herb Ellis (g), Pee Wee Erwin (tp),
Carl Fontana (tb), Jake Hanna (d), Milt Hinton (b), Peanuts Hucko (cl), Cliff Leeman
(d), Jack Leshberg (b), Dave McKenna (p), Flip Wilson (ts), Bucky Pizzarelli (g), Ed
Pulcer (tp), Lou Stein (p), Buddy Tate (ts), Clark Terry (tp & vcl), Bob Wilber (cl, sop s)
*Odessa, Texas, 1977*
**Yellow Dog Blues**                          Odessa Sound 1001
**I Gotta Right to Sing the Blues**
**Black and Tan Fantasy**
**Lady Be Good**


PAN AFRIKAN PEOPLE'S ARKESTRA – THE CALL
Horace Tapscott (cond, arr, p), Jesse Sharps, (bnlder, ss, ts, bamboo fl), Linda Hill (p),
Adele Sebatian (vcl, fl), Lester Robertson (tb), David Bryant (b), Everett Brown Jr. (d),
Herbert Callies (alto cl), James Andrews (ts, b-cl), Michael Session (as), Kafil L. Roberts
(fl, ss), Archie Johnson (tb), Red Callender (tu, b), William Madison (perc, d), Louis
Spears (cello, b), Kamonta Lawrence Palk (b)
*Los Angeles, 1978*
**The Call**                                  Nimbus 246
**Quagmire Manor at 5 A.M.**
**Nakatini Suite**
**Peyote Song No. III**


EARL HINES – 'FATHA' – HITS HE MISSED
Earl Hines (p), Red Callender (b), Bill Douglass (d)
*Los Angeles, 1978*
**Birdland**                                  Real Time RT–105
**Blue Monk**
**Humoresque**
**Squeeze me and Ain't Misbehavin'**
**Sophisticated Lady**
**Old Fashioned Love**
**Misty**
**The Preacher**


THE BINGO LONG TRAV'LING ALL STARS
Music from Original Motion Picture Soundtrack
William Goldstein cond, Red Callender (tu, b)
Film starring Richard Pryor, James Earl Jones, Billy Dee Williams
*Los Angeles, 1980*
**Main Title-Signifying on the Diamond**      Motown MCA 2094
**Leon in High Gear**
**Bean Bale Blues**

**Polka Dot Jitterbug**
**All Stars on Parade**
**With Love from Sallie Potter**
**The Bingo Long Song (Steal Home)**
**Baseball Magic**
**Enter the Goons**
**The Amazing Esquire Joe Catch**
**Steal on Home**


JAMES NEWTON – THE MYSTERY SCHOOL, Music for Wind Quintet
James Newton (fl), John Carter (cl), John Nunez (bassoon), Charles Owens (eng. h,
oboe), Red Callender (tu)
*Los Angeles, 1980*
**Introduction**                                India Navigation 104
**Clarinet and Basson Duo**
**Dirge**
**Dreams and Remembrances**
**Eulogy** (English Horn)
**Tuba Solo**
**Tuba 7 Flute Duo**
**Flute Solo**
**Dirge Recapitulation**


DAUWHE – THE JOHN CARTER OCTET
John Carter (cl), Bobby Bradford (crnt), Red Callender (tu), James Newton (fl), Charles
Owens (ss, oboe, cl), Roberto Miranda (b), William Jeffrey (d), Luis Peralta (water-
phone, perc)
*Los Angeles, 25, 28 February and 8 March 1982*
**Ode to the Flower Maiden**                     Black Saint BSR 0057
**Enter from the East**
**Soft Dance**
**The Mating Ritual**


RED CALLENDER – GERALD WIGGINS
Gerald Wiggins (p), Red Callender (b, tu, vcl)
*Los Angeles, 1983*
**Sonara**                                       Hemisphere Records 1002
**Night Mist**
**Wind and Rain**
**Lush Life** (tuba solo)
**Edie Was a Sweetie**
**Merry Go Round** (Callender comp)
**Blues**
**The Way You Look Tonight**
**Baby I'm Gone** (Callender comp)


JAMES NEWTON
James Newton (fl), Red Callender (tu), Charles Owens (fhr, as, oboe), John Carter (cl),

John Nunez (bassoon), Anthony Brown (d) + others
*Los Angeles, May 1984*
**Loan Hill** Grammavision Records

JEANNIE CHEATHAM + JIMMY CHEATHAM – SWEET BABY BLUES
*Los Angeles, 1984*
Jeannie Cheatham (p & vcl), Jimmie Cheatham (bs & b), Red Callender (b & tu), John Harris (d), Charles McPherson (as), Jimmie Noone (s sax, cl), Curtis Peagler (as, ts), Snooky Young (tp)

Concord Records CJ-258

# Index